P9-DYZ-641

THE POWER OF A GOOD FIGHT:
Executive Edition

Lynne Eisaguirre

LITERARY™
ARCHITECTS

Copyright © 2007 Lynne Eisaguirre

All rights reserved. No part of this book shall be reproduced, stored in a retrieval system, or transmitted by any means, electronic, mechanical, photocopying, recording, or otherwise, without express written permission from the author. No patent liability is assumed with respect to the use of the information contained herein. Although every precaution has been taken in the preparation of this book, the author and publisher assume no responsibility for errors or omissions. Neither is any liability assumed for damages resulting from the use of information contained herein. For more information, contact Literary Architects, 1427 W. 86th St., Ste 324, Indianapolis, IN 46260.

International Standard Book Number: 1-933669-05-5 (softcover edition)

International Standard Book Number: 1-933669-84-5 (ebook edition)

Library of Congress Catalog Card Number: Available upon request.

Printed in the United States of America.

The author and publisher specifically disclaim any responsibility for any liability, loss, or risk, personal or otherwise, which is incurred as a consequence, directly or indirectly, of the use and application of any of the contents of this book.

For information on publicity, marketing, or selling this book, contact Bryan Gambrel, Marketing Director, Literary Architects, 317-462-6329. For information on becoming a Literary Architects author, contact Renee Wilmeth, Acquisitions Director, 317-925-7045.

www.literaryarchitects.com
www.workplacesthatwork.com

Cover design: TnT Design, Inc.
Interior design: Amy Hassos
Copyediting: Kim Cofer
Proofreading: Julie Campbell
Index: Angie Bess

Table of Contents

Introduction

There is nothing I love as much as a good fight.

—Franklin D. Roosevelt

Franklin Delano Roosevelt did not issue this challenge in his presidency but rather long before he got there. Willingness to embrace conflict and his legendary confidence made Roosevelt a dynamic, resilient, and successful leader. Before he ever sat in the Oval Office, he ran for the New York State Senate as a Democrat in a district that hadn't elected one since 1884. He defended the rights of farmers in his district, who were mostly Republicans, and he fiercely fought corrupt politics of the Democratic political machine in Manhattan known as Tammany Hall.

Roosevelt continued fighting throughout his life. His presidency—which spanned four terms and twelve years—was unparalleled in scope and length. Under the shadow of the Great Depression, Roosevelt mobilized the unprecedented numbers of poor Americans, including minorities, and he organized labor and others to forge a political revolution that launched economic recovery with the social programs of the "New Deal." He also catapulted the United States into international leadership, committing the country to defeat fascism in World War II.

In 1944, Roosevelt faced Thomas Dewey in his bid for a fourth term as President. His opponents waged vicious attacks, calling him "a tired old man" and accusing him of sending a battleship to Alaska to retrieve his beloved dog Fala who was rumored to have been left behind accidentally. Roosevelt, in a speech to the Teamster's Union blasted the Republicans, saying, "I am accustomed to hearing malicious falsehoods about myself…But I think I have a right to resent, to object to libelous statements about my dog."

Roosevelt had no tolerance for malicious fights, but he also had no compunction about fighting the good fights. Just as important, he was savvy enough to walk away from the bad fights. And that is a critical skill that often separates an exceptional leader from an ordinary one. It can be the difference between being a legendary leader and a CEO wannabe.

Why You Need to Know How to Fight the Good Fight

As a senior leader, you've probably read more than your share of management books chock-full of leadership principles, quality initiatives, and strategies for organizational greatness. It's all good stuff, but the elephant in the room is organizational tension. It's all the small resentments, the inter-departmental tussles, and the "personality conflicts" among managers that get in the way of success, no matter how that success is benchmarked.

Before an organization can implement pillars of success, create blue oceans of opportunity, go from good to great, become a big fish, keep buckets full, or soar with its strengths, it must know how to use creative tension. Healthy conflict is a tremendous internal asset that when properly harnessed unleashes the potential of a company.

If you already use conflict to drive innovation, you're a step ahead. You need all the employees capitalizing on the "Big C." This book will give you the tools to reframe your own approach to conflict management and teach your employees to use conflict constructively. If you can manage a few hours alone with this book on your next business trip or early morning train commute, the ROI will be well worth it.

There really is such a thing as a good fight and more importantly, good fights are potent organizational assets. A good fight is one that builds trust, fosters strong relationships, keeps a work group or an entire company on point, and actually helps to lead an organization. A good fight reveals the value of conflict. A good fight can drive innovative solutions to issues that would never have been discovered without working through the dispute. The question then becomes, *How can we encourage more good fights and fewer bad fights?* I've devoted most of my professional career to helping Fortune 500 companies, individual executives, and mid-sized firms answer that question.

What's in It for You?

Simply put, the modern workforce is more diverse than ever before, and the competition isn't always the 800-pound gorilla across the country. It could be a one-person band with an Internet connection and a great idea half a world away. Just look at how a few college kids knocked the music industry on its ear with downloadable music.

Workplace conflict isn't the exception—it's the reality of today's business climate. There's on-the-job violence, harassment, ethnic tensions, plain vanilla dysfunction, gender issues, religious wars, and hostile work environments. You want to hit your budget numbers, enhance customer loyalty, improve quality, and reduce turnover? This is the golden ticket. You want to ease that tension in your neck and shoulders and sleep like a baby? Embrace conflict. You want to lose ten pounds? Sorry, can't help you there. Harnessing the creative power of conflict isn't a panacea; it's just good business. I spent ten years in front of federal judges trying cases as an attorney. I learned more than a thing or two about good fights and bad fights.

A Workforce Forced to the Brink

The extraordinary increase in workplace conflict really skyrocketed in the 1990's. Downsized, right-sized, re-organized, and demoralized, many employees have become more suspicious than productive, ready to file internal grievances or sue at the least provocation.

And no wonder. Most had been loyal, hard-working, integral parts of an enterprise. They expected some measure of security in exchange for their hard work. In today's workplace they find that they could be terminated on a moment's notice, frequently after being reassured the day before that their jobs were secure.

Mergers, acquisitions, and devastating corporate scandals have created more *Working Wounded*, as author Bob Rosner calls them. Even though research revealed that 70 percent of mergers fail—usually because of the failure to address people issues—organizations continued to pursue them. The working wounded who stayed with the company viewed their leaders with distrust. Organizational mission statements, the latest "program du jour," and *Dilbert*-style consultants were greeted with equal disdain. Dozens of new "trainings"—from sexual harassment to new computer programs—were launched by harried human resource departments who struggled to keep up with the legal realities of the changing workplace climate as well as the continuing demands for new skills.

The irony is that an intensely competitive business environment creates even more of a need for innovation, yet many business leaders choose to avoid conflict and foster conformity, as author Gary Hamel argues in his book *Leading the Revolution*.

Leaders need to offer a different attitude toward employees—one of partnership and alliance rather than parental arrogance. Employees need to be educated to understand the real-world requirements of the organization, and executives must have the tools to teach their employees that conflict is a normal part of the workplace.

What leaders need to do is give workers a new set of skills and a new way of thinking about conflict—a more creative approach—one that neither avoids disputes nor fans the fire of anger in destructive ways. Executives need the ability to harness the energy of conflict to fuel innovation.

No matter whether you're a finance wiz, a marketing genius, an accountant extraordinaire, or an operations magician, your success is actually less connected to your college degree than it is your ability to manage creative conflict and build consensus. Welcome to the worldwide market. There are plenty of people eminently qualified to hold your title. What will separate you, and your division or company from the pack, is the power inherent in a good fight. While you may have studied other approaches, this book is truly a powerful roadmap for yourself and your organization. If you don't think that's true, answer this question:

What is your business plan for effectively dealing with conflict?

If your answer is "We'll work it out," think again. Most organizations are spending more energy dealing with dress codes or what's served in the company cafeteria than with having a functional plan for inevitable conflict.

The great news for you is that dealing with conflict effectively requires a skill set that is learned. It's not about having good instincts, or being extroverted, or being a born people person. Driving a car is a learned skill. Reading a balance sheet can be taught. Playing a sport requires practice—so does navigating conflict.

A recent survey of recruiters and CEOs ranked good people skills as the number one attribute they sought in employees. Other research has pointed to "interpersonal conflict" as the reason most people leave jobs. An American Management Association study found that managers spend 25 percent of their time refereeing conflicts. As individuals, we spend 50 percent of our time each day negotiating. Yet, what resources are devoted to giving people the skills to do that effectively? How much time do leaders spend demonstrating and teaching employees how to harness the force of creative contention?

In order to survive and have a chance to thrive in what has become a wobbly work world and an intensely difficult business climate, both you and those you lead must be able to embrace and use conflict. You must develop the ability to build broad support for your work and ideas through the use of strong consensus-building skills. Leaders must also learn to be *confrontable,* to welcome others' feedback and criticism in order to drive innovation and creativity.

This book takes you through the essential attitudes, skills, and systems you need to instill in your organization.

How to Have a *Good* Fight

There are three critical elements to having a good fight:
1. Assume leadership.
2. Be on purpose.
3. Prepare.

This book will demonstrate how those three key factors create the creative synergy for a good fight that adds value to your organization and advances its mission. Briefly, the first element, *assume leadership,* is all about assessing the costs and benefits of raising a particular conflict. It's crucial to recognize that difference between productive and destructive conflict. Healthy conflict is a normal, natural, and productive part of life, unhealthy and *destructive* conflict is not. The central question to ask repeatedly is, *how important is the conflict?* If the issue is important, it's equally important to be proactive. Take the lead in improving your own approach to conflict and model for others in your organization the power of doing the same. Embrace conflict as a healthy chance to change what's not working into something more successful.

The second key, *be on purpose,* is the power that drives through obstacles that need to be overcome in order to embrace the conflict. Allow the broader purpose, the higher meaning to be significant enough to fuel the effort required to transform the conflict. There is no doubt that conflict innovation takes work and skill. Skills are honed by practice; there is no substitute for rolling up your sleeves and doing the work while your eyes are focused on the prize—the larger goal. It is purpose that helps to sustain the challenging effort necessary to skillfully and elegantly harness the power of contention. That purpose will also allow you to look for the creative edge that exists in good conflict.

The third key is to *prepare for conflict.* Every noteworthy strategist plans for the conflict before it ever happens, and then, in the midst of a dispute, pauses to prepare more. It may not seem reasonable, but actually, it's very rational. It's just that pausing to plan is counter to the typical knee-jerk response that conflict often evokes. There are ten steps to conflict success outlined in Chapter 11, "The Top Ten Steps: How to Use Conflict to Your Advantage," and these are virtually foolproof when put into practice.

A Practical Approach

There are some other helpful books on conflict resolution available. Many, such as *The Mediation Process* by Christopher Moore, focus on third-party conflict resolution. While *The Power of a Good Fight, Executive Edition* will briefly touch on that issue, this book primarily focuses on *direct conflict resolution*—the situation in which you, as a leader, are directly involved in the conflict. There are some excellent academic books that dissect conflict very well; they are also rather lengthy tomes that are impractical for most overextended executives!

Other useful books, such as Fisher and Ury's *Getting to Yes*, focus on negotiation and assume that you can walk away if the deal doesn't work. The problem with these approaches is that most leaders assume that negotiation is something different from the every day conflict processes in which most of us engage. I prefer to believe, *conflict is simply a negotiation that we don't know we're having.* These so-called negotiation skills are of limited use for most leaders since they assume the involved parties can simply walk away from the conflict. While technically true, an executive who repeatedly leaves posts because of destructive conflict skills or an inability to confront conflict is destined for a short career ladder. Moreover, books such as these focus on resolving the conflict rather than using the conflict to drive creativity.

> This book focuses on *using conflict as energy to mold problems into innovation solutions.*

In this book I offer practical strategies and skills that will assist you in fostering an environment in your own organization that values conflict and productively embraces contention. It won't happen overnight, but there are numerous tips to incrementally, but steadily, move the needle. The book is a "user-friendly" overview of the issue with a strategic view you can begin using today to immediately improve both your attitude about conflict and your own approach.

Conflict Resolution Options

There are many ways to approach conflict. Certainly one of the most popular options throughout history has been to resort to war or other forms of violence. At the opposite end of the spectrum are those who simply surrender rather than face conflict. Along the spectrum in between is the "California Method," in which the disagreeing factions spend time in a lovely hot tub together with the misguided assumption that warm "bonding" will mitigate the issue. Appealing to a higher authority—manager, leader, mediator, or judge—is also a popular, although costly, approach.

This book focuses on options that offer more ROI through learning to value conflict and create productive disputes. The *interest-based* conflict approach is the concept that a skillful and productive conflict process can actually create new and more innovative solutions that would not have been possible without the conflict. The interest-based conflict approach is different from conflict resolution or negotiation systems that operate on a zero-sum premise in which one party necessarily loses and another party wins. Those methods seek to provide ways to gain the most advantage and, thus, win the most in the situation.

This book avoids *third party decision-making,* which usually involves the use of a judge, arbitrator, leader, or other decision-maker who has the power to mandate a decision. More viable alternatives are explored that promote methods of cooperative decision-making. Cooperative decision-making differs from *third party assistance,* which requires help from a therapist, trainer, or mediator in the negotiation.

If you can challenge your own attitude toward conflict and recognize the creative edge your organization will gain through skillful conflict management, you and your company stand to reap very rich rewards, but don't take my word for it—read and learn!

Acknowledgments

Books are written by authors, but actually delivering a copy into a reader's hands takes much more than one person's work. I'm indebted to my agent, Michael Snell, who saw the potential of this book early on and guided me skillfully through the proposal process. Renee Wilmeth at Literary Architects helped me shape and refocus the book, while remaining cheerful and optimistic—everything a writer wants an editor to be.

On the home front, my hard-working and upbeat assistant, Shannon Duran, typed footnotes and proofed endless versions of this book without complaint. O.C. O'Connell offered last minute research. I'm thankful to my many clients who trusted me with their personal stories.

Long-time friends Peter Clarke and Susan Hazaleus helped shore up my attitude. My fellow "villagers," residents of my co-housing community in Golden, Colorado, offered in-the-trenches-training on the realities of dealing with thorny conflicts and the consensus process.

My parents, Joe and Wilma Eisaguirre, and siblings, Kim Jones and Lew Eisaguirre, provided moral support and their usual unflagging belief in my abilities—as well as teaching me much of what I know about good fights!

On the home front, Allison King helped care for my children with devoted attention so that I would have the time and energy to work. John Evans provided moral support as well as extra child care. And of course my kids, Elizabeth and Nicholas, worked cheerfully on their own books so that I would have the time to write mine. I love you more than any of my writer's words can ever express.

Chapter 1
Leading the Way: How to Leverage Conflict into Success

If two people on the job agree all the time, then one is useless. If they disagree all the time, then both are useless.

—Dale Carnegie

A group of eight senior managers gather around the conference table to discuss the merits of several companies vying to become the new IT provider for the division. Not ten minutes into the meeting, things turn ugly. The accounting manager sulks because billing functions aren't even among the top ten system features being evaluated. The IT manager is indignant that the operations people keep interrupting her presentation to explain the kinds of reports they need in order to measure performance against budget. When the IT manager directs the discussion in favor of a particular system, the vice president of operations lashes out that his staff is not getting the chance to participate in the selection process. The CEO detaches himself from the fray. The meeting ends in disarray and open hostility.

And the person who contributes most to the deadlock? The CEO. His style of conflict resolution is to avoid it. He refuses to assume leadership in conflict. As a result, not only do conflicts continue to fester without resolution, but his organization is losing its creative edge and its most innovative employees who resign in disgust at the lack of forward progress on their projects.

1

Sound familiar? Unfortunately, you're not alone; scenes like these are repeated in the hallways and offices of workplaces everywhere.

According to the American Management Association, your best people are spending about 25% of their time dealing with unproductive conflict in the workplace. That's about two hours a day your staff is burning up fussing about disagreements instead of creatively approaching and harnessing conflict to focus on core objectives, sales numbers, production schedules, or bonus triggers. Can your organization afford that?

The more teamwork your organization needs in order to function, the higher the number of potential unproductive conflicts. In the information field, for example, large companies such as AT&T—with different business units making up the whole—have to knit together the pieces a customer needs. This requires an agonizing amount of teamwork. AT&T estimates it expends 80% of its energy in responding to a customer's request for complex systems with fighting, negotiating, and jawboning internal stakeholders into line. Only 20% is devoted to actually listening to and selling to customers. These ratios are not unusual for many companies.

If you want your organization to thrive, you and your management team must learn to expect conflict, confront it, and skillfully harness the power. You must learn how to have *good* fights and how to teach others to do the same. If you're an executive, you may have instinctively learned how to do this but may lack the strategies and skills to pass your approach on to others. This book will help you do both. Contrary to popular misconception, these are learned skills and attitudes more closely related to leadership not personality. If you learn to harness conflict and practice the skills, you can become one of the most respected leaders in your organization. Why? Because innovation and productivity will improve, collaboration will increase, staff members will feel valued, turnover will decline, and you'll beat the budget.

It's that simple. Move toward success by recognizing and understanding the causes of destructive conflicts.

If you're going to be viewed as a *leader* in your organization and survive and thrive at work into the next century, you must develop your own conflict approach *and* develop a reputation for leadership in conflict management and consensus building. Today, unproductive conflict increasingly disrupts most workplaces, lowering productivity and morale.

What this book asks you to do is to assume *leadership* in conflict resolution. By that I mean I will encourage you to be the person who first steps up to the plate to embrace conflict. In order to do that, you'll need to change your most basic attitudes about the role of conflict in the workplace.

Many professionals tell me that they chose their profession—HR, sales, marketing, or information technology—because they like people *or* because they want to avoid dealing with people.

Either way, they view conflict as the enemy. I constantly hear my clients complain about wanting to move to a job where there is "less conflict" or where "things are less political." My experience is that conflict-free organizations are rare. Even if you do find one, an apparently calm organization may not deliver on the professional's true needs. Conflict—skillfully resolved—tends to develop more creative, innovative, and vibrant organizations. As Jim Aubrey, former president of Meredith Corp. emphasizes:

> If you think managing conflict and managing diversity are loaded with problems, then you haven't thought through the problems of managing sameness. I'd far rather be faced with trying to achieve harmony and good will among people who are at one another's throat than try to square an ounce of innovation or creativity or risk out of a company full of photocopies of each other.

We need to move toward embracing conflict as a friendly force to be directed and used, not avoided like the enemy. Leadership involves learning to value conflict.

The Value of Conflict

Why should we value conflict? Because research has shown it's necessary in order to drive innovation and creativity. According to author and business expert Gary Hamel, in *Leading the Revolution*, fostering innovation is the number one issue most businesses must face in order to stay competitive today.

What is the relationship between constructive conflict and innovation?

Many researchers have found a direct link. For example, Robert I. Sutton, professor of management science and engineering at Stanford University, author of a *Harvard Business Review* article titled "Weird Ideas that Work: 11½ Practices for Promoting, Managing and Sustaining Innovation," notes that most experienced executives would reasonably expect that creativity would flourish in a fun, low-stress workplace where conflict is held in check, managers keep a close watch on how money is spent, and people use their time productively. Yet, after studying creative companies for more than ten years, Sutton has found them to be "remarkably inefficient and often terribly annoying places to work where 'managing by getting out of the way' is often the best approach."

He finds that managing for creativity means "taking most of what we know about management and standing it on its head . . . . It means taking perfectly happy people and goading them into fights among themselves."

His research and decades of other research prove that good fights succeed by increasing the range of a company's knowledge, by causing people to see old problems in new ways, and by helping companies break from the past. These conditions produce the rich soil for creative work.

Start with Hiring

Researcher Sutton emphasizes that creating constructive conflict needs to start during the hiring process. In fact, he suggests hiring people who make you uncomfortable—even those you don't like—in order to find a few useful misfits who will ignore and reject the organizational code, increasing the variety in what people think, say, and do. This is exactly the opposite of what most people do, which is to hire people who "fit in" based upon a manager's chemistry with them.

Taking a risk on hiring at the executive level can be a bit more difficult. Many senior managers come up from within the firm. Sometimes CEOs have to examine the possibility of hiring from outside even if there's a good candidate internally, just to mix things up a bit. Taking a risk on a hire at the executive level becomes more difficult. If the hire doesn't work, the greater the potential for damage to the company, the team, the morale, and most importantly, the balance sheet. Yet because the need for creativity and innovation in today's competitive environment is so great, even that risk may sometimes be worth taking.

I remember, for example, the hiring process we used at the large Denver law firm where I was a partner. We received many resumes from young graduates of prestigious, traditional east coast law schools who thought it would be fun to move to Colorado to ski. We doubted, however, that they would fit into our litigation-driven law firm environment, which tended to favor smart aleck, entrepreneurial self-starters. In order to screen out any suspected wimps, or to be polite, candidates who we knew over time wouldn't have the chops to cut the day-to-day pressure and be effective in legal situations, we would, after formal interviews of the most promising candidates, take them to dinner at an old Denver restaurant called The Buckhorn Exchange.

This colorful eatery features animal heads on the walls—from anteaters to elephants—and an exotic menu ranging from snake to Rocky Mountain Oysters. We would sit in the bar drinking shots of tequila with worms in it and munching peanuts, throwing the shells on the floor. This interview-screening tactic resulted in hiring many people like us, but we lacked diversity and ultimately, I believe, limited the creative potential of the firm.

Today, it's generally not considered professional or acceptable to take a senior-level candidate out and order him or her tequila shots, but these sorts of interviews served a purpose. They made us feel like we were hiring someone who would fit in—someone who was "one of us." Today, while we might not interview an executive over beer and peanuts, we weed out diverse candidates in many more subtle ways. We make hiring decisions based solely on whether or not the candidate has good chemistry with the interviewer or dresses well—or that they "think like us." But the problem is that if we only hire people who think like us, we're hiring people who lack innovation, diversity, and creativity—or people who can force it through the conflict of simply being different.

Creativity researcher Sutton mentions, for example, a toy company where managers kept hiring people who pretended to "think like us" during the job interviews, but showed their true colors after being hired by pointing out how bad the company's products were. Although irritating, the complainers turned out to be crucial to the company's success because they kept coming up with innovative ideas for new toys ("probably just to spite us," in the words of one manager). The toy company got lucky by finding their managers were hiring employees who turned out to be helpful. But what would have happened if the CEO had a team of "yes men" on his senior management team? Would he have been so lucky? CEOs have a smaller margin for error, but if they can manage the conflict that difficult people may create, the business will have more opportunity to bring in employees who can offer true innovation to the business.

Provoke Good Fights

Sutton has other ideas for managing for creative sparks. For example, he suggests you should encourage people to ignore and defy superiors and peers—and get them to fight among themselves. You should also reassign people who have settled into productive grooves in their jobs and start rewarding failure, not just success. He cites the example of 3M's former CEO William McKnight, who once ordered a young employee named Richard Drew to abandon a project he was working on, insisting it would never work. Drew disregarded the order and went on to invent masking tape, one of 3M's breakthrough products. Drew's perseverance also laid the foundation for 3M's defining product, Scotch tape.

Similarly, in *The HP Way*, David Packard brags about an employee who defied a direct order from him. "Some years ago," he writes, "at an HP laboratory in Colorado Springs devoted to oscilloscope technology, one of our bright, energetic engineers, Chuck House, was advised to abandon a display monitor he was developing. Instead, he embarked on a vacation to California, stopping along the way to show potential customers a prototype."

House was convinced he was on to something so he persisted with the project, even persuading his R&D manager to rush the monitor into production. The resulting $35 million in revenue proved he was right. Packard continues: "Some years later, at a gathering of HP engineers, I presented Chuck with a medal for 'extraordinary contempt and defiance' beyond the normal call of engineering duty."

Such scenarios could never have occurred if Packard and HP hadn't created an environment that welcomed good fights.

One of Professor Sutton's most well-supported ideas for managing creativity is that you should find some *happy* people and then get them to fight. He emphasizes that he's not talking about provoking personality conflicts or relationship issues; battles between people who despise one another squelch innovation. *The fights you need to cause are all about ideas.*

Bob Taylor, a psychologist turned research administrator, first encouraged this kind of conflict among the computer scientists from various universities he funded while at the U.S. Department of Defense's Advanced Research Projects Agency (ARPA) in the 1960s and later at Xerox PARC in the 1970s. These scientists and engineers, perhaps more than any others, are responsible for the technologies that made the computer revolution possible, including personal computers, the Internet, and laser printers. The computer scientists Taylor funded through ARPA met at an annual series of research conferences, as retold by Michael Hiltzik:

> The daily discussions unfolded in a pattern that remained
> peculiar to Taylor's management style throughout his career.
> Each participant got an hour or so to describe his work. Then
> he would be thrown to the mercy of the assembled court like
> a flank steak to a pack of ravenous wolves.

"I got them to argue with each other," Taylor recalls with unashamed glee. "These were people who cared about their work. If there were technical weak spots, they would almost always surface under these conditions. It was very, very healthy."

All of this healthy conflict, Sutton found, generated a lot of new ideas. And every bit of solid theory and evidence demonstrates that it is impossible to generate a few good ideas without also generating a lot of bad ideas. Successful leaders reward the generation of ideas themselves. Former Time Warner chairman Steve Ross had a philosophy that people who didn't make enough mistakes should be fired. That's an anomaly, though. Few companies tolerate failure, let alone reward it. Ross used the power of creative conflict strategically.

How Creativity Springs from Conflict

Many other researchers agree about the link between conflict, innovation, and creativity. For example, authors Sy Landau, Barbara Landau, and Daryl Landau, in *From Conflict to Creativity*, point out that going all the way back to Hegelian philosophy we find the assertion that a new idea emerges as the "*synthesis*" of a battle between a *thesis* and an *antithesis*."

Similarly, Peters and Waterman in their book *In Search of Excellence* cite the example of Procter & Gamble, which has encouraged the idea of "creative conflict" since 1931, encouraging competition among its various brands. Peters and Waterman cite other innovative companies such as Exxon and Citibank, pointing out that their meetings were far from tame affairs:

> The difference between their behavior and that of their competitors is nothing short of astonishing. They make a presentation, and then the screaming and shouting begin. The questions are unabashed; the flow is free; everyone is involved. Nobody hesitates to cut off the chairman; the president, a board member.

How, you may be wondering, can something that feels so terrible to most people and make many so angry, actually be good for the organization? Because when you allow conflict, you encourage employees to be themselves.

CEOs have had various names for this created conflict. Jerry Hirshberg, president of Nissan Design International in San Diego and author of *The*

Creative Priority, calls it "creative abrasion" and encourages creative contention on projects by purposefully putting together people from different professional and cultural backgrounds. Hirshberg's innovative design shop has created some of the most interesting cars and other designs in the market by focusing on each team's creative edge and encouraging the kind of ripe and juicy conflict that leads to innovation.

Professor Kathleen M. Eisenhardt and her colleagues, publishing in the *Harvard Business Review*, examined the determinants of performance and innovation in technology-based companies. Some companies experienced virtually no conflict. They tended to have little group diversity, created fewer options, and generally suffered in effectiveness, such as time to market. Other companies had lots of conflict, but it was often *personal* in nature. These companies were also relatively ineffective because their interactions (when they occurred) were divisive and angry. A final group of companies was able to minimize interpersonal conflict while effectively managing *substantive* conflict. "Such conflict provides executives with a more inclusive range of information, a deeper understanding of the issues, and a richer set of possible solutions." As a result, they emerged as the most productive and innovative.

As she emphasizes:

> A considerable body of academic research has demonstrated that conflict over issues is not only likely within top-management teams but also valuable. Such conflict provides executives with a more inclusive range of information, a deeper understanding of the issues, and a richer set of possible solutions. Among the companies in our studies, the evidence also overwhelmingly indicates that where there is little conflict over issues, there is also likely to be poor decision making. 'Groupthink' has been a primary cause of major corporate- and public-policy debacles. And, although it may seem counterintuitive, we found that the teams that engaged in healthy conflict over issues not only made better decisions but moved more quickly as well.

Eisenhardt found that without conflict, the groups she studied lost their effectiveness. Managers often became withdrawn and only superficially harmonious. She found that "the alternative to conflict is usually not agreement, but apathy and disengagement." The teams in her study that were unable to foster substantive conflict ultimately achieved, on average, lower performance. Among the companies she observed:

> . . . . low-conflict teams tended to forget to consider key issues or were simply unaware of important aspects of their strategic situation. They missed opportunities to question falsely limiting assumptions or to generate significantly different alternatives. Not surprisingly, their actions were often easy for competitors to anticipate.

There are many more examples of the benefits of managing conflict at the employee and managerial levels throughout business literature and research, regardless what you call it.

This kind of creative friction helps organizations avoid the dangers of "groupthink," a term coined by Irving Janis. Janis described this phenomenon as "a mode of thinking that people engage in when they are deeply involved in a cohesive in-group, when the members' strivings for unanimity override their motivation to realistically appraise alternative courses of action." The groupthink tendency is really troublesome for creativity. Groups have illusions that everyone else is in agreement, self-censor doubts, and pressure dissenters. As a result, the group aborts divergent thinking and seizes too quickly upon options. Many of Janis's observations came from examining critical decisions of U.S. foreign policymaking where groups critically needed creativity.

The Bay of Pigs disaster was one of his examples. Pulitzer Prize winning historian Arthur Schlesinger, Jr., called the 1961 invasion of Cuba by 1400 ex-patriots one of the "worst fiascoes every perpetrated by a responsible government." Within three days, all of the invaders had been killed or captured. The major assumptions President Kennedy and his National Security Council held were entirely misguided. They believed that the Cuban population would spontaneously rise up to support the brigade of invading ex-patriots. They underestimated the ability of Castro's large, well-trained army and airfare to respond. And—to add insult to injury—the invaders landed in a big swamp.

How could a group of such smart people make such a dumb decision? At least part of the answer lies in the groupthink. Schlesinger, a member of Kennedy's group, later berated himself for his silence during the meetings:

> Though my feelings of guilt were tempered by the knowledge
> that a course of objection would have accomplished little save
> to gain me a name as a nuisance, I can only explain my failure
> to do more than raise a few timid questions by reporting that
> one's impulse to blow the whistle on this nonsense was simply
> undone by the circumstances of the discussion.

Interestingly, Kennedy himself later analyzed the fiasco and appointed his brother and attorney general Bobby Kennedy to be a special "devil's advocate" during all such future discussions. Historians credit his recognition of the problem with his success in handling the Cuban missile crises.

Richard Tanner Pascale's study of innovative companies found that they embraced paradox and tension. He points to Honda as an illustration of a company with "a contention-management system that facilitates, rather than suppresses, conflict." Because Honda is decentralized, it has conflict between its separate companies and departments. It decided to manage this contention in a productive way.

One of many approaches Honda used is called *waigaya*, which means "noise" in Japanese. During these regular meetings, subordinates are encouraged to openly though politely challenge their bosses.

With *waigaya*, Honda has cultivated communication skills of the participants and the facilitator to keep the meetings productive.

Honda also intentionally creates cross-functional teams composed of young and new employees who have the right blend of personality and knowledge and are likely to see the problem in new and creative ways.

Assuming Leadership in Conflict

As these examples of successful conflict illustrate, if you want to change the way you are perceived in your organization, you need to plan for conflict, improve your own skills, and assume leadership in modeling conflict management and consensus-building skills.

In order to succeed, you must first examine your own view on conflict: do you avoid conflict and, therefore, allow disagreements to fester?

Be careful if this is your personal conflict resolution style. Conflicts can devolve into a *negative spiral of conflict*. When we reach the bottom of the spiral, some important psychological changes occur: we're unable to see the opposing party or parties clearly; our perceptions of others will be clouded; we'll suspect every action, no matter how innocent. Psychologists call this *selective perception*. If, for example, I'm having a conflict with Jane and I walk down the hall and see Jane talking to Jim, whom do you think I will assume they're talking about? Me, of course!

What's significant about this change to selective perception is that we don't even realize this is happening. We'll continue to insist that we see the situation accurately. At that point, conflict is difficult to manage creatively and frequently results in personality clashes, litigation, or escalates into violence—tragic, unnecessary, and expensive outcomes. Therefore, the key is to assume leadership and be the first to try to embrace the issue.

A hundred years ago John Dewey, the great thinker, writer, and the founder of our modern education system, wrote: "Conflict is the gadfly of thought. It stirs us to observation and memory. It instigates to invention. It shocks us out of sheep-like passivity, and sets us at noting and contriving . . . . Conflict is a *sine qua non* of reflection and ingenuity."

If you triangulate conflict, you may need to learn to talk directly to the person with whom you have the problem, rather than to others. Complaining to third parties about the conflict results in what I call *triangulation strangulation*: the conflict process is *strangled* rather than resolved. If you need to ventilate, choose a trusted advisor—coach, counselor, or priest—outside the organization. This style is another way of avoiding—rather than valuing—conflict. We will return to a more extensive discussion of style in Part II of this book.

Consider the possibility of welcoming conflict and developing the balanced approach outlined in this book. Try to discover the *needs* and *interests* of all parties involved and invent creative solutions that address those needs rather than becoming polarized on *positions*.

Learning to work skillfully with conflict and to add consensus-building skills in your organization will help move you into leadership as a strategic business partner and leader in your organization. With this approach, you'll also be able to help those you lead do the same. One of the first jobs you need to assume is to uncover what causes good and bad fights.

Chapter 2
The Leader as Detective: How to Uncover the Causes of Good and Bad Fights

Too often we enjoy the comfort of opinion
without the discomfort of thought.

—John F. Kennedy

Mark Jacobs stared out of his office window into the darkening light. It was after 6:00, but he hadn't moved since he returned from the staff meeting at 5:00. All his management team today did nothing but squabble over things that seemed insignificant to him. Didn't they understand that he was a senior VP now and didn't have time to hear them squabble over when they would have the next meeting, why some reports went before others, or who would get to choose the new software providers? He couldn't get them to focus on the real issue: they were behind on their production schedule, and what were they going to do about it? Why couldn't they work together to solve the problem? Why did every little dispute ignite a new round of warfare? What was all this conflict about, really? Why did every discussion degenerate into person sniping?

Mark's musings and confusion over causes are not unusual. He understood his managers were trying to get as much mindshare for their teams as possible. But he felt frustrated that they didn't recognize his problems, too. He had less time than ever before and had to report to a CEO who expected him to just get the job done. He needed his team to work together. He needed to understand how to lead through conflict and manage it. In order to lead with conflict, we need to discover the causes in our organization. If we don't, it's much more difficult to value conflict. Instead, we will continue to think that life is unfair or that people are just too difficult. We especially need to uncover masked conflict.

What kind of conflict causes good fights instead of bad ones? Productive conflict concerns ideas, not personalities. Productive conflict is open instead of hidden.

The Causes of Conflict

Why do we have so many bad fights in the workplace today? Let's consider some contributing factors. Certainly media violence, including movies and the Internet, is one cause of more conflict. So is an increasing self-awareness of young people and women, both of whom are more able to assert themselves in contentious situations. At the executive level, we're also seeing the results of multiple generations of managers who grew up with an awareness and often exposure to conflict and pressure in the workplace.

Change in the workplace is another reason. We're working in a time where mergers, acquisitions, sales, and creation of entire new enterprises occur at lightning speed. All this change and the resulting conflict is not necessarily a bad thing. In fact, as psychologist Harville Hendrix has written, "Conflict is an indicator of growth trying to happen." Yet, when we resist the change, we fail to embrace the conflict and we become mired in it. Many people fear change, and fear spawns more conflict.

The increasing diversity in most workplaces also creates conflict because we have not effectively trained most workers to work with people who are different than they are. In addition, the use of email and other technology—and lack of training and communications skills—also causes conflict. People will often make comments or express sentiments in email that they would never say in person. When we fail to talk face-to-face, we miss subtle nuances of emotions and expressions that help us understand what the person talking really means. Abrupt statements by email or fax can create more unproductive conflict.

As psychiatrist Edward Hallowell has postulated in his book, *Connect,* many executives now spend their day staring at computer screens rather than having human contact. He started researching this issue because many of his successful executive clients were all dealing with clinical depression. For Hallowell's practice in Boston, this was a change. He asked them what was different about their work life. They all gave him versions of the same explanation: "I used to spend my day mentoring people, talking to my team, coaching my managers. Now I spend most of my day dealing with email or voice mail."

Hallowell's research found that this is actually causing chemical changes in our brains, leading to depression and mood swings. People in this state frequently have more unproductive conflicts.

Many executive teams are also moving toward a less hierarchical structure and toward a more team-oriented environment. This can be a good thing and yet it requires a more sophisticated set of skills, especially conflict management and consensus-building skills. Finally, most executives are forced to do more with less, in these days of shrunken budgets and downsizing. They simply may not have the time or energy for productive conflict.

All of these reasons point to more conflict in the workplace and yet, after the participants in my workshops have listed all of these reasons, I frequently list one overwhelming cause: life.

Life causes conflict, especially because life isn't fair and we all have to deal with change and loss. When we're not conscious about our own grieving process, we may project our feelings onto others in the workplace and cause unproductive conflict. We all have different needs and interests than those with whom we live and work. Most of us have been raised and educated with the idea that we cannot embrace conflict, work through it, and have all of our different needs and interests met at the same time.

Yet more often, if we're willing to be honest about our needs and creatively explore ways of meeting everyone's needs, we can satisfy many of our interests much of the time. We can actually develop a more creative idea than what we planned before working through the dispute.

The bottom line: we can't wait until we move to an organization without conflict, until the difficult people leave or until the current emergency is over to improve our own approach to conflict. And as managers and executives, we often have to lead not only by talking to key employees about this fact, but we have to lead by example. We have to presume that it's up to us to assume leadership in conflict. We have to assume it's up to us to serve as models of skillful and creative conflict management. In addition, we have to insist that those we lead develop good conflict management skills and take the lead in their own teams by demonstrating creative conflict resolution.

The Mask of Conflict: Identifying Conflict in Organizations

One of the first steps in assuming leadership in conflict is to learn to identify issues before they escalate out of control, because other issues often mask conflict. If conflict is masked, we're not really seeing the value of conflict.

For example, can you identify the hidden expressions of conflict in the following:

Why can't they do their jobs?

Why do we always have to clean up their messes?

That's not my job!

Because we're all dependent upon each other in the workplace, and each worker's efforts impact the success of another, unresolved conflict creates a climate of blaming, whining, and griping.

Our department always gets the shaft. We have to get our share!

No one appreciates our effort.

The sales guys get whatever they ask for!

All organizations have limited money and resources. If leaders fail to address and skillfully embrace these issues, turf battles and perceptions of unfairness and favoritism emerge. Every department will feel that it needs more than it's getting.

Don't bother to complain. No one listens.

You know what happened to the last person who spoke up!

Just stay away from him and you'll do fine.

Expressions of apathy and cynicism infect organizations where conflicts around limited promotional opportunities, small pay raises, or ineffectual leaders are the norm. When individuals aren't rewarded for creative conflict management and collaboration, they'll spew forth negativity.

If they weren't so difficult (or stubborn or gossipy), we'd have a better place to work.

Negative judgments about co-workers or managers are expressions of unproductive conflicts. If people don't respect each other, they'll blame and complain. These kinds of attitudes are long running spirals of conflict.

Can you see the *masked* conflict in the examples above?

What we mean by a masked conflict is one that doesn't express itself directly. Instead, it may appear as a specific complaint or more generalized whining, as in the preceding examples. If, for example, as a leader, you hear someone complaining that their department always "gets the shaft," you need to ask the obvious questions about why they believe that to be true. If they provide specific examples that seem plausible to you, you need to investigate to see if the resource allocation indeed makes sense given the goals of your organization. If you find that the division of money and resources is in line with your goals, you need to go back to the complainers and make sure that they understand the reasons behind the allocation. Once they do, the complaining may die down or they may present valid reasons to you for why the priorities need to change. If they do, as a leader, you need to consider whether their assumptions are correct.

All organizations must struggle to resolve issues of limited resources, time, abilities, and personnel, yet the conflict-skilled organization with strong models of collaboration and creativity can find direct ways to master these challenges. Leadership involves recognizing conflict and embracing it even when it's masked. Masked conflicts create simmering and ultimately bad fights.

Why Fairness Is Not the Issue

When I suggest to people that they need to welcome conflict and embrace its creative potential, I frequently hear a chorus of "it's not fair." People believe, "I'm not really the problem, it's *those* difficult people over there."

We assume that those employees or managers or executives labeled as "difficult" people are the problem. We see them creating conflict and seemingly getting away with this. But what many employees, managers, and even executives don't recognize is that "difficult" people who are effective at leading may just have a different conflict management style than we do. And if we're honest, we'll find that most successful "difficult" executives are successful because they are effective with many of their managers and employees. Not everyone sees them as difficult. Those who are aggressive about confronting people, for example, tend to point to those who avoid conflict as the problem. Folks who are loyal and accommodating sometimes see people who are always raising issues as the "difficult people."

Mostly, we all seem to think that it's simply *not fair* that we should be the one to have to assume leadership and develop the skills to lean into conflict.

We believe that it's not fair that we work with people who cause conflicts or who avoid conflict. We haven't really accepted the reality that *life causes conflicts*.

For example, I was asked by our law firm's managing partner to coach a woman who was brilliant (and billed a lot of hours) but who was creating significant personality problems within the firm. I'll call her Esmerelda. Esmeralda came across to co-workers as highly critical, and I suspect that she was one of those people who sat in the first row in fourth grade, constantly yelling: "Call on me, call on me, call on me!" She was a tiny woman with a tall personality.

While it's good to give people feedback and offer suggestions in most organizations, it's better to wait a while when we're new. Additionally, Esmerelda was the kind of person who would not only advise you on how to write your brief, but would also tell you how to wash out your coffee cup and, when you were in the bathroom trying to have a little peace and quiet while you combed your hair, she would be telling you how to fluff it.

After a few sessions with Esmerelda, I was ready to give up. "It's not fair!" Esmerelda would wail. "I'm not the problem! I work harder than anyone else and I'm brighter than anyone else. I shouldn't be the one who has to change."

I made no progress. Everything I suggested was met with stubborn resistance—"it's not fair" and the cry that others, not she, were the problem. Finally, when her disruptive personality overcame the value of her work, the firm fired her. Esmerelda could not believe it. She was stunned. She arrived in my office when she'd been given the news with a fresh round of "it's not fair. I worked harder than anyone else. I'm smarter than anyone else and I even washed the coffee cups!"

She finally got to me. I lost patience and said something that wasn't very diplomatic: "Esmerelda, most of us learn at about age four that life is not fair. What happened to you?"

This was not a nice thing to say, but it got her attention.

After that, I started thinking, was that true? Did I really learn at age four that life isn't fair? I decided that my own epiphany came at age eleven when I had one of those life-changing experiences.

I attended the kind of small rural school where if you weren't at the Friday night football game, there was nothing else to do. Not exactly the end of the world, but you could see it from there.

I had a lot of energy as a child and I didn't think it would be fun to sit in the stands on Friday night. So, from the time I was in kindergarten, I decided that I would become a cheerleader. My friends and I practiced all through grade school.

Finally, we reached junior high and could actually try out for cheerleading. We were so excited. We practiced even harder. The big day arrived. The gym at school was full of kids, teachers, and the principal.

I did my cheer and I was great. Perhaps not as great as Esmerelda, but I was great. The next day the judges posted the list and my name wasn't there. I was devastated.

Even worse, at least one girl who had been selected was nice, but she was not as good of a cheerleader as me. I went home sick. My mother put me in a hot bath to calm me down. I cried for three days.

When I finally stopped crying, I realized that I still did not want to sit in the stands every Friday night. So, I looked at my options and decided to become a baton twirler. The only problem was, I didn't know how to twirl a baton. But I spent the summer practicing and in the fall was selected to be a majorette. I pranced out in front of the stands at least some of the time.

Life isn't fair. People in authority make bad decisions—such as the teachers in this case. How often has someone in authority made a bad decision about you? Instead of complaining about their unfair assessment, what did you do about it? Did you examine what was behind the problem? Or did you investigate other options—other creative solutions to overcome the problem? I may have been happy as a cheerleader, but if I hadn't failed to make the squad, I never would have learned to become a majorette—an experience that ultimately was better for me and made me learn and practice more new things than cheerleading would have.

Even though life isn't fair, we still need to take responsibility for assuming leadership in our life and in conflict. Believing that "it's not fair" is one of the primary hurdles to using the energy of creative contention.

We need to realize that both others and ourselves in our organization are constantly battling these feelings of unfairness and loss, and that these unrecognized and unaddressed feelings can frequently lead to unproductive and uncreative conflicts. We need to provide leadership so that our organizations can address these issues directly and skillfully.

How many corporate executives have stories about failures that led to great success? How many of your star employees have been fired or failed at jobs in the past? The key to managing conflict is to first recognize it, and then figure out what's causing it. Whether or not it's fair, it's reality. Learning to lead through it—and use it to your advantage—will result in success for you and your organization.

We need to stop avoiding conflict and welcome the creative potential in dealing skillfully with thorny issues. We need to change our thinking and attitudes about conflict and assume leadership. If we do, we will build trust, relationships, and creativity in our organizations.

Chapter 3
The Power of Purpose: How to Use Your Mission and Values to Embrace Conflict

I have fought a good fight, I have finished my cause, I have kept the faith.

—2 Timothy 4:7

In 1945 a young inventor looks around the ruins of his homeland. He takes $1,600 in savings, hires seven employees, and rents a room in a bombed-out Tokyo department store. They spend weeks sitting in the rubble trying to figure out what kind of business the new company should pursue. They brainstorm, fight, and sit until they agree upon a path. With that, Masura Ibuka founds Sony Corporation. Today, that global entity reveals the power of purpose.

A clearly articulated mission paves the road to organizational success as surely as the yellow brick road illuminated the way back home for Dorothy and the gang. It's easy for you or your organization to become hopelessly lost in destructive conflict without a landmark to guide it back to its focus. A defining focus serves as an organization's global positioning compass and gives it the drive to do the hard work of moving from conflict to connection, and then from connection to creativity. Creating a strong network of connection is a safety net that allows people to take risks, embrace conflict and challenges, and raise the performance bar.

That's why the first key to valuing conflict is perhaps the most important—being on purpose. It's difficult to change your attitude and embrace conflict without a clear sense of values and purpose. You may be thinking: *This is a lot of work, Lynne. All this conflict management stuff. I don't have time for this! I've got 99 voicemails to return. I've got 110 emails to return. I don't have time to redefine my organizational values.*

20

The only way I find of staying clear in order to effectively lead through conflict is to have a deep understanding of what I'm about, both in my work life and my personal life. It's also important to make sure our organizations are clear about how conflict relates to the mission.

Organizational Goals and Conflict

Conflict and creativity researchers agree that common goals, missions, objectives, and values are necessary to use conflict to fuel innovation and productivity. Researcher Eisenhardt, for example, in studying companies that managed conflict well, found that these teams minimized destructive conflict by framing strategic choices as collaborative, rather than competitive. "They did so by creating a common goal around which the team could rally. Such goals do not imply homogeneous thinking, but they do require everyone to share a vision." Steve Jobs of Apple and Pixar has said, "It's okay to spend a lot of time arguing about which route to take to San Francisco when everyone wants to end up there, but a lot of time gets wasted in such arguments if one person wants to go to San Francisco and another secretly wants to go to San Diego." Teams that can't find common goals can be hamstrung by unproductive conflict.

Similarly, creativity researcher Dorothy Leonard found that a "thoughtful, common mission statement does serve to unite people" during the conflict process. She warns, however, against the kind of generic mission statement— "to be a world class company"—for example, that many organizations create, but that have no real meaning for people.

The kinds of mission and purpose statements that help make conflict constructive are those that are specific and distinctive, Leonard found. Those, for example, that unite the group against a common enemy such as earth-moving equipment giant Komatsu's slogan, which was "Beat Caterpillar." Similarly, during World War II, the British produced radar, faster airplanes and computers in an unprecedented collaboration born of the common mission to defeat Hitler.

My own client, Sun Microsystems, has an informal mission: "to kick butt and have fun." Having clear missions helps keep these organizations on purpose during the inevitable conflicts. If you're going to encourage the sparks of creative abrasion, your organization must be clear about its values and purpose in order to build a creative synthesis.

Using Conflict to Fuel a Turn-Around:
The Sunflower Case Study

In fact, one of the best ways to turn an organization around is to both embrace conflict and to be clear about your values, mission, and purpose while doing so. That's what drove a major change effort and the resulting success at Sunflower Electric Power Corporation in the 1990s. I read the story of Sunflower's turnaround as a brief report in a small magazine and became very interested and researched it as a case study. It was clear to me that the twin drives of welcoming conflict while staying true to their purpose and values created success. Sunflower's experience can serve as a useful template in constructive conflict management.

Sunflower Electric Power Corporation was a cooperative power company based in western Kansas. In 1987, it was the first of several generations and transmission cooperatives (G & Ts) to default on critical debt obligations. Sunflower had to renegotiate its financial obligations; the debt restructuring agreement was signed just days before CEO, Chris Hauck, was hired in 1988. Sunflower and its eight members faced a plummeting local economy, double-digit interest rates, and the problem of what to do with their brand-new $500 million coal-fired Holcomb, Kansas power plant. The morale of employees was at an all-time low as they faced an uncertain future and criticism by the local press, and even feared cashing their paychecks in the local communities as they believed they were being blamed for the situation. Clearly, the company needed an infusion of creativity and innovation to manage its problems. The new CEO came in committed to redevelop and change the culture; he was specifically committed to breaking down organizational walls between work units as well as opening up decision processes to encourage participation from everyone.

CEO Hauck's predecessor had enforced an intense command-and-control culture that encouraged bad fights over protecting turf. Power was used to advance the self-interests of this previous CEO and some managers who followed his lead. One of his senior executives, for example, was a particularly abusive manager—utilizing an aggressive confrontational style I call "the pit bull." The manager frequently engaged in the practice of berating one supervisor until the man became physically sick. This supervisor and his group were so fearful of the executive and his predictable reaction to any mistakes they might make that they avoided taking the reasonable risks necessary for them to succeed. Their work performance was dismal and creativity was non-existent.

Hauck dismissed the executive and made clear to all employees that he counted on them to use their judgment, including taking thoughtful risks. While at first glance, it appeared Hauck had just fired his biggest problem employee, it was an example of looking at conflict through the eyes of his mission. Was the conflict valuable? Was it a good fight? In this case, no. After the executive was gone, and as the group came to believe that it really was part of their "job description" to risk reasonable mistakes, their performance improved dramatically and these improvements led to significant and much needed rate reductions. Dismissing the abusive manager and setting a different tone sent a message about the company's values and mission, and set the stage for building a better work climate.

As Hauck soon discovered, however, Sunflower's entire executive management was also seriously misaligned as evidenced by unproductive conflicts over decisions, recurring turf issues, and the withholding of information by managers.

Hauck initially defined the management difficulties as "people problems" that would go away if individuals could just be given the right psychological assistance to help them "fix" their personal shortcomings. Yet outside consultants convinced him that organizational development isn't just a matter of changing individuals; rather, they explained the importance of assessing the entire culture to grasp how effectively it functioned in decision-making, combination, and utilization of human capital. The consultants explained that to attack the most aggravating symptoms, such as "misalignment" and "dysfunctional behavior," without an understanding of what triggers and perpetuates them can lead to changes that make the problems worse rather than better.

What they found was that while the practices of the old regime had been renounced, people were not clear on what to do instead. The work environment didn't include any new coherent mission, cultural values, or norms of expected behavior. Rejection of old values had created a vacuum. Personalities had filled in the rest.

Hauck decided that his purpose was to hold himself and all Sunflower executives accountable to Sunflower as stewards in a much larger community. He and the executive team began to approach their jobs as being responsible for managing the assets of their members and helping employees do their jobs. Their jobs were to help people get their work done. Hauck laid out new ground rules—from now on everyone in Sunflower was to hold him accountable to act consistently with his stated values and purpose; and if anyone disagreed with his decisions, they were to confront him directly. He invited conflict, but *constructive conflict.*

Consistent with their purpose, senior managers decided on an overriding core value for how Sunflower would conduct business: above all else, people were to be treated with dignity and respect. Hauck's vision involved an organization where people at all ranks and in all positions took initiatives to solve problems creatively without fear of reprisal. He initiated a management leadership program where the goal was to promote a more open participatory style and to put an end to the turf battles and micromanagement that had stifled employees. He encouraged good fights. Follow-up assessments revealed that employees felt they were listened to more and that their input was solicited, but they were unable to tell whether their input made much difference.

Even though individuals were given training in conflict resolution, it wasn't enough. It became apparent that there was conflict within the executive team, including sensitive interpersonal conflicts. These bad fights were not getting addressed, much less resolved. An underlying "hot" issue was Hauck's own management style. While endorsing a more open, participatory work climate, his fellow executives often felt intimidated and unable to confront him when they had serious differences of opinion. Ironically, Hauck's management style was triggering significant personal conflict for some managers and executives. The more open process required a higher level of personal responsibility than most were used to and required them to assume leadership in conflict. Other executives also criticized Hauck for moving so quickly that he didn't give people enough time to absorb ideas. Personal style differences compounded the problem, leading to communication conflicts that led them to question each other's motives. They were not sure how much to trust each other. The focus was now on building a greater degree of trust among executives and managers. The solution was to openly address their styles and differences.

Addressing the interpersonal issues within the executive team was, at times, uncomfortable, but it enabled them to create the kind of team they wanted. Decision-making was more efficient; they were quicker to voice concerns or differences of opinion; they spent more time inquiring about one another's ideas and perceptions; and they had a better appreciation of their individual differences, needs, and perceptions, resulting in more productive conflicts. The executive team now had a shared vision and created more good fights and fewer bad ones.

This shared vision and new culture created better decision-making where the free flow of ideas was expressed and valued. Their creative collaboration and conflict management produced astounding rewards leading to a business arrangement that led to more than an $8 million annual reduction in Sunflower's rates. None of this could have been accomplished without the combined focus upon vision, purpose, values, and conflict management processes.

Now, as Sunflower learned, this is hard work—to be on purpose no matter what we're doing. But if we are, we won't get involved in petty conflicts and we'll go through the work that we need to go through to embrace and value the big conflicts.

Integrating Your Personal Mission and Values

What questions do you as an executive ask yourself every day?

How can I be on the road again? Why do I leave my family so much? What makes me keep sacrificing my personal life? My health? My freedom? What is going to happen when I burn out? Why do I bother to get up in the morning to go to work? What is my purpose in life? How is what I'm doing today serving my larger purpose? These are the questions I and every senior manager out there ask themselves every day in order to stay on purpose. Some of the answers? Because the company is important, because no one else can do this and I have good number twos in the office. Because if we invest this time on the road now, the company will be much healthier in the future. Because I am proud of the job I do and want to do it well. Because doing this job will ensure my family's security. Staying "on" our personal purpose helps us to constructively use conflict. But there may be some messages in there that aren't part of your personal purpose.

I would suggest to you that you need to have a purpose that is big enough to serve you in both your work life and in your home life, so there's no conflict of values between who you are at work and who you are at home. Now I'm not saying you should go into your boss tomorrow morning and start sobbing about your personal problems. But we need to have a goal that's important enough that we are on purpose no matter where we are.

I'm clear that my life's purpose is to limit the distance between you and me. If I'm involved in a conflict with you, my purpose is to close the space between us; to see us both in relationship. I ask: How can we use this conflict to enhance our relationship? My purpose, if I'm working with a group, is to look at how we can all come together as a community. How can we create more community at work and at home? How can we make the conflict work for the organization to create more innovation and creativity?

My twelve-year-old twins are going to be around in 2050. I want them to have a planet where people can talk to each other; where people can close the space in relationships; where people can have a real community at home and at work; where people realize that conflict can be embraced and managed and need not tear groups and nations apart. And if we practice conflict management and consensus-building skills, we can create more connection and community and find more creative solutions to our deepest problems. We can learn to value conflict.

There are, of course, many different models for determining purpose. The best one, I find, focuses on process, not outcome. Instead of having a purpose that we want to grow the business to $50 million in sales by 2010, for example, a process purpose would be that "I want to build a business where employees are proud and happy to come to work every day and our customers are proud and happy to recommend us." We might even have more subtle process purposes, for example, such as "I want to make sure that I focus on every person with whom I'm speaking today—my family or my employees—so that they will feel that I've really connected with them."

A process purpose allows us to integrate our lives. We no longer feel the same kinds of pulls between work, family, and community. We know that whatever we're doing or saying, no matter who we're with, we can be "on purpose." Such a purpose also protects us from feeling tossed about by the vagaries of the stock market, business sales, or family troubles.

The best way to find such a process purpose is to answer the question: What is true for the person I want to be in all situations and with all people?

Look for Role Models

To help you stay on purpose, it's important to look for models. Models help us realize what we can do. Certainly, there are the famous models of conflict transformation—people like Gandhi and Martin Luther King, Jr.—who were faced with enormous conflicts, but were so clear about their purpose that they never forgot what they were doing no matter where they were. They were able to embrace the creative potential in conflict.

Consider Queen Elizabeth I, for example. She ascended the throne in 1558 when England was in shambles. Impoverished, shackled by runaway inflation, and lacking both an army and a navy while facing rebellion in Ireland and enemies in Scotland, the English found a woman on the throne to be just about the last straw. They presumed that, as a woman, Elizabeth was unsuited for leadership and intellectually inferior to men.

Despite the widespread doubts about Elizabeth, she proved more than capable. Enemies and power-hungry lords regularly sought to overthrow her. She surrounded herself with extremely competent advisors, retaining some from the past and adding some of her own choosing. Elizabeth transformed crises into opportunities.

Her approach to conflict was unique in an "age of absolute monarchy, when many rulers were nothing less than dictators who would brook not debate over their decisions, Elizabeth was remarkably liberal. Typically unafraid of disagreement, she invited debate on the most important questions."

Another famous example of creatively managing conflict by staying on purpose is, of course, Mahatma Gandhi, the leader in the Indian struggle for independence in the 1930s. He pioneered the notion of passive resistance (successfully used again by Martin Luther King, Jr., in the 1960s) and organized a campaign of non-cooperation. Because of his efforts, India's public officers resigned, government agencies were boycotted, Indian children were withdrawn from governmental schools, and he orchestrated a complete boycott of all British goods. He called upon Indians to refuse to pay taxes, particularly on salt. (He chose salt because it was used as the basic commodity at the time, but was controlled by the British.) Gandhi led a historic protest march from Ahmadabad to the Arabian Sea and made salt by evaporating seawater.

Due to Gandhi's relentless and creative management of the conflict that crippled India, the Indian people gained independence in 1947.

In our own country, think of how radically our own path would have been changed if not for the willingness of Abraham Lincoln to embrace conflict. Lincoln was able to move beyond the bitter contention that had divided a nation. His moderate politics and oratory powers of persuasion kept the union intact. During his second inaugural address, he stated:

> With malice toward none, with charity for all; with firmness in the right as God gives us to see the right, let us strive on to finish the work we are in; to bind up the nations' wounds; to care for him who have borne the battle and for his widow, and for his orphan—to do all which may achieve and cherish a just, and lasting peace among ourselves, and with all nations.

Other examples of plunging into conflict because of a powerful purpose include Elizabeth Cady Staton, Susan B. Anthony, and Lucy Stone, who stormed into the center of controversy by seeking to secure voting rights for women. Protestors heckled and physically attacked and threatened their quest. After splitting from the abolitionists who refused to fully embrace the rights of women to vote, the suffragists sought to change the law state by state. In 1869, Wyoming passed legislation giving women the right to vote. Over the course of the next 50 years, 13 states followed suit until finally, in 1919, the 19th Amendment to the U.S. Constitution was passed. The courage of these women to embrace conflict radically shifted the course of American history.

All of these historical examples can help keep us on purpose during our own quest through conflict.

One of my personal favorite models is someone who might not be as well known—a woman named Elizabeth Glasser. In the '80s she found out she was HIV positive. She received the virus through a blood transfusion. Glasser passed it along in the womb to her two children before she knew she had the virus.

Although it was a devastating blow, Glasser took on AIDS as a cause. Not many people knew at that time that children could be HIV positive and that kids could get AIDS. So Glasser found that doctors, hospitals, and schools discriminated against her precious children. She sought out the discriminators and started forums where they could meet, share their fears, and creatively resolve their conflicts. She went on the road and started speaking about AIDS. Glasser brought the term "pediatric AIDS" into our vocabulary and raised millions of dollars for this particular cause.

It's interesting because she was a tiny person—under five feet and less than 100 pounds—a shy wife and mother who never worked outside the home. Yet she learned how to speak publicly because she was on purpose and believed in her cause. In fact, Glasser was asked to speak at the 1992 Democratic Convention. I'm told that before she spoke, she looked out—there were 20,000 people in the live audience, 20 million more watching on TV—and was absolutely petrified. Glasser was afraid that she wouldn't be able to talk. They had to put a step behind the big podium because she was so tiny that she couldn't see over it without one.

Glasser wrote that just before she stepped up she thought she might not be able to find her voice, but she felt someone grab her hand and help her up the steps. She was able to give a powerful speech and influence many lives. Glasser realized later that it was the hand of her daughter who had died two years earlier.

If you're on purpose, I promise you—no matter what conflict you're in, no matter what challenge you're facing—someone will step up to hold your hand and help you do whatever you need to do.

So, what's your purpose? Please get clear about it if haven't already.

One of the most useful tools for conflict transformation is for us to clearly hold a purpose to build partnerships, alliances, and communities. If that goal is a part of our purpose, both as individuals and organizations, we will be able to stay more committed to embracing the conflict instead of running away or seeking to flatten the opposition.

A Suggested Purpose: Community Building

Is anyone else as sick of networking as I am? When I attend a function I tend to zero in on the people I want to talk with professionally. If not, I try to leave them alone—after all, they're trying to do business as well. If someone is overly solicitous to me and wants to "get to know more" or set up an "informational meeting" just to "exchange contacts" or "see if we can find a way to do business together," I'm turned off. I don't have time to brainstorm ways I can help them. Do they just want to add me to their "contact management program"?

Stop "managing your contacts." I know this is contrary to every bit of career advice you've received in the new millennium, but trust me. The future does not belong to networking; it belongs to partnerships/alliances/communities. Building these kinds of relationships is a skill that successful leaders naturally have.

Let the difference in those words sink in. *Network* has a cold, metallic ring. *Networking* has acquired a superficial meaning. It's the word linked to using people; it's the word of takers. I know many bright, capable people whose careers have stalled because—even though they believe they should engage in networking—something in their soul rebels. These are caring, connecting kinds of people. The idea of networking leaves them cold.

The future, I believe, will not reward superficial connections. If you want to thrive in your industry or profession, think deep, think long-term, think partnerships, alliances, communities, and education. Giving back by helping educate the next generations of people in your industry is a great way to foster a long-term community and culture of change and be a leader. Think giving, not taking.

Creating more opportunities for people to get to know one another will automatically, as Deborah Tannen writes in *The Argument Culture*, create more productive dialogue and fewer uncreative arguments. "One of the most effective ways to defuse antagonism between two groups is to provide a forum for individuals from those groups to get to know each other personally. What is happening in our lives, however, is just the opposite." Yet, in our high-tech culture, when many of us spend both our work and our private time staring at computer screens, we are going in the opposite direction.

Partnerships, alliances, and communities imply equality—especially equal initiation and participation—as opposed to *networking*, which implies one person latching onto or using another. These words symbolize long-term, deep commitments to other people and organizations.

I don't mean to suggest that you must stay with your present employer, boss, or co-workers for life. But even if you leave, would it serve you and them to leave on the best terms with a commitment to maintain your relationship, to continue to include them in your community?

I must confess that my bias on this issue comes from a philosophical perspective. I believe that we have a responsibility to respect and serve and assist others in our pathway through life. We are all connected in a fragile web—whether we like it or not. I view the Internet as a wonderful (if flawed) reminder of this truth. If we don't take care of our connections with others, these precious, connecting strands tend to tangle or break. When we disconnect from someone—because of creative conflicts or lack of attention—we are both lessened.

Dr. Edward Hallowell's book, *Connect*, makes this point brilliantly. A respected psychiatrist, he details our need for connection on a physiological as well as an emotional level. His clinical practice, especially his work with depressed patients, has proved to him that our modern age, where so many of our contacts are with screens—TV, videos, computers, and movies—rather than with each other, is causing us physical and emotional pain. He came to his conclusions after studying his executive patients: successful men who had the jobs, power, and material wealth that many people envy. Yet, they were increasingly suffering from clinical depression, Hallowell found, a huge change in his practice from ten years before.

When he asked them what had changed about their jobs, they all said the same thing: "Ten years ago I spent my days meeting with groups, coaching people, mentoring people. Now I spend my days staring at a computer screen." This experience, in addition to his review of experiments with animals, has convinced him that the lack of human contact causes damaging chemical reactions in our brain. Literally, we connect or die. And, ironically, one of the best ways to connect is to work through a conflict with someone.

Creating connection and community isn't just a "touchy-feely" idea; there's hard evidence that it creates real productivity gains.

Researchers William Judge, Gerald Fryxell, and Robert Dooley conducted extensive interviews at eight U.S. biotech firms. They assessed innovation through an analysis of the "cycle times" of the companies' patents—the shorter the cycle time, the faster the new technology is brought to market. They divided the companies into fast and slow groups. They found striking differences between the cultures of the two groups. The "ability of management to create a sense of community in the workplace was the key differentiating factor. Highly innovative units behaved as focused communities, while less innovative units behaved more like traditional bureaucratic departments."

There are, of course, many ways to build communities. A virtual bazaar of online groups, blogs, and communities explodes daily for every business and interest. When used judiciously, and without using these groups as an excuse to avoid human contact, valuable communities can result. The phenomenal success of My Space, for example, has shown us a new way to connect. The site has changed the music industry, for example, by giving new bands a revolutionary way to gather new listeners. Businesses are now adding to this community by building their own sites, blogs, and online communities for customers, users, and potential clients.

In the innovative companies, leaders provided overarching goals, but allowed the scientists autonomy in reaching them. In the less innovative firms, leaders granted either too much or too little autonomy.

I'm convinced that the most powerful need we share as human beings is the need to move from *conflict* to *connection*, and then from connection to creativity. If you can make it a part of your individual purpose as well as your organization's purpose to constantly look for ways to create *connections*, many conflicts will evaporate and those you do have will be embraced and creatively transformed more quickly. Consider including *connecting* through partnerships, alliances, and communities in your own purpose.

How Do We Develop Partnerships/Alliances/ Communities?

When you meet someone new and interesting, or when you hear about a great team or organization, think: How can I help this person or group? What do I have to offer that could help their long-term needs and mission? What kind of partnership could we create together? How can we work together to contribute to the larger local and world community? How can we embrace and transform our inevitable conflicts in order to build more creativity? How can we have more good fights and fewer bad ones?

Try to respect everyone, but if you can't respect him or her, let that person pass out of your life. Don't build partnerships with people you believe are dishonest or evil. If you can't find a way to embrace conflicts and respect your coworkers, bosses, or owners as fellow human beings, leave.

If we think we can hide these feelings and they won't hurt us in our working relationships, we're fooling ourselves.

That's my rule. I simply don't work with people or organizations that I don't genuinely like and respect. I don't try to get to know someone unless I can see the potential for a long-term partnership/alliance/community. Luckily, I have learned to view life as a cultural anthropologist, appreciating many diverse thinking and working styles, and most people interest me—even when their values and personalities differ from mine—more than they irritate me. A kind of detached amusement at the flaws and personality quirks we all share as fellow humans bumbling along this strange path called life is an attribute we can all develop, I've discovered.

People today in our mobile, disconnected, distracted society are hungry for community. If you lead with your heart—and have cultivated the heart of a warrior so that you're not injured by every slight—you'll see opportunities to build community everywhere. Do it, even if you can't see any immediate payoff for your career.

Thirty years in the world of work in many different kinds of jobs, professions, and businesses has convinced me that *soul leaders*—those who build deep connections with people no matter what their skin color or their position, and regardless of whether they walk or wheel themselves into a room, come out winners—both personally and professionally—in the long run.

And really, what do you want on your tombstone: *"She Was a Great Networker"* or *"She Was a Great Community Builder"*?

Having this kind of attitude toward life will make your job of embracing and valuing both everyday and more difficult conflicts much easier. It will help propel you and your organization through the hard work of transforming conflicts into creativity and building innovative consensuses.

Chapter 4
Five Beastly Conflict Coping Styles: Identifying Your Animal Instincts

---

The reptilian brain is hidebound by precedent.

—Paul MacLean

Bill looks out the window of the plane as it banks over the San Francisco harbor. He's just been promoted to Executive Vice President of the Prestige Hotel Group. After 9/11, the business suffered historic downturns, and he needs to turn it around fast. First on his agenda will be to encourage his new team of direct reports to work more productively together: Tom, whose response to the downturn has been to bark at his team to work impossible hours; Glen, who has been missing meetings and escaping early; and Susan, who, as the head of HR insists on bringing in catchy slogans on placards for every meeting, such as "There's a reason for everything," "Do your best every day," and "Use the Force." All of these styles lead Tom to demand why they keep hiring "kindergarten teachers" as executives.

Tom and the rest of the crew typify five basic coping styles that people use when faced with a conflict. Some choose to respond like a pit bull that's been taunted or dash away like a roadrunner. Others will wag their tails like happy golden retrievers, lay in wait like cobras going for the kill, or respond gracefully and swiftly like eagles. Each style has significant advantages and disadvantages.

While each of us is naturally inclined to a particular style, with practice we can adapt our style according to the situation and improve the outcome. In addition, with an awareness of the styles others use, we can learn how best to respond to them.

A key to embracing conflict and harnessing its creative power is to understand these different styles. Once you identify your own and others' styles, you'll be able to acknowledge and utilize differences to your advantage and value conflict as an opportunity to explore those differences and welcome diverse views as a key to creativity. You'll also be able to choose the style that assists you best in using the energy of the conflict.

Most of us, however, have not thought about how style influences our approach to conflict. In fact, the first time a pit bull attacked me, I was totally unprepared. I had no idea how to deal with other styles of conflict resolution.

How and When Do We Raise Conflict?

The answer to the question of how and when we raise conflict will tell us many things. One issue it will reveal is how much you value conflict as reflected by your conflict resolution style, and how skillfully you deal with conflict management styles that are different from your own. The answer will also tell us how likely the conflict is to be embraced and creatively used.

It's a delicate balance, I've learned. If we raise dispute too often, we run the risk of generating unnecessary emergencies or of seeming petty.

If we don't raise issues soon enough—if we're a classic conflict avoider—we may spin into the *negative spiral of conflict*, which means conflicts are less likely to be embraced. Conflict—skillfully embraced—builds trust, builds relationships, and builds our reputations as leaders in the organization.

What Is "A Good Fight"?

When I worked in law, I had a particularly nasty run-in with a very aggressive managing partner. When he verbally harassed me one day for no apparent reason, everyone suggested I chalk it up to "his style" of communication. But I couldn't let it go. I was so upset by the conflict that I called a "Johnnie Walker Red" session with a friend to ask for advice. None of my options seemed easy or risk-free and after a night of tossing and turning, I awoke the next morning with a queasy stomach.

When I got to work, I sat in my office drinking coffee and trying to work up my nerve to approach Claude. Finally, I took a deep breath and approached the lion's den.

Claude sat alone at his desk working on some papers. He didn't look up. I sat down on the couch in his office because my knees felt shaky.

"Claude, I need to talk to you about what happened yesterday."

He looked up from his desk and grunted. He wasn't breathing fire, but he didn't look pleased to hear from me.

I took another deep breath and continued. "Claude, you're my boss. You have a right to give me feedback. In fact, I welcome feedback. But I need to have criticism conducted privately, without yelling or profanities, and I need to have a chance to have a dialogue about it because, Claude, that mistake you were yelling at me about wasn't my fault. The client forgot to send me the form, and I'd been calling him for days trying to get it and he hadn't returned my phone call." There! I'd said it, all in a breathless rush. I sat back on the couch, exhausted.

Claude wasn't going to take this sitting down, say "okay," and apologize. He leapt up from his chair and started trotting around the room, ranting and barking: "Well, if you don't want anyone to yell at you, the way to avoid that is to not make any mistakes, and if you hadn't screwed up, I wouldn't have been yelling at you and I'm just going to have to talk to that *&^% hiring committee about how they keep hiring incompetent new associates and . . . ."

He was getting more and more agitated as he talked, stalking around the room in circles, talking, yelling, barking "rrrup, rru, RRRUP!" Finally, Claude yanked his phone out of the wall and threw it across the room.

Luckily, he missed me. I jerked back in my seat, took a deep breath, and repeated what I'd said earlier, using what I call the *broken record technique*. Claude just stared at me, frowning so deeply his eyebrows were practically touching, and then he started shouting and trotting again.

"You will never make it at this firm or any other if you have that kind of attitude! This is a tough business and you have to toughen up! We sometimes yell! This isn't a charm school . . . bark, bark, rrup, rrrrup, RRRUUP!"

I sat glued to my chair, eyes wide, trying to breathe and calmly repeat what I'd said before. This time I added, "You know, Claude, if I have to wait tables again I will, but I need to be treated with respect at work."

We went through several more rounds like this: Claude yelling, barking, and trotting around the room; me calmly repeating how I wanted and needed to be treated. Finally, he ran out of steam. He sat down at his desk, and we were able to have a real conversation.

From that day on, he treated me with respect. We had disagreements, conflicts, and many discussions, but he never again yelled or swore at me. We developed a highly creative and successful approach to our cases. He became a wonderful mentor to me, both at the firm and after I left. In fact, he remains a mentor to me today.

My discussion with Claude was what I call a good fight. And I think that conflict was the beginning of my interest in research on conflict. By accident, I negotiated the tricky terrain of handling what I now call a pit bull, and I managed to embrace the conflict by following most of the conflict management techniques I describe in the book.

The Five Basic Conflict Management Styles

Over many years in my consulting practice and research, I have come to categorize most managers into one of five style categories. While they may sometimes seem to fit some common social style indicators, mine are thinking style preferences, closely related to how we handle conflict. Through a combination of genetics and our personal history, these thinking styles seem to be "hard wired" into our personalities and reinforced by years of working environments. Just as we instinctively seem to prefer certain food or clothes, we have habitual ways of thinking and reacting that we don't often analyze. These ways of thinking are ingrained over time and difficult to change.

Many workplaces utilize complex social style typing systems to help managers identify and work with various personality types. However, the problem with these more complex systems is that they are difficult for most people to remember and use effectively. Most of us have trouble enough remembering our own four letters in the Myers-Briggs system, for example. We're hopeless when we're asked to recall and respond to the letters of all of our direct reports.

By contrast, my own "beastly" conflict resolution styles are vivid and easy to remember—since each style is likened to an animal whose traits it exhibits. Most users find that these types are easy to remember, coming to mind immediately when we need to identify and respond to someone who is using a different style. They also assist us in being more self-reflective about our own style.

While some people use more than one style and some a mixture of several, most of us fall into one style, especially when we're under stress and our backs are against the wall. Each style has advantages and disadvantages. Each has a different level of ability to truly value and embrace conflict.

The five styles are:

- **Pit Bull:** Attacks conflict, likes to argue and debate, threaten and intimidate. Highly competitive. Avoids concessions. Can be useful in all-out wars.
- **Golden Retriever:** Usually accommodates. Can be extremely loyal and has a need to please people and to be liked. Useful for team building and raising morale.
- **Roadrunner:** Avoids conflict. Can be difficult to pin down to determine interests. Can be useful in avoiding unimportant disputes or petty disagreements.
- **Cobra:** Triangulates conflict, talks to other people rather than the person or persons directly involved. Can be useful in building consensus among groups with little power.
- **Eagle:** Approaches conflict with skill and balance. Uses other approaches only when necessary after much thought. Truly understands the value of conflict. Constantly applies the ten steps of conflict management.

Is There One Right Style?

As you'll notice, every style has its pros and cons. Not any one style is ideal all the time, and no style on its own is always the right answer either. In managing conflict, we have to be careful to remember that we need to *all* use *all* of these styles at different times and in different situations in order to be successful.

The key to success is understanding what style you tend to use the most and under what circumstances you tend to use it. Most executives are good at managing conflict when things are calm. But when stressful situations occur or company circumstances call for quick action, many often use an unproductive style. We also use unproductive styles when we're responding to conflict in an automatic, emotional way. Why do we do this? The answer lies in what physical anthropologists, who study the development of our brains, call the reptilian brain.

Emotional Versus Thoughtful Reactions

What these anthropologists tell us is that we all have an old part of our brain that resembles that of a reptile. When reptiles are stressed, they respond with an instinct for "flight or fight." Humans still retain this instinct as well. To understand how this might work, imagine an avocado.

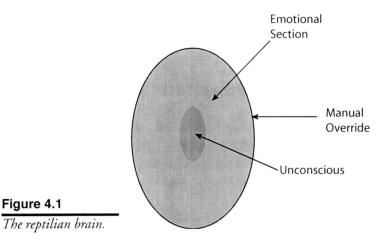

Emotional
Section

Manual
Override

Unconscious

Figure 4.1

The reptilian brain.

The fleshy part of the avocado is our regular emotional and thinking brain. The skin is that small part of our brain, the pre-frontal cortex, that serves as a manual override, pure instinct. The pit represents the unconscious part of our brain—basically, we have no idea what's going on there. Our task is to try to develop and access the thinking part of our brain, to override the emotional part and react with thought during conflict.

What we have to step back and understand during stress and conflict is the difference between emotional reaction and thinking reaction. When we react emotionally during conflict we're frequently generating and sustaining *personality* conflicts instead of productive conflicts over ideas, theories, and programs.

If we take a look at our beastly styles, we see that the styles of conflict management that avoid conflict—roadrunners, golden retrievers, and cobras—are simply accessing the flight mode of their reptilian brain. Those styles that tend toward aggression during conflict—pit bulls, especially—are simply reacting to stress with a fight mode. None of these extreme styles truly value and embrace conflict. Aggressive styles simply steamroll over others' needs and interests. Conflict avoiders also do not understand the creative potential in conflict.

Most of us primarily use one style in conflict situations. We use this style when considering new ideas and problems of conflict within ourselves as well as when we interact with others. What we need to do is learn how to utilize the right style for the right situation—and the right person we're dealing with. We need to learn to take the most useful characteristics from various styles and put them together for an innovative and productive solution.

Three Steps to Changing Your Style

For example, because of my training as an attorney and my innate personality (it's no accident that I became an attorney), I tend to use an analytical, argumentative, and critical conflict resolution style. If someone presents a new idea to me, I imagine all the reasons why it won't work. I will argue. I am a pit bull.

If I don't guard against this tendency, without thinking, I will begin to debate instead of discuss. Although this is a useful skill when engaged in an actual debate, courtroom battle, or a dispute with the plumber, this style creates disadvantages in personal and most professional relationships. I'm not seeking the creative spark in conflict, I'm simply running over the needs and ideas of others. This may make conflict management sometimes seem easy, but what I don't always notice is that others shut down or tuck their heads in to avoid having them torn off. It doesn't foster creative ideas or problem solving. Like a karate chop, it gets the job done but doesn't require skill to use it. Plus, if overused, I'm no better than the senior partner, Claude, I mention above. I've had to learn to reign in my pit bull tendency when it's inappropriate and to use other conflict styles.

Changing our conflict resolution style takes three things:
1. Developing an awareness of the style we primarily use.
2. Consciously choosing to use a different style when appropriate.
3. Finding the discipline to practice.

Most of us have not really thought about developing or using conflict styles other than our habitual mode.

1. Developing an Awareness of the Style We Primarily Use

How do you determine your own style? The following questions will help you assess your usual approach.

Pit Bull

Do you enjoy the give and take of a good argument?

Are you competitive—even in situations where the results aren't very important to you?

Do co-workers frequently give in to you because it's too much trouble to work things out?

Are there some people in the organization who avoid you or fear interacting with you?

If you answered "yes" to two or more of these questions, your habitual conflict management style is that of a pit bull.

Golden Retriever

Is loyalty one of your highest values?

Is it important to you to have your co-workers like you?

Do you give in during disagreements—even when you think you have a better idea—because you believe it's best for your team or organization?

Are you constantly trying to take care of the feelings of others or to make them feel better?

If you answered "yes" to two or more of these questions, your habitual conflict management style is that of a golden retriever.

Roadrunner

Do you generally avoid conflict even when the issue is important to you?

Are you frequently unsure about where you stand on a particular issue that others seem to feel strongly about?

Do you avoid certain people in your organization who have an abrasive or competitive style?

Do you prefer to have time to think before you speak or answer questions?

If you answered "yes" to two or more of these questions, your habitual conflict management style is that of a roadrunner.

Cobra

When you're upset with a co-worker, do you feel a need to talk to someone else about the issue?

Does the idea of confronting someone directly with your issues intimidate you?

Do others at your level of the organization come to you to talk about their problems with their co-workers?

Do you need to talk extensively about your feelings with someone before you're sure what you think and feel?

If you answered "yes" to two or more of these questions, your habitual conflict management style is that of a cobra.

Eagle

Do others frequently ask you to mediate their disputes?

Do you consistently step back from the emotion of a conflict and think before responding?

Are you able to see the big picture during disagreement?

Are you able to remember and consider your own goals as well as your organization's goals during an argument?

Do others tell you you're a good listener?

Do you understand how to use and value conflict?

If you answered "yes" to two or more of these questions, your habitual conflict management style is that of an eagle.

2. Consciously Choosing to Use a Different Style When Appropriate

This step requires us to develop the "manual override" thinking part of our brains. We need to learn to practice stepping back from the emotion of a dispute and to react with the most skillful response.

I'm not suggesting that we should "stuff" or ignore our feelings—emotions must be acknowledged and released—but we need to learn the proper time and place for that release. Frequently, it's not appropriate to dump our feelings during the heat of a debate. Perhaps we need to talk with a trusted advisor instead of the person we're upset with, write out our anger, or go for a walk around the block to cool off instead.

The following five chapters will help you decide when and how to use a style different from the one you normally use.

3. Finding the Discipline to Practice

Contrary to what may be a popular belief, a skillful conflict approach, one that values conflict, is a skill that can be learned, just as you practice a new computer program, your golf swing, or a new cooking technique.

The key is to find non-threatening situations to practice your new skills so that you'll be able to draw upon them during a more emotionally charged situation.

Some people naturally use different styles in different settings. A working mom, for example, may be a roadrunner in the office while dealing with a difficult boss, yet act like a pit bull drill sergeant at home when trying to organize her family for dinner.

There is nothing wrong with using different styles in different situations. The key is to examine whether the style we're using for a particular situation is the one that serves our goals as well as the goals of our organization.

How Do You Think and Approach Conflict?

If you only use one style, you may be limiting your future success. Looking at the way we think and react and learning how to approach conflict more creatively and effectively will be one of the most important skills you can learn.

If we recognize which conflict resolution style we're using at any given time, we can help improve our conflict management mode and clarify both the problem and the solution. We can consciously choose the appropriate style. Also, if we recognize that someone else primarily uses or reacts under stress with a specific conflict style that may be different from our own, that insight can help us step back from personality clashes and creatively solve the problem.

It's important to realize that none of these styles are right or wrong, better or worse. They are simply examples of style. The key is to try to increase the different styles we use to skillfully resolve conflict, solve problems more creatively, and prepare more effectively for the future.

If we open ourselves to the idea of thinking about style—of reflecting on how we think, react, and negotiate—we'll develop the ability to face whatever challenges we have in conflict with renewed vigor and with new and more powerful tools. This system also helps us depersonalize our conflicts with others by helping us detach from their personality and conflict style instead of judging them as "right" or "wrong" on any particular issue. Understanding that another's style is "hard-wired" helps us take their actions less personally. It helps us use the energy of the conflict to spark creativity and innovations instead of sinking into the murky waters of a destructive dispute.

Chapter 5
When the Pit Bull Attacks: How to Soften the Bite

You must watch your fear. Fear leads to anger, anger leads to hatred, hatred leads to suffering.

—Yoda

Steve Jansen is in his office working late. As the newest member of the senior management team, he wants to make sure his first financial review for his retail division goes well, so he's taking extra time to prepare. His comptroller ran additional year-over-year breakdowns that he thinks will shed some light on overall company performance. In order for some of the other vice presidents to look at their own comparisons, he sent some of the data out this afternoon. Just then, the senior vice president of the production division roars into Steve's office and slams the door. "Just what the hell do you think you're doing with these numbers?" he screams. "No one ever presents this sort of data without giving us all a chance to run numbers. It makes everyone look like fools." It even doesn't matter that a few of his direct reports are still in the office and hear the tantrum. The excitement about his year-over-year numbers that could spur some productive discussion and action has just evaporated, and he's now decided to just keep his head down, present his financial review, and not try to rock the boat. After all, he's new and doesn't know the political landscape yet. This pit bull could scuttle his executive career before it's started.

It's a dog-eat-dog world when a pit bull attacks. The fur flies, the growling turns deep, the fangs come out, and the intensity stirs up the adrenaline of everyone within hearing range. When it's over, the devastation takes its toll. The era of the aggressive, confrontational style of management that leaves in its wake a victor and the vanquished disguises organizational dysfunction. There are no sustainable spoils for the victor. In today's diverse workplace and global business environment, successful organizations are built from collaborative teams who value conflict, manage it creatively, and actively build a consensus. Pit bulls need to be understood and tamed. Unfortunately, the upper echelons of corporate America are full of them! Many people have risen to the top by using this style, because they may be viewed as decisive hard-charges who produce results. Most executives never realize the damage pit bulls can do since their attacks are often so effective, they stop discussion and ideas before they ever see the light of day. In today's competitive world, good ideas must be nurtured, not squelched.

Understanding Pit Bulls

Pit bulls appear angry. The number one tool to cope with a pit bull and move from conflict to creativity is to look for the emotion behind the anger—usually fear, hurt, or loss. *In the workplace, this translates to a worry that a valued position, or standing, or even perk might be lost, fear of not knowing something, or blustering through an uncertain situation, worry that someone will figure out a pit bull's lack of knowledge or understanding, or even loss of a small, seemingly inconsequential issue or argument that has an emotional value to the pit bull.*

To do this, you need to remember a bit about how our brains work.

Remember the emotional part of our brain that physical anthropologists call the reptilian brain? What this means is that when a threatening stimulus comes at us—through what we see, hear, or feel—we immediately react as a reptile would: flight or fight.

This is our knee-jerk reaction to fear. So, what's most important to know when you're facing an angry, attacking, debating pit bull is that underneath the anger is fear. Fear frequently leads to hurt or stirs up memories of past hurts. Frequently the fear involves the fear of loss, especially a loss of status, power, or his or her image.

Ask yourself of what this person might be afraid. Are they afraid of change? The perception that they're facing someone potentially more powerful? Do they fear losing face or their own power? If you can identify a potential fear or fears, you can answer that question, and it will help you measure your own response.

One of the best ways to cope with a pit bull is to allow them to ventilate, to talk themselves down from their fear/anger high. Pit bulls are like a balloon full of hot air. If you can provide the space for them to talk, they will simply run down.

Psychotherapists call this trying to talk the person *through* his or her emotions, rather than trying to talk him or her *out* of them. You do this by using techniques such as "active listening," which is paraphrasing back what someone has said to confirm, clarify, and pursue his or her train of thought.

A psychotherapist tries to help parties explore how they feel. They accomplish this feat by mirroring what's said rather than minimizing it. What this means is that even if the anger/fear seems petty or insignificant to you, you must validate his or her feelings. (Not as justified, but as real to them.)

For example, in the case of a boss who is mad that his work hasn't been completed, the assistant might say: "You're angry because your work didn't get priority. Is that correct?"

The surprised boss, expecting an argument, rather than snapping back, may respond: "Yes, I thought we agreed that you would do my work first rather than Bill's. If I don't get this to *my* boss today, I'm really going to be in hot water." Or he might engage in a host of other explanations below the feelings. This way you can find out what is really going on. It may take several rounds of questions and mirroring before you get to the crux of the fear.

By paraphrasing what people say without trying to talk them out of it, cheer them up, or immediately solve their problems, psychotherapists help clients become conscious of what's really bothering them.

It's important to learn to paraphrase rather than parrot. This means that rather than just repeating what someone says, you search for the meaning underneath his or her angry words and ask if you *understand* what is being said. This sincere effort will help you to defuse tension and anger and use the energy of the conflict to creatively solve issues.

Usually, when people are upset, they have a legitimate reason to be so. Try to acknowledge what they've said and move on to the creative solution to the underlying cause.

In cases where it's not appropriate to agree with someone, at least acknowledge his or her emotions and be willing to take helpful action by asking, "How can I help?" "What can I do?" "How can I make the situation better?" "I think I understand your *complaint* now, do you have a *request* of me?" Sometimes people fall into the habit of complaining about things without really asking for what they need to improve the situation.

Such gracious behavior defuses the complainer's emotions and prevents the situation from becoming explosive. By focusing on what can be done *now*—instead of what should have been done and wasn't—you can often remedy a problem or a mistake before it gets blown out of proportion.

This is skillful conflict management. This is the way an eagle would approach the problem.

The worse thing to do with a pit bull is to argue, attack back, defend, and debate. This just continues to pump up their already over-stimulated adrenal glands and leads to intractable conflicts. One of you needs to stay in your sane mind. By looking for the fear underneath the anger, you may be able to generate compassion for the pit bull rather than anger or fear.

You might also try humor. This often works with a pit bull if you're skillful. Be careful, the best humor to use is not something that pokes fun at the other party. Instead, use self-deprecating humor: poke fun at yourself or the organization.

Mainly, you need to be patient. If you allow pit bulls to ventilate, they will—like a balloon full of hot air—wear down. As a last-ditch effort when nothing else is working, try *emphatically* agreeing with them.

Be mindful of the effect of our communication habits. Some pit bulls are so used to defending, debating, and arguing that they will launch into attack mode without even thinking about whether the issue merits a vigorous debate. They may even believe that they like arguing or find that it is the only way they know how to attract people's attention and connect with them.

Transforming Your Own Pit Bull Tendencies

We all have our pit bull moments. Whether or not you find pit bull is your dominant style, when you find yourself launching into an unproductive attack, stop, breathe, count to ten. Ask yourself: *What am I afraid of here? Especially ask What am I afraid of losing or what loss have I already suffered? Am I feeling hurt or is what's happening reminding me of past pain? Is there a more skillful way to handle grief?* If you can't think of anything, spend some time by yourself or with a trusted friend, mentor, or counselor, trying to understand the underlying fear or hurt feelings. You might try writing all of your thoughts about the issue. Keep asking yourself: *What am I afraid of here? What hurt am I feeling here?* Then just write, keeping the pen moving on the page until something comes up.

Once you've identified the fear or hurt, ask yourself: Is this the best way to solve the underlying problem? Am I willing to use this conflict to spark creativity instead of indulging in my need to run over others' interests? Can I learn to engage in a creative dialogue instead of a win/lose debate? Will what

I'm doing alleviate my fear? Usually, the answer is no. Yelling, attacking, and arguing work only in the short run. You may win the battle and lose the war. The other problem is the harm this response does to your own body and health. When the adrenals work overtime, the stress response in our bodies leads to high blood pressure, ulcers, clinical depression, and heart attacks.

Pit bulls often consider themselves courageous. If you really are courageous, ask yourself the following: Am I courageous enough to reveal the underlying fear or hurt to the person with whom I feel angry? Usually, the very idea of doing this is enough to make strong men weak in the knees. You may be amazed to find, however, that if you do this, a miracle will occur in your communication.

For example, I coached an attorney, Joe, who was a powerful partner in a major law firm. All of the associates and many of his partners were afraid of him. Yet, when I talked with Joe I sensed a great sadness. After many probing questions, he finally admitted: "None of the associates like me; they won't even talk with me. They call me the 'prince of f------darkness'!"

This powerful person, like most of us, had a deep need to connect. For some reason, Joe had it wired that even arguments created some sort of attention and connection with people. He needed to learn another way: basically, being vulnerable and revealing his fears.

Do you think this was easy for him? Of course not. He resisted and persisted in arguing that to do what I was asking would be tantamount to professional suicide. I'm familiar with this fear. Again, it's our animal brain taking over and telling us that to reveal the soft underbelly of our emotions would be to leave ourselves open to wounding. What these people don't realize is that they already wound themselves in small ways every day by failing to connect with other people. They also injure their organizations by failing to harness the creative power of conflict because they simply run over the ideas of others or inhibit their co-workers from even offering a new suggestion.

I kept suggesting that Joe try responding my way by starting with small, perhaps unimportant interactions, and then notice what happens. Taking small risks and small steps is a good way to move along this path.

He did and was amazed at the results. Rifts with partners that went back years were healed. He learned to embrace conflict instead of attacking it. He was able to use his energy to work with others to manage his cases innovatively instead of spending his time in destructive disputes. He became a mentor to young attorneys at the firm. Rather than reducing his real power and strength, he increased his influence in ways Joe could not have imagined. This is the power of transforming conflict into creativity.

Chapter 6
When the Roadrunner Revs Up: How to Stop Others from Fleeing the Scene

---

Were we to fully understand the reasons for other people's behavior, it would all make sense.

—Sigmund Freud

Maria sighs as she walks into the CEO's office. As the Vice President of Corporate Communications, she's in charge of company public relations and outreach. She wants to start sending out targeted information to certain press contacts about the upcoming product delays. Based on more than thirty years of experience, she knows it's better to take the hits in small doses, instead of waiting until the press finds out and screams the headlines in the Wall Street Journal. *Yet every time she proposes the idea to her boss, he finds an excuse to take a phone call, talk with his assistant, or end the meeting to catch a plane. Maria vows that if she can't get him to focus on the issue today, she'll quit and accept the offer of a competitor who's been courting her for months.*

Maria's boss is a typical roadrunner. While a pit bull invites conflict, the roadrunner bolts at the first sign of trouble. Not only does every workplace have its share of roadrunners, just about every family has one. When a potentially controversial topic comes up for conversation at the dinner table—grades, in-laws, curfew, family, finances—the roadrunner slips away to do something that suddenly can't wait. Like the pit bull, the roadrunner responds to conflict with one of the most basic survival instincts known—fight or flight. However, the roadrunner prefers to take wing instead of taking heat. The problem with the roadrunner's strategy is that the conflict can't ever be creatively managed.

The user of this style doesn't value conflict or know how to harness its power to innovate. Since the roadrunner refuses to acknowledge the disagreement, there is no way to move beyond it. The conflict festers and frustrates colleagues, enmeshing them even more.

Working with Roadrunners

When I conduct workshops on conflict, a question frequently asked is: "Which style causes the most problems in workplaces?"

My participants are surprised to learn that roadrunners cause as many (if not more) problems than pit bulls. Avoidance and denial of conflict can be just as detrimental to using the creative spark of conflict as is the attacking, argumentative style of a pit bull.

Why do roadrunners run from conflict? The surface reasons are many, but the underlying reason (surprisingly) is the same as pit bulls: fear, hurt, or loss. Roadrunners are just demonstrating the flip side of our leftover reptilian brain: flight or fight. Instead of fighting, they choose to flee. Somehow, they have it wired that escape is easier than facing the issue head on.

The problem with this response is that problems do not get embraced and creatively addressed with this strategy. When people avoid conflict, it festers; it doesn't disappear and relationships deteriorate. At some point, when the conflict can no longer be avoided, the other people involved will become more and more frustrated and exhibit more unproductive confrontational behavior and more emotions. In a kind of weird conflict symbiosis, what some avoid will be demonstrated by others in the group. In fact, the pit bulls usually become even more pit bullish out of sheer frustration and the triangulators triangulate more. Instead of operating creative discussions about ideas, the entire conflict becomes even more unproductive and personal.

What Can You Do If You Work with a Roadrunner?

First of all, never chase a roadrunner. Chasing simply leads to even more frustration. Instead, you must tell them directly that you know they do not want to talk about the conflict. Do not speculate with them about why they are avoiding conflict or accuse them of hiding. Instead, the best approach is to ask them what you can do to make it easier to come to you directly. The first time you ask a roadrunner this question it is unlikely they will give you a response. But if you keep asking every time this conflict avoidance behavior happens, eventually they will give you some valuable information about how to work with them.

If they refuse to discuss the real issues with you, simply accept your lot, remind them that you're ready to talk whenever they are, and go about your business. It's important to act happy and productive when you do this so that you don't give them the impression that you're reacting to what they're doing. In addition, you should periodically circle back into their orbit and ask them if they're ready to talk about the issue.

I was hired by Bob, a CEO who always seemed to have several messy, unproductive personality conflicts brewing with his executive team and upper managers. Before I knew him well, I could not understand why such a nice, fair, and reasonable man kept creating so many conflicts around him. I did a lot of work mediating among the various warring factions below him. He seemed to be relieved to hand over the continuing problems to someone else. Finally, I discovered what was happening.

Bob avoided conflict, avoided making the difficult decisions his executive team needed him to make about people and policies. He tried to wait out conflicts, hoping that they would blow over. He did not understand the power of embracing the creative potential in conflict.

Every once in a while, conflict-averse roadrunners get lucky and find they can just wait the issue out. Sometimes the problem employee quits (without having to be confronted with a work performance plan) or the CEO decides to close the underperforming division, instead of addressing the turnaround issues head on. One thing about roadrunners, they do not make a big deal out of small matters.

For a CEO, the roadrunner attitude doesn't work. Decisions need to be made. Consensus management can be effective in the right situations, but this style can lead to an endless delay in what gets accomplished. Creativity is stymied. And continual avoidance can also leave the people affected by the conflict steaming with hostility. They want problems solved and they want them solved now. At the very least, they want someone to communicate with them on a regular basis about how the conflict is going to be managed. A conflict-avoider isn't going to be willing to keep confronting issues on an ongoing basis. They want to have the conflict disappear and not have to face the issue.

Bob spent a small fortune on my services, hiring me to come in to manage conflict among his executive team. Along the way I tried to coach him on how to be a better CEO, addressing what I thought was the underlying problem. But it didn't seem to work. Bob wasn't open to my gentle prodding about how his style might be causing the continual issues.

Finally, the head of their global conglomerate made an interesting suggestion: he sent Bob to a week-long leadership school at the Center for Creative Leadership, one of the country's premier leadership training programs. One of the hallmarks of the program is that they require feedback from each member of the leader's staff before they go. That way, they have that data and can present the results to the executive during the week. They also have structured exercises that help them understand their own style by having psychologists watch them during interaction and then give them feedback on their style.

After that week, Bob came back and told me that the sessions had helped him tremendously. "What did you learn?" I asked.

"I learned that people don't know who I am. I learned I needed to be more vulnerable with people and let them know who I am and what I *need* and want. I learned that people think I'm indecisive, avoid conflict, and fail to deal directly with issues."

This was an amazing leap of honesty from this man. *What does a fear of our vulnerability have to do with conflict avoidance? Everything!*

What's important to understand is that roadrunners run from conflict for the same reason that pit bulls start fighting: fear. One of everyone's major fears is that someone will find out who he or she really is and what he or she needs. Most of us, as children, have been given messages from the world in some way that who we are and what we need is not okay. When we become adults, it's understandable that this hiding has become so much a part of who we are—even those of us who are successful CEOs—that we don't even realize what we're doing.

Learning to value conflict, however, requires that we reveal ourselves and let others know what we need and think about the issues. If we don't, it's simply impossible to creatively work with the spark of conflict.

Bob's admission to me and his team was a major step forward in helping embrace the issues that constantly swirled around them.

What to Do If You're a Roadrunner

First, admit that this is your style and ask yourself whether this style is really working for you. Most people find the answer is no, at least if they use this style too often. It may seem easier in some ways to avoid conflict, but avoidance can wreak havoc with your relationships. All of the emotions you're avoiding expressing—that you're *repressing*—will be acted out in spades by the people around you. You may constantly wonder how you manage to attract so many angry, resentful, sad, or worried people. Here's why: they're simply expressing the emotions that you don't own. And they will continue to do so until you start appropriately revealing and owning your own feelings.

Every human being has emotions. There's no escape from this. Feelings pass through our bodies like changes in the weather. We can learn to appreciate all of them just as we welcome a change of seasons. The trick is not to deny that we have them, but to acknowledge them and find ways to appropriately express them. This is *Emotional Intelligence*, as brilliantly described in the book by Daniel Goleman. Goleman argues that people succeed, not because of their intellectual I.Q., but because of their emotional intelligence or E.Q. He provides a very important look at how to go about accessing and improving your own E.Q.

Until you're willing to take this step of owning and thoughtfully expressing your emotions and needs, you'll find it difficult to harness the power of conflict.

Next, learn to value conflict. As we explored in Part I, the conflicts we need to encourage, value, and use creatively are all about ideas, not personalities. Learn to appreciate different styles and embrace their contribution to the creative fuel of conflict. Learn to manage your own emotions so you can sustain your own participation in the messy process of working through a disagreement. If you can do that, you'll be able to use conflict creatively instead of feeling abused by its very existence.

Chapter 7
When the Golden Retriever Wags Its Tail: How to Teach "Just Say No!"

What's important in communication is to listen for what's not being said.

—Peter Drucker

The vice president of a Fortune 500 company conducts a performance appraisal with a key member of her management team over a wonderful lunch at an avant-garde restaurant near the office. She gives the employee a nice raise, catches up with the latest news about their respective families, and talks about future career plans. The lunch meeting is productive, upbeat, and enjoyable. A month later the vice president is stunned when she opens a letter of resignation from that employee. The vice president thought she had a great relationship with the manager. The resignation letter stings. The fact that the employee chooses not to tell her, but instead leaves her a letter, adds salt to a big wound.

Golden retrievers bounce around the office with an infinite supply of loyalty, innocent eyes, and energy. They seem happy, easy-going, trustworthy, and supportive of every decision. That's a great pet—not a great worker. Obedient dogs are to be treasured—no one wants a dog testing its creativity in the living room. However, an employee who always marches cheerfully to the corporate drum is an ambush waiting to happen.

Golden retrievers tend to say yes to everything—they take on extra assignments, they come in early, they agree with you *all the time*. Success is stymied because the golden retriever doesn't give honest feedback, explore creative alternatives, or challenge the status quo. This contributes to organizational stagnation, stifling innovation. Furthermore, in an effort to please, retrievers can burn out because they take on too much. Because they abhor disagreement, they can become passive/aggressive when the strain becomes too great.

55

Working with Golden Retrievers

What could be wrong with working with a golden retriever? Loyal, trustworthy, cheerful—aren't these the characteristics of an ideal worker? Yes, but . . .

The problem is that golden retrievers—like roadrunners—have a problem revealing who they really are and what they're thinking and feeling. The first you may learn that a golden retriever is unhappy and is leaving, for example, is when his or her resignation letter appears on your desk.

The other problem with golden retrievers it that they tend to say yes. *Yes, I agree with you. Yes, I'll take on the extra assignment. Yes, I'll be there early.* Agreeing with you all the time might seem like a gift, but the problem is that this style doesn't give a leader or co-worker the creative feedback he or she needs to be successful. What this leads to is a problem for organizations: they stagnate and can't keep up in a global market that constantly demands a proactive stance and new, creative ideas. Many old, slow organizations tend to be full of people who can't tell their leaders what they really think. This organizational dysfunction inhibits invention and growth.

A recent *Fortune* magazine article, for example—"Why CEOs Fail"—found that leaders don't stumble for lack of smarts or vision. Most unsuccessful CEOs stumble because of one simple, fatal shortcoming: the failure to put the right person in the right job and the related failure to fix people problems in time. *Fortune* claimed that the failure is one of "emotional strength," usually a mechanism for conflict avoidance and a misguided sense of loyalty.

Second, golden retrievers are highly susceptible to burnout. They may start engaging in passive/aggressive tendencies—saying one thing and doing another—as a way to be able to get some rest from the constant demands of work.

If you work with this kind of person, you need to constantly be asking them how things are going and what they need from you. If you're their boss, I recommend weekly one-on-ones where you ask two questions:

1. What do you need from me (or from anyone else in our organization) in order to be more successful at work?
2. Is there anything I'm doing or that anyone else here is doing that is interfering with your success?

Now, the first time you ask these questions, I doubt you will receive any useful answers. Most golden retriever types will simply stare at you like a deer frozen in headlights and insist that everything is fine. If you keep asking these questions week after week, however, you will eventually receive answers. Once you do, you can start giving this person what they really need. If you can't give them what they need, you must find a way to manage their expectations and directly address their disappointment.

Ironically, I've found even more golden retrievers on executive teams. Sometimes, leaders seek to surround themselves with people who reflect their ideas and attitudes. In addition, leaders in some organizations—especially traditional hierarchical ones—have risen to the top because of their enthusiastic way of not making waves. Retrievers also tend to over-commit, which can lead to burnout, stress, and the predictable health problems. At the executive level, the potential damage from leaders who discourage fresh thinking or simply take on more than their mind, bodies, and spirits can bear, spells disaster for an organization.

If You Are a Golden Retriever

You need to take care of yourself. You will find that you are highly susceptible to burnout. You need to constantly monitor your reactions to make sure that you are doing what you want to do and what you're capable of doing.

You need to learn to reveal who you are and to ask for what you really need. If you can't do that, you won't be able to creatively embrace the conflict. While using this style some of the time is fine—some disputes are not worth taking a lot of our time and energy to manage—if we use it too often, we will deplete our energy and ultimately fail to achieve what we want.

If you're protesting that you really are a golden retriever—constantly cheerful, loyal, etc.—beware! No one is. It's great to have those qualities as a part of your natural tendencies, but you need to recognize and admit your humanness.

All of us have unmet needs and interests that are different from the interests of those with whom we live and work. Learn to explore, identify, and creatively honor yours. Learn to value conflict as a creative fire for you and your organization and to actively participate in the process of innovative dialogues.

If you have unmet needs and unexpressed creative ideas, the organization will ultimately suffer. Your group needs all of your fresh thinking, as well as your most authentically passionate self. If you're suppressing problems, the organization's political landscape tends to become confused.

Chapter 8
When the Cobra Strikes:
Tangling with a Triangulator

When dealing with people, remember you are not dealing with creatures of logic, but with creatures of emotion, creatures bristling with prejudice and motivated by pride and vanity.

—Aristotle

Janet Olafson's team produces the company's quarterly report. She's responsible for working with an outside advertising agency, SG, to write the final copy. Henry, the president of SG, takes Janet to lunch at quarter close to discuss how things are going. In between glasses of an excellent Pinot Noir, Janet praises his team's work. Thrilled, Henry returns to the office and announces that they are a shoo-in to win the contract for the next quarter. Three days later, Janet delegates the job of firing SG to her director, Mark. The reason? Because SG's copy for the last quarterly report "reeked."

Janet is a cobra. Cobras have the perception—which may or may not be factual—that they lack power in the organization or with specific individuals. In order to feel more powerful they go around the person with whom they have a conflict to a third party. Cobras triangulate because they are *afraid* to talk candidly with others. Triangulation is a particularly insidious problem because it can impact numerous staff members, promote rumor-mongering, cause a host of repercussions, and divert time, energy, and productivity. For these reasons, cobras can be deadly. Powerful people who command attention in the corporate jungle are unlikely to be cobras. It's difficult for cobras to continue to climb the corporate ladder using solely their "end run" style. However, even executives sometimes have cobra-like tendencies when under stress. And all managers have to learn how to deal with cobras in their midst.

If You Work with a Cobra

Why don't they just talk to me face to face? Why is he always going behind my back?

These are the questions I'm frequently asked about triangulators. The answer? In a word: power. It takes having your own sense of personal self-confidence or the ability to be in control of your situation to be comfortable talking to the people involved in a conflict—or other business situation such as hiring or firing—directly.

Cobras—the term I use for people who do not resolve conflicts directly with others—do so because they're *afraid* to confront people directly.

Once you understand this dynamic, it may make it easier for you to deal with them. If you think in terms of our "fight or flight" comparisons, cobras are in the flight category; their behavior is a way of avoiding the direct resolution of the conflict because they can't manage the intensity of their emotions—how they feel—about a particular situation. If you are the leader or manager of a triangulator, you must make it clear to them that you will not tolerate that kind of behavior. Make talking directly to the person who can solve the problem a part of *their* job description. Otherwise, you will find yourself leading a group full of personality conflicts, politics, backbiting, and unproductive gossip.

If you work with people who triangulate conflict, first understand why they are doing what they do. It's not because they are sneaky, malicious, or untrustworthy—although they may also be all of these things—it's because they are *afraid* to talk with you directly. The good news is that with proper leadership and communications training, many cobras can be trained to become better communicators and change this style.

True triangulators can be rare at the executive level. But often senior managers and executives must manage large workforces where this style can infect and paralyze a team. Triangulating can also sometimes be the chief strategy of women and minorities, who tend to have the least amount of power in most organizations. (Think about historically how women and minorities have banded together into effective groups such as civil rights movements or women's groups before they've talked with anyone directly.)

And history has proved that they were correct in their approach. Most people in these groups have not had the power to talk honestly with anyone. These techniques led to the formations of large groups such as labor unions. Historically, workers have had less power than owners and, therefore, it has made sense for them to talk with each other first, organize, and then face management as a collective.

Once you understand what drives a triangulator, you can take constructive action. And you must act. If you just allow this kind of behavior to go on, the conflict becomes strangled—what I call *triangulation strangulation*—and becomes unresolvable. Triangle patterns can be complex and confusing. Once they form, they can be difficult to dismantle.

Why Triangles Stubbornly Persist

Interestingly, triangles tend to persist because they're stable. If people deal with conflict directly, yet lack a creative approach, the relationship may become too intense and perish. With a triangle, the third leg creates stability. The three can endlessly circle around each other. The conflict isn't managed creatively, but the relationship remains in place, although stagnant.

In fact, as explained by psychologist Dr. Roberta Gilbert in her book, *Extraordinary Relationships,* "a two person relationship is a delicate thing, prone to collapse in several different ways. Triangulating—bringing into focus a third party rather than solving the relationship problem of the original twosome—is only one of many ways primary two person relationship problems can be avoided."

Breaking out of the triangle is possible, however, Gilbert asserts, if the partners in a triangled relationship first see the triangle and how it enables the primary partners to avoid each other.

Why do we triangulate? Gilbert asserts that when anxiety rises between two people, they turn to a third and include that person in the situation in some way. This triangular arrangement seems to be more stable, it will continue longer, and contain the anxiety better than can the twosome. "Triangles are ubiquitous and automatic in emotional systems." In fact, Gilbert finds, they are the molecule, or basic building block of any system of people—family, an organization, or society itself. Therefore, the goal isn't how to escape them, but how to manage ourselves in triangles.

Triangles in organizations tend to rise when anxiety is more intense, and when the system is calmer, triangles are less noticeable. Managing oneself in a triangle takes "considerable mental effort." Basically we need to step back from the emotion of the situation and become more neutral.

It is important to become aware of all the forms that triangles take. In everyday life, they turn up in innocent activities, such as asking a third person to settle a disagreement between two others. In churches, workplaces, or social groups, triangles are ever-present, but they are more apparent and intense when anxiety is running higher.

How to Stop Triangulating

Once we realize we're in a triangle, Gilbert suggests, we need to ask ourselves questions such as:
1. What is my contribution to this pattern?
2. How am I triangulating?
3. How do I go about changing my part of the triangle?
4. What do I have to do to get emotionally more neutral and still communicate with both other parts of the triangle?

After you've considered your own part in the triangle, you're ready to approach the other person. These same strategies work if you're observing those you lead who are caught in a triangle.

The best approach is to ask to talk to the person in private and state the problem directly and empathetically. Take some responsibility in the conversation that acknowledges their fear. Consider what might be increasing the emotional intensity in the organization as a whole. Is there some threatening change taking place, for example? Is the business suffering through financial problems or reorganization? You might ask, for example, what it is that you have done to make it difficult for him or her to talk with you directly and what you can do to make it easier to talk with you.

Expect that it will take some time to gain this person's trust. You may have to have several sessions or several incidents before he or she will work with you to resolve the problem.

Be sure you name the game. Say, for example, "I heard you talked to Mary about 'x'. In the future, if you have a concern about 'x' and me, I'd like for you to talk with me directly. What can I do to make that easier for you? What can we do to resolve 'x' right now? If you need some time to think about possible solutions, when can we get together to talk about it?"

When you do persuade cobras to talk to you, you will need to make sure you practice all the skills in this book to embrace the conflict: be sure you listen to their point of view, restate, and look for creative solutions that meet everyone's needs. You will gain trust with this person by embracing a number of conflicts with them—not by avoiding the conflicts. Strengthen your own resolve by learning to value conflict.

If You Triangulate

If you triangulate, you need to work to develop courage. You need to utilize all of the strategies in this book to learn how to talk to people directly. You may even need to have a coach to help you work through matters. What you cannot do is continue to avoid these issues. The gossip train in most organizations is faster than the Intranet. People will hear what you say about them—and you may be quoted incorrectly or out of context. A more effective strategy is to find a way to talk with the person or persons involved in the issue.

A few years ago, I was hired to coach a woman named Lily who worked for a large corporation and had long-standing conflicts with two men—very powerful people in the organization—that she had never resolved. She had managed to work her way up to a vice presidency, and these two men also ended up being vice presidents in this organization. Lily didn't like them. In fact, she couldn't stand them, but believed she was hiding her feelings. However, over the years Lily's whisperings and complaints behind their backs had made the rounds. Even though she discreetly expressed her disapproval to others in the organization, Lily thought these men wouldn't hear. What she didn't realize was that everyone in the organization—including her boss and her colleagues—knew how she felt.

When I began her coaching, I told her "You know, you really need to work with them because I know the CEO expects all the VPs to work together as a team." And she would reply, "Oh, they don't know how I feel. I'm sure they don't know how I feel." Eventually, unbeknownst to Lily, her two male colleagues worked politically to force her out of the organization. And they succeeded. Lily was shocked.

When the CEO asked her to leave, the reason he cited was that she was difficult to work with, she wasn't "nice" enough. Since when is "niceness" a requirement for success in most corporations? The reality was the two VPs—and many others—knew that she didn't like them and had difficulty working with them. We really do telegraph how we feel to people in the workplace.

One of my favorite quotes is from Emerson, who said, "Who you are speaks so loudly, I can't hear a word you're saying."

What do power imbalances in organizations have to do with how cobras triangulate? Power imbalances—or even perceived power imbalances—create situations where people feel like they have to find another way to gain power. Add to that equation the emotional intensity and an inability to confront colleagues, managers, and direct reports about problems, and you have a breeding ground for cobras. Historically, women and minorities tend to be most likely to fall prey to the circumstances that foster cobras, but they're not the only ones. (There's a reason why there are only 11 out of 500 women CEOs of Fortune 500 companies. It's not the only issue, but there are still power imbalances at the top, sometimes much larger than at lower levels of management.)

I'm not suggesting that anyone—like Lily—should turn a blind eye to the power imbalances found in most organizations. I'm also not suggesting that you reveal your innermost feelings and fears during every workplace conversation; that strategy isn't skillful or smart. There is no doubt that most organizations have people who have more power than others and that there are those who sometimes abuse authority. But you need to recognize that differential and still find a way to skillfully communicate your needs and interests.

If you refuse to do so, you're failing to value the conflict and ignoring its creative potential. In addition, even if you do not personally behave in this manner, understanding why people triangulate will help you mentor those you lead. This kind of understanding is an essential part of eagle behavior, the subject of the next chapter.

Chapter 9
When Eagles Take Flight: The Sight and Skills to Soar

Eagle: any of several large, diurnal, accipitrine
birds of prey, noted for their size, strength,
and powers of flight and vision.

—Random House Dictionary

*Some 200,000 miles above earth's atmosphere an explosion rips through an oxygen
tank, and within three hours, the Apollo 13 spacecraft loses all oxygen stores, water,
electrical power, and the use of the service module propulsion system. Adrift in space
with only a glimmer of hope for survival, it would be easy for hysteria or a bad fight
to take over. Instead, command module pilot Jack Swigert calmly utters his famous
understatement, "Houston, we've had a problem here."*

*With lives hanging in the balance and an international audience watching the
rescue efforts, NASA departments could start blaming each other for the catastrophe.
However, calmer heads prevail. Under the skilled direction of Eugene Krantz, the
Apollo Flight Director on the ground, mission control assembles in a room to find
creative solutions before time runs out. Ultimately, ingenuity, collaboration, and
good fortune create the most dramatic and successful space rescue mission in history.
Using tape, cardboard, plastic bags, and parts of a lunar suit, the crew fixes the
life support system responsible for removing carbon dioxide from the spacecraft.
Navigating by the stars, they use the moon's gravity to slingshot back toward earth.*

None of these brainstorms would have happened if not for the superior
leadership and creative conflict management skills essential to success. Not
your everyday office dilemma, that's for sure.

We've all experienced death knells of a project or a budget request, but
barring extraordinary circumstances, we've never had to put our creative

conflict management skills to the supreme test. The lesson of Apollo is that with the eagle style, and that bird's powers of flight and vision, performance and results can soar far beyond the ordinary. Krantz, the Apollo Flight Director, soared with the best CEOs, even though he directed from the ground. Krantz consistently galvanized his team to solve the plethora of puzzles that bedeviled the historic flight. Eagle behavior is courageous, creative, disciplined, and highly functional. Using the eagle style, like Krantz, you will be able to take command of any situation with exemplary leadership.

Working with Eagles

If you doubt that successful leaders with eagle style welcome conflict, consider the case of Jack Welch, the legendary former CEO of GE. When he took over GE in 1980, the stock had lost half its value over the previous ten years. Welch told his managers that he wanted "a revolution."

He burned the "blue books," the five volumes of guidance for every GE manager that discouraged innovative practices. He launched the famous workout process, in which employees at all levels would gather for "town meetings" with their bosses and ask questions or make proposals about how the place could run better—80% of which must get some kind of response then and there. Welch created a cultural revolution. In an article by Geoffrey Cloven for *Fortune* magazine, an electrician put it this way: "When you've been told to shut up for 20 years, and someone tells you to speak up—you're going to let them have it."

Welch created a lot of good fights. The workout sessions' most important effect was to teach people they had a right to speak up and be taken seriously. Welch rewarded those who created new ideas as well as those who implemented them. He also encouraged good fights in his behind the scenes people practices. According to *Fortune* magazine: "When a manager meets with Welch, the exchange is candid, not scripted. There may be shouting. The manager will almost certainly have to stretch his mind and do new thinking on the spot."

The results of Welch's revolutionary style were startling. He transformed GE and multiplied its value beyond anyone's expectations: from a market capitalization of $14 billion to more than $673 billion in 2006. Today, GE is the second most valuable company on earth, behind Microsoft. And Welch is the most admired, copied, and studied CEO.

Many less-recognized eagles soar in other institutions. Consider, for example, a vice president of a large regional health care system that I interviewed. The organization was at war with its nursing staff in its home health division. Tensions escalated to the point that the nurses mobilized to unionize. Fanning the flames toward an unproductive conflict, one middle manager strangled the dispute by triangulating: she gave the nurses misinformation while concealing her acts from her own supervisor. The vice president successfully intervened.

She went directly to the nurses, called a meeting, laid out the ground rules for a productive discussion, and turned the situation around. She listened to their concerns, acknowledged the errors the organization had made, addressed the unfair pay scales, and made commitments about the future. The group brainstormed to create innovative solutions for the issues, the inequities that had simmered below the surface for many years, but that would never have been resolved without the conflict being directly and creatively addressed.

Two years later, the organization underwent a survey by Gallup and that division had the highest level of employee satisfaction in the entire hospital system. Moreover, Gallup said their rating put them at the top of all industries.

Author and business innovation expert Gary Hamel in his most recent book, *Leading the Revolution,* writes that businesses who want to create wealth must focus on "creating heretics" and get out of the trap of thinking conflict is poison.

Eagles do this instinctively. Heretics are welcomed into the fold as harbingers of change, virtual "canaries in the coal mine" who warn miners that they're low on air by dying before them. Can you view heretics with interest instead of irritation? If so, you are on your way to developing an eagle style. You are learning to do what you need to do to foster creative sparks.

It can take enormous courage to listen to controversial opinions or complaints, yet failure to do so can lead to disaster. Consider, for example, the managing partner of a large Midwestern law firm, Lewis, who sought my advice after a young associate complained of sexual harassment by one of their most prominent, successful, and politically connected partners. Because the young woman had a reputation of being "emotionally volatile," as well as "a bit seductive," the other partners and associates refused to believe her claims. In addition, the firm was proud of its record of hiring and promoting women so they were loathe to admit that there might be any problems.

Lewis brought me in and allowed interviews of all the women associates, despite intense criticism from his partners who insisted that he was over-reacting and stirring up a stew of problems. His partners felt so strongly about the issue that Lewis faced a near mutiny.

In true eagle style, Lewis held seemingly endless meetings with his partners and me, explaining to them why we needed to do a thorough investigation, despite their belief that the associate's claims were incredible and that the accused partner couldn't possibly have acted the way she claimed. He listened patiently to all his partners who stomped into his office, taking apart their lawyerly arguments one by one.

After talking to the other women, three of them revealed that they also had been sexually harassed by the same man, claims that never would have seen the light of day if Lewis had not been willing to listen to one brave and unpopular woman. Because he tolerated the one "canary in the mine," he averted an entire negative chain of events—including lawsuits. Lewis also adopted my suggestion that we conduct meetings with all the associates to explain what we were doing and why, in order to hold down the rumors and gossip. This move also raised his partners' hackles since they were convinced that we should try to hide the process from the associates. Based on my advice, he finally convinced them that whatever rumors the other employees were hearing were more inflammatory than the truth.

After the sexual harassment claim was resolved, Lewis led the firm through a painful self-examination. They were forced to consider whether their own perception of themselves as a great place for women to work and thrive was consistent with reality. Once Lewis began the dialogue, the floodgates opened and the women partners and associates detailed other, more subtle problems of unequal treatment. We held a series of workshops on gender issues for all employees where their underlying beliefs and prejudices could be explored. Although sometimes painful and contentious, the process ultimately resulted in a better working relationship for all employees. None of this could have occurred for the firm without Lewis' willingness to embrace the conflict and see the ultimate value in working through the process.

Consider, for example, the eagle-style CEO of one of my clients, the CEO of a manufacturing company. Bill inherited a management team riddled with conflict. He hired me to facilitate an executive retreat with his team. We did an exercise that I frequently use with groups where we draw a time line for the organization and have each person chart their own high and low on the time table. Bill was astounded to hear that many of the low points on the others' time table involved descriptions of his associates suffering through one of his blistering attacks. As the head of his operations department put it: "Listening to feedback from Bill about the Casey project was not only the lowest day at the firm, it was the lowest day of my entire life."

Before my eyes, Bill grew wings in an instant. After a moment of silence while he dealt with his shock, he jumped up and announced that they were going to do another exercise. He ripped out pieces of flip chart paper and started plastering them around the room. "OK, guys, here's what I want you to do. I want you to give me three things that you think I do well and three things where I need to improve. Don't hold back, I want to hear the best and the worse of it. The rules are that I can't say anything in response, and I need to write down what you say right here so that I won't ever forget it. Then I'm going to have it typed up, framed and hung in my office so that I focus on what you've said on a daily basis."

The quiet in the room was deafening. Finally, Linda, the V.P. of P.R. found her voice and started listing his strengths: he was decisive, visionary, and good with bottom-line issues. Weaknesses she saw were that she and others frequently didn't feel as if he heard what they said, he was impatient, and he didn't really seem to want to get to know people on a personal level, limiting, she thought, his ability to harness their strengths and weaknesses.

The other eleven subordinates followed Linda. Bill listened and wrote, saying nothing. When he was finished he thanked them, sat down, and said nothing. The team squirmed in the silence. Finally, the head of their global marketing team asked if he could go next. Bill agreed and that led to the entire team moving through the spontaneous feedback process.

Bill made good on his promise to frame his feedback in his office; the others followed suit. The lists became a proud company tradition and—far from avoiding feedback—led to the practice of executives actually welcoming suggestions and input and actually feeling left out of the process if they had yet to receive their lists.

Doing so will help you develop your own creative conflict skills.

Managing an Eagle

If you're managing an eagle, promote them! That's a joke but the reality is that they are rare birds. Be humble enough to realize that you can learn, even from your own subordinates. Ask, as Bill did, for their feedback, advice, and suggestions for improvement. Encourage them to serve as coaches, facilitators, and mediators for the others in your group. Study Chapter 17, "The Dogfight Referees: How to Mediate, Facilitate, and Survive," with them to help them develop those skills.

Interestingly, studies show that most managers spend 80% of their time dealing with the 20% of their people who are unproductive and create problems for the organization. In order to increase the productivity and innovation of your group, however, you should spend most of your time encouraging the upper 20% to be even more creative. The most successful CEOs in the world have realized this secret.

Les Wexner, CEO of the specialty retailer Limited Brands, realized this after the stock of his company plunged during the 1990s. Determined to uncover where he was making mistakes, Wexner decided to study the most successful CEOs. He shadowed director Steven Spielberg; Jack Welch, CEO of General Electric; and Jack Callaway, the CEO of Pepsi. Les Wexner found, to his astonishment, that they all spent their time very differently from the way he used up his days. While Wexner reviewed budgets, approved deals, and put out fires, Jack Welch told him that he didn't do those things. Instead, Welch and the others he studied spent most of their time encouraging their best people in doing their best work. With good teams working under them, these CEOs simply let their people do the things that Les Wexner found himself mired in. He changed his focus, and stock for his company, then named after their clothing store flagship, The Limited, rebounded. In 2003, Limited Brands was named the most admired specialty retailer by *Fortune* magazine. In 2005, the company increased its annual dividend 25% to $.60 per share and had 40% growth in the second quarter of 2006.

As a manager of eagles, you should spend most of your time learning how you can help them do their own jobs better. If you help make your best people even more productive and innovative, the effort will rebound to the entire organization.

What to Do if You're an Eagle

If you're an eagle, whether CEO and mid-level manager, you need to recognize your own strengths. Use your skills to influence your organization and to mentor and grow others.

Study the tactics and suggestions in Chapter 17 to learn how to expand your own natural conflict management style by offering your skills as a mediator and facilitator to your organization. Offering to serve as a facilitator for groups outside your own hemisphere of influence is a good way to showcase your talents.

You may not have realized how unique and valuable your style is. Honing these skills and taking the opportunities to use them with others can both propel your career forward and help your organization grow.

Chapter 10
A Creative Menagerie:
How to Harness the Unique Styles

The opposite of a correct statement is a false statement. But the opposite of a profound truth may well be another profound truth.

—Neils Bohr

Michael Johansson sits on the train headed to work, examining his Blackberry with a sigh. He is scheduled to run his weekly division meeting today with his direct reports, then he has to prepare a presentation, finish a marketing report for the senior VP, and fly to Minneapolis tomorrow. But his direct reports just bicker constantly. Sometimes he feels working with them is like mediating squabbles among his three kids; his technically talented team seems to have the social skills of a bunch of seven year olds. And he doesn't have time for it with everything else he has to do. Today, they have to discuss resource planning for next year's budget, and he can already predict how the meeting will go: Linda will charge in armed for combat with stacks of papers to buttress her department's extra fund requests; Manny will say nothing, but whine to Joe afterwards that his department never got a fair shake; and Tom will smile and agree to whatever anyone proposes yet will strike back later by procrastinating about requests from anyone he feels abused him in the budget process.

How is Michael somehow supposed to create order and teamwork out of this chaos?

Michael is struggling with a classic leadership dilemma: how to encourage different styles to utilize each others' strengths during conflict instead of pouncing on their weaknesses. He's also struggling with a factor increasingly becoming important to today's executives—time, or rather, lack of it.

Let's just admit it right up front: most of us think the way we operate is best. We think the world would run better, be better, even resolve conflict more creatively if others thought and felt the way we do. We don't really want to understand and work with the styles of people who behave differently. We just want them to conform to our expectations. Stubbornly, they refuse.

So we are left with a dilemma: we need to find a way to harness the creative strengths of others, respect their styles, and believe in their creative potential. Not an easy task for most of us. One way to begin is to understand that diversity actually creates more vibrant, creative, stronger organizations and to educate your co-workers to value diversity. A plethora of research points in that direction.

Diversity in the workplace comes in many guises: cultural, generational, professional, thinking, and conflict styles. A mix of all these diverse elements tends to make group dynamics more effective and creative—as long as the members have been encouraged to value differences and work well with those who are different.

There may have been a time when diversity just meant ethnic differences, but in today's workplace diversity must be addressed from a much broader perspective. Different generations, sexual orientation, national origins, new lifestyle choices, or even simple work/life issues like working remotely can all bring both positive and negative forces to the organizational mix. Today's successful executive needs to not only recognize that the "goth chick with the lip ring" might be a brilliant financial analyst, but also know how to make his team see past differences. He needs his team to embrace all excellent members regardless of their background, how they look, or even how they work because as an executive, he's also faced with managing their local employees as well as the groups in India and Scotland. Buzzwords such as "valuing differences" and "embracing diversity" may have been corporate luxuries at one time. In today's global environments with the looming labor shortage, they're critical executive skills.

The Creative Value of Diversity

Researchers have identified three primary reasons to value diversity in the workplace:

1. Diverse workplaces are more interesting;
2. Workplaces whose members reflect the broader community can better understand and meet the needs of increasingly diverse potential customers;
3. Diversity brings with it a variety of opinions and ideas that enhance creativity.

Laboratory research has consistently demonstrated that groups that are diverse with respect to abilities, skills, and knowledge perform more creatively than groups that are more alike.

To verify this finding in work groups, researcher Dr. Susan E. Jackson, Professor of Human Research Management and Director of the Doctorial Program at Rutgers University, contacted the CEOs of 199 banks and asked them to assess the level of innovation in their organizations and to identify up to eight people who are key players in their top management teams. Jackson found a significant relationship between the extent of innovation (in products, programs, and services) and the degree of diversity in "functional background" in the top management teams. That is, teams made up of people with different professional backgrounds, experiences, and thinking styles were more creative than those made up of only engineers, for example.

Diverse groups are more likely to avoid "groupthink," the dynamic identified by Irving Janis we discussed in Part 1, and thought to be responsible for foreign policy fiascos like the Bay of Pigs invasion. If loyalty to the group becomes too strong, members will quickly agree to decisions that the rest of the group seems to support. As Janis states, the unspoken norm in groupthink is, "Preserve group harmony by going along uncritically with whatever consensus seems to be emerging." In the disasters Janis explores, a handful of people with similar views were isolated from diverse thinkers and were discouraged from voicing dissenting opinions. Their decisions led to tragic outcomes.

To avoid these results and harness a group's creative power, we must think about how we build teams. Researcher and professor Teresa Amabile, writing in the *Harvard Business Review*, found that if you want to build creative teams, you must pay careful attention to the design of such teams. That is, you must create mutually supportive groups with a diversity of perspectives and backgrounds. Why? Because when teams comprise people with various intellectual foundations and approaches to work—that is, different expertise and creative thinking styles—ideas often combine and combust in exciting and useful ways.

She emphasizes that leaders must ensure, however, that political problems don't fester. Information sharing and collaboration support creativity:

> The more often people exchange ideas and data by working together, the more knowledge they will have. The same dynamic can be said for creative thinking. In fact, one way to enhance the creative thinking of employees is to expose them to various approaches to problem solving. With the exception of hardened misanthropes, information sharing and collaboration heighten people's enjoyment of work and thus their intrinsic motivation.

Most organizations don't follow this model, however, Amabile found. In fact:

> "creativity is undermined unintentionally every day in work environments that were established—for entirely good reasons—to maximize business imperatives such as coordination, productivity and control."

Amabile found that creativity demanded three facets:, expertise, creative thinking, and motivation. Harnessing conflict into creativity through diverse groups requires that we consider all three areas.

Area 1: Expertise

Expertise encompasses everything that a person knows and can do in the broad domain of his or her work. Take, for example, a scientist at a pharmaceutical company who is charged with developing a blood-clotting drug for hemophiliacs. Her expertise includes her basic talent for thinking scientifically as well as all the knowledge and technical abilities that she has in the fields of medicine, chemistry, biology, and biochemistry. It doesn't matter how she acquired this expertise, whether through formal education, practical experience, or interaction with other professionals. Regardless, her expertise constitutes what the Nobel Laureate, economist, and psychologist Herb Simon calls her "network of possible wanderings," the intellectual spaces that she uses to explore and solve problems. The larger this space, the better.

Area 2: Creative Thinking

Creative thinking, Amabile believes, refers to how people approach problems and solutions—their capacity to put existing ideas together in new combinations. The skill itself depends on personality as well as on how a person thinks and works. The pharmaceutical scientist, for example, will be more creative if her personality is such that she feels comfortable disagreeing with others—that is, if she naturally tries out solutions that depart from the status quo. Her creativity will be enhanced further if she habitually turns problems upside down and combines knowledge from seemingly disparate fields, especially if she is willing to consult with other experts in these fields. For example, she might look to botany to help find solutions to the hemophilia problem, using lessons from the vascular systems of plants to spark insights about bleeding in humans.

Area 3: Motivation

Motive is what drives any project. For some, it can be internal—our individual drive to discover something new and the excitement and reward that comes from thinking differently. For others, it can come from financial payoffs or status within the organization. External rewards can also arrive in the form of feedback from someone whose praise is meaningful. A combination of internal and external motivators drive the most successful creative teams. When a successful executive is motivated to succeed, he or she will work harder to drive a team to find solutions. Employees with a direct interest in the outcome—or those personally motivated by chance of advancement, recognition, or ambition—are often most interested in how to look at differences and find ways to innovate.

How Conflict Drives Creativity

Amabile's research points to creative solutions for workgroups. For this hypothetical scientist, if she is comfortable with disagreeing with others—and, in my experience, part of that comfort comes from appreciating different styles—she will be more creative. Also, the idea that she "turns problems upside down" and "combines knowledge from seemingly disparate fields" can be aided by an organization that supports and encourages the creative ferment of having diverse experts from different fields clashing and creating together.

In studying the differences in creative teams and those who were not, Amabile found that those who were the most creative had the most diverse professional and ethnic backgrounds. Although occasionally that diversity led to communications difficulties, "more often, it sparked new insights and allowed the teams to come up with a wider variety of ways to accomplish their goals."

In the teams in Amabile's study that were not so creative, managers damaged creativity with their approach. They were routinely critical of new suggestions. One employee told the researchers that he was afraid to tell managers about some radical ideas that he had to develop his unit of the business; he was wildly enthusiastic about the ideas, but knew that each one was studied for all its flaws instead of its potential. Surrounded by classic pit bulls, whose competitive nature leads them to criticize instead of embracing the conflict, he retreated, withdrew, and refused to share his own creative potential.

In addition to putting the right people on the teams with the make-up that leads to creativity, leaders must make sure to avoid squelching the very creativity they want to foster. So, in addition to building diverse teams as Amabile suggests, leaders need to then harness their unique style and allow enough time for them to clash and hash through the conflict to creative breakthroughs.

Building Diverse Teams

Building a team from a number of individuals with different work styles can be an important factor in your success. Can you can imagine the chaos created by a team full of pit bulls? Many law firms find themselves overburdened with pit bulls, creating endless personality conflicts and turf battles instead of the creative tensions more diverse styles may bring. The opposite extreme, however—a group full of golden retrievers and roadrunners—is also uncreative since people are afraid to express their issues and ideas openly and skillfully. The ideal? Teams and organizations with a balance of styles to foster the creative abrasion of success. What works is to emphasize that leaders and others must be willing to openly discuss the differences in style, ideas, and opinions that team members use to consider conflict.

What's especially useful is to encourage your team members to consider the advantages and disadvantages of different styles. Once they do, that will help them embrace the value in working with those who are different from them.

As you build your teams to capitalize on the best of each of our five beastly styles, think over them again and imagine what benefit having each on the team could provide. Imagine also the drawbacks and what will have to be managed with an open eye. If you get the mix right, you'll find that you have not only an innovative and productive team, but that all your team members will learn to moderate their styles using the most effective tools when necessary.

Pit Bulls

Ask yourself what might be the advantage of working with a competitive, abrasive pit bull. There are advantages. If you're engaged in an all out war, an aggressive and quickly moving conflict or problem that needs to be solved, where you've tried everything else and you're quite convinced that nothing else will help you resolve the issues, that's when you *want* a pit bull on your side.

Certain kinds of lawsuits, for instance, that you're convinced will have to be tried, not settled, or maintaining operations during a major crisis or disaster might be described as a war for your organization. At that point, you want someone who is geared for all out combat. The problem, of course, as we've previously explored, is that people who operate in this mode tend to do so all of the time without considering the long-term consequences of their actions. You'll have to constantly remind the pit bulls on your team that most instances don't call for armed combat, and that they need to cultivate an eagle style in order to utilize the creativity inherent in conflict.

Pit bulls also make good devil's advocates, a technique that assists groups in avoiding the pitfalls of groupthink. In addition, one reason many organizations put up with pit bulls is that they are sometimes some of the brightest members of the group. They can, in fact, be true geniuses who need your careful guidance in order to fit into the team. Although they can be notoriously prickly and not suffer fools gladly, fiercely individualistic and not team players, their inner lives can be fragile and vulnerable.

Because everyone needs the true geniuses to survive in the competitive world of the 21st century, not to mention creative and professional talent, many top managers spend time bolstering the fragile egos of their exceptional pit bull people, yet not in an obvious way. Says Mark Morris, choreographer and leader of the renowned Mark Morris Dance Company:

You've got to guide these very talented individuals without actually intruding. In addition, you can't be fake. There's no use in saying something like, "You are so fabulous; you can do no wrong." Such general praise might work with ordinary people, but that's no way to manage a gifted artist. With them, you've got to be honest and say, "Hey, you were a little bit flat there, so let's fix that." Of course, nobody wants to tell a big star to crank things up, because he *is* such a big star. But the fact is, real artists or geniuses or whatever you want to call them especially need the truth. They're not fooled by false praise and empty encouragement. Only honest recognition of their real accomplishment means anything to them at all.

Morris emphasizes that his own ambition is not about his individual career, but that "I am totally ambitious in getting something right: I must have excellence." Managing such a creative genius on your team requires you to both respect their unique contribution and help them interact more successfully with other team members.

Roadrunner

The obvious advantage of roadrunners and others who avoid conflict is that you don't have to worry about them creating unnecessary and destructive disputes. They are not the members of your team who will plague you with pettiness, raising issues that are not worth the team's time and energy. Discussing this style openly can help them and others see that a certain hesitance in rushing into the fray can sometimes be an advantage. These are the thinkers, the philosophers, and careful engineers among us. We can learn to appreciate and use their ability to research and mull through an issue. The problem, of course, is that these team members need to be encouraged to speak up when it's clearly necessary for them to do so.

Golden Retrievers

These friendly critters are so lovely to have around that it's easy to see why everyone wants to welcome them on their team. They will consistently volunteer to help out, and to be there when you need them. The advantage of this style is obvious; who wouldn't want to have someone on their team with such a loyal way about them? Again, openly talking about the value of loyalty and obedience can help these members be more appreciated by the entire team. As a leader, however, you need to foster an atmosphere where they feel comfortable speaking up and offering their feedback, advice, and even criticism. Otherwise, you'll be leaping off the cliff before you realize that the golden retriever failed to bark about the dragons lurking below.

Skillfully utilizing golden retrievers requires a leader to harness their energy and enthusiasm while keeping a close watch on them to make sure that you're getting all their ideas. Use constant check-ins to make sure that they're feeding you the bad news as well as the good. You'll probably need to ask more probing questions than you might with another style. After a retriever has embraced a new venture, for example, ask them to also identify the pitfalls and roadblocks. You'll need to constantly coach them to bring you issues they might naturally withhold.

Cobras

Hard to think of an advantage to having cobras on your team? Consider this: they serve as an early warning device that something is wrong with the balance of power in your organization and it needs to be addressed. Remember, cobras triangulate because they feel they lack the power to address the issues directly and because triangles are stable. Talking openly about how and why individuals triangulate can help those who constantly use this technique to become more conscious about what they're doing, as well as helping others be more open to hearing about what's happening. Cobras also signal that the intensity in the group is increasing. You need to help people to manage their own intensity so that direct relationships feel more stable and they don't have to rely on the "third leg" of the triangle. Leaders can also educate people that triangles are ubiquitous—we all triangulate when we feel weak or unable to face the fire of a particular interaction. Asking others to mark when they triangulate can help them appreciate those who use this technique more habitually. They can remind all of us to notice and correct unproductive power differentials.

Embracing the Dragon

Working skillfully with these different styles, then, requires that you recognize the necessary diversity up front, discuss your differences openly, and talk about the ways in which various styles would be useful to the team.

It's useful to begin the process of appreciating different styles at the hiring stage. As described by authors Dorothy Leonard and Walter Swap in *When Sparks Fly: Igniting Creativity in Groups*, when Jerry Hirshberg first set up the Nissan Design International studios in San Diego, he designed the organization for creativity. Resisting the temptation to hire only people in his own image—intuitive, big-picture, visually oriented right-brained individuals—he instead also deliberately hired a few left-brained individuals who sought structure and always questioned "why" before proceeding. These thinkers frequently avoid conflict. Initially, these "different" individuals annoyed him. They seemed to be "anticreative" and threatened by novelty. He soon realized that instead, "They simply come to the table with a different set of preparations and expectations." He needed such individuals to complement his own inclination to leap first and ask why and how later. Hirshberg describes himself as:

> Somebody who is likely to leap off a cliff with a joyous intuition and halfway down, scream up to the rest of the group, "Hey, let's build a parachute—*now!*" and thanks God, the [left-brained] people were there. I might have told them beforehand that I was having this impulse, and I thought we were going to jump off a cliff tomorrow morning about seven. If I did that, they would say "thank you, Jerry," and they would go home that night and think about it and come in with some ideas about how to make it work.

Under his leadership designed to facilitate *creative abrasion*, he hired designers in complementary *pairs*—as unlike as possible "so we keep from becoming a harmonious choir, all singing the same tune." So, for example, they hired a "breathtakingly pure artist who is passionate about colors" the same year that they hired a "Bauhaus, Tectonic, rational, clear-headed" designer with a "function-form orientation," who is "passionate about clarity and logic." He invited dissent, but also guaranteed conflict. Hirshberg did so deliberately, believing that conflict would generate energy that could be channeled into creativity instead of destructive anger.

If we can appreciate the value of other styles of thinking and conflict management, we can construct more creative solutions to problems. In another example from Leonard and Swap, when Fisher-Price moved to a cross-functional team structure, a thinking-style preference diagnostic was part of the training. The Director of Marketing, Lisa Mancuso, found understanding others' preferences enlightening. "One man on the team had been driving me nuts," she said.

He wanted to give me every little detail about why a schedule had slipped or what was going on in the factory—all I wanted was the bottom line . . . . it turned out that he had thought me really rude because I wasn't interested in all the details, and just wanted him to get to the point. It really helped us to communicate to understand that we just approached things differently.

In encouraging groups to appreciate diversity, it helps to remind them that creativity involves different types of intelligences. Psychologist Robert Sternberg in his book *Successful Intelligence* considers it a balance of three types: creative, analytical, and practical. *Creative intelligence* is the ability to generate new and unique ideas. *Analytical intelligence* is the ability to analyze those ideas and make decisions based on that analysis. *Practical intelligence* is the ability to see the connections between the ideas and real-life situations. It is possible, but not likely, that one person might have all three. Therefore, the best way to insure a creative group capable of elaborating novel ideas and seeing them through, is to have all three types.

The key for a leader is to encourage the group to appreciate these different styles of intelligence, which inevitably result in different conflict resolution styles. As Hirshberg put it:

> It seemed to me that exceptional and varied individuals brought together with a common goal and appropriate leadership could inspire rather than intimidate each other. The least appealing kind of staff I could imagine for any business was a congregation of like-minded yea-sayers, cozy, comfortable, mutually reinforcing, and nonthreatening to top management. Achieving consensus might have been easier, but unprecedented concepts would have been far less likely. Furthermore, consensus itself is considerably more powerful when reached from different worlds via different routes."

Hirshberg calls this process of honoring different thinking and conflict styles *Embracing The Dragon*. For the individual, it requires "a willingness to adopt an alien, even threatening viewpoint to gain a fresh, re-orienting take on an entrenched position. This process is specifically involved with 'the other hand,' as opposed to the interaction between two of them."

Hirshberg recalls the first time he realized the value of this process when he was trying to persuade the president of Nissan, Takashi Ishihara, that they should integrate a group of engineers into the design team. This was considered a radical approach because of the long-standing tension between architects and builders. "From the viewpoint of traditional engineers, designers are decorative artists with little grasp of what it takes to build a car or make it work. To the designers, engineers are technicians so lost in the parts and pieces they are blind to the expressive power of the fully integrated whole."

Ishihara was concerned that integrating the two would interfere with the pure design center he had envisioned, asking at one point: "But why would you want the enemy with you?"

Hirshberg responded: "They're *not* the enemy . . . . And even if they were, *with us* is exactly where we'd want them!" In that moment of dialogue, Hirshberg discovered that he didn't want the typical engineer, but engineers of "the concept, engineers whose responsibility it would be to find a hundred ways we might be able to do something new rather than a thousand reasons why we couldn't."

Harnessing Diverse Styles

Encourage team members to value the strengths of different styles and to even try them on, when appropriate. Harnessing diversity also requires those of you who are leaders to harness the different styles and use different people for different projects, as appropriate. If you have a situation where you know that only open warfare is possible, or you need a devil's advocate, for example, it's good to have a pit bull on your team. If you already have a bunch of warring pit bulls, sprinkling the mix with a few golden retrievers will cool things down and prevent unproductive meltdowns. If you've created a team full of brilliant prima donnas who seem to leap destructively into the unknown, inserting some thoughtful roadrunners into the fray will force the group to consider the implications of their actions. Finally, holding the concept of an eagle style out there as a model for you all will give the entire group something to work towards. Most of all: model eagle style yourself; the vision and strength are catching.

Chapter 11
The Top Ten Steps: How to Use Conflict to Your Advantage

In a culture that tends to leave the resolution of conflict to lawyers and law enforcement officers, few people have experienced the rewards that can come from working openly and skillfully with disagreements.

—Carolyn R. Shaffer and Kristin Anudsen

A software development team files into a conference room, laptops in hand, for its weekly meeting. They are designing a new program that was supposed to hit the streets three months ago. Over budget and behind schedule, the manager has no idea when the product will be ready. The frustrated VP of development strides into the meeting unexpectedly, announcing that he's going to sit in along with his outside consultant to see "what it's going to take to get this team off their collected asses!" The meeting starts and the attendees have their laptops and PDAs fired up. However, they aren't taking notes or checking schedules. When a team member presents an idea or offers a comment, the other people in the meeting shoot off instant messages that disparage the idea and the person. One message says, "Dog breath! That is the stupidest thing anyone's every said." Remarkably, this behavior was so ingrained in the culture that both the VP and the division manager didn't even notice the collective emailing and lack of constructive attention.

I was the outside consultant in this case, and the conflicts were so deep I pulled out all the stops. That meant using the entire "Top Ten" list of conflict management steps. It also required confiscating the laptops, cell phones, and PDAs. Following these steps provides a logical road map to navigate through a tense situation to use conflict creatively.

In Parts I and II of this book, we've talked about the *what* of conflict: what it is, what makes it valuable, what we need to do to assume leadership. In Part III, we need to focus on *how* we go about using conflict to fuel innovation. Changing our attitude about conflict will take us a long way, but we also need the power of skills.

In this chapter, you'll learn these ten steps:

1. Don't Despair, Prepare!
2. Follow the Yellow Brick Road.
3. Reveal, Don't Conceal.
4. Tackle the Problem, Not the Person.
5. Play Within the Bounds.
6. Stir Up a Storm.
7. Take a Time Out.
8. Talk Until You Drop.
9. Circle the Wagons.
10. Write to Avoid Bad Fights.

Remember the first key to assuming leadership: *plan for conflict.* Don't be surprised when it comes up. As a part of planning, educate yourself about the elements of conflict and the types of conflict.

Every conflict has two elements: the content—the facts of a disagreement—and the process—the patterns and style of dealing with the disagreement. The content is "what" the argument appears to be about. The process is "how" we deal with it. The content is often easier to focus on and deal with than the process problems. As explored in more detail in the next chapter, learning to have good fights requires us to learn to map conflict and to think about both content and process. We also need to teach ourselves and educate our organizations to recognize the difference.

Moving from conflict to creativity requires learning new skills. While we're learning, it's helpful to focus on the ten steps that encapsulate many skills. Although you'll seldom use all of these in every conflict, understanding all of them will help you when you need a more innovative approach.

1. Don't Despair, Prepare!

Perhaps the most important part of your preparation is understanding the styles and identifying your own style and the style of your team. Learning to value the creative spark of conflict, assume leadership in conflict and appreciate the diverse styles of others will take you far in your preparation.

How many different ways can you prepare to manage a conflict? Certainly, thinking through the ten steps, especially step two, is important. The other way is to do as much research as possible on the other party's needs and interests. Perhaps you can interview their associates or clients. Find out what style of conflict management they practice and what is most important to them about the issue.

Review whether this is a substantive or a process conflict and map the conflict as outlined in the next chapter: is it data, relationship, or structural? The other important step is to think clearly and completely about your own needs and interests. Why do you care about this issue? How important is it? Is the problem the type of conflict that can fuel creative sparks? Is the issue really something you want to spend your time on? Conversely, are you intervening soon enough or has the situation begun to spiral into a negative one?

Identify your own "exit point." This is the point at which it makes more sense to walk away from the conflict than it does to work creatively to manage the issue. Ask yourself, what will happen if you don't resolve the conflict amicably? What will you do? What will the other party do? The answers to these questions are helpful, but often not even considered. Some people simply go into a negotiation or try to talk to someone without wondering why it's important. Sometimes, your best option is to walk away, especially if you've already made skilled and extensive attempts to resolve the issue, or if you can come to a better solution on your own.

Finally, rehearse. Find a trusted friend, coach or other advisor. Ask them to role play various scenarios with you and brainstorm ways to talk through the problem. Explain to them what the other person's style is likely to be, the impact you believe this will have on the negotiation, and then ask them to role play that style. This practice is an invaluable and often ignored step.

2. Follow the Yellow Brick Road

As part of your preparation, identify goals for yourself. Then, when you actually sit down with the person or parties to manage the issue, start here. If you can agree upon a common goal—to creatively solve a problem, to generate a new idea, to sell more product, or to achieve the goals of the organization—you will have a clearer chance of harnessing the conflict. Many times, in fact, the root of a conflict may be that you do not even agree upon what the problem is or that you are struggling to address different issues.

Sometimes, there are many difficulties to address. Having a path to follow can help you identify and sort through those issues. Try to list them in order of importance. You may want to start, however, with the one that you feel you have the best chance of managing or the one that addresses a relatively minor issue. Successful conflict management breeds success and builds trust. If you creatively solve a small issue, you'll build the energy to move forward.

Another useful approach to identifying goals is to sort problems into historical, new, and beyond issues. Historical issues are those that are no longer relevant but may need an airing just to clear the slate. Current issues are those still on the table. "Beyond" issues are those beyond the ability of those present to solve the problem. Structural problems, for example, may be beyond issues when you need input or a decision from a higher up.

For example, I was hired by a large law firm to mediate a dispute between two associates. The firm valued both women for their hard work and intelligence, but the two constantly tangled instead of working as a team.

Bill, the managing partner who hired me, had brought in Carol, an associate in her seventh year of practice, to support Debra, an associate in her sixth year of practice. Debra worked directly with Bill to help him with his successful, but hectic legal work. Both Debra and Bill thought they had clearly explained to Carol that she would need to take some direction and supervision from Debra, since Debra had been with the firm longer and knew Bill's clients and work. When I spoke with Carol, however, she held an entirely different view of her role. She whined that it was "inappropriate" for a sixth year associate to supervise a seventh year associate and that she took the job to work with Bill, not Carol. Debra complained that she rarely even saw Bill and that Carol "micro-managed" her in a way that was "insulting" for a seventh year associate.

After meeting with the women individually, I talked to Bill to deliver the common, but unpopular news: I could mediate between the two associates forever, yet the issues wouldn't disappear. The real issue was a "beyond" issue, one that was beyond the two parties in the room and that Bill needed to solve it by delineating the roles and working relationship of the two parties.

Step two requires that we identify our own needs and interests and avoid positions. This is the most important step in what is called *interest-based* conflict management and negotiation. The whole premise of this system is that it is possible for people to gain most or all of what the disputants want if they are willing to continue talking until they come up with a creative solution. This is the most powerful tool in your ability to use the conflict.

3. Reveal, Don't Conceal

While step two focuses on interest-based negotiation, other kinds of negotiation systems focus on helping you win the most for your side. Those systems tend to focus on short-term gain for one party rather than long-term gains for both parties and for the relationship or the entire organization. In a workplace, it is best to assume that you will be there for the duration and, that, therefore, creating a good working relationship is an important goal. Although you can leave a job where you can't creatively manage the conflict, this is an expensive solution—both in terms of emotion and money.

In addition, even if you exit a job because of destructive conflict, in many industries, you may meet again. The world is becoming a very small place. In step three, we have to focus on revealing the real reasons for conflict—and coming up with creative solutions for working relationships.

Underlying needs or interests are often the reasons we think we must have our way in any dispute. It is the reason why we think our solution is the best. In this form of conflict management, you must agree—to at least some extent—to be vulnerable, to *reveal* why you want something, and to declare what's really important to you about an issue. Many people are afraid to do this, especially at work. We're fearful that if we acknowledge underlying need or interest, the issue will be used against us.

Could this happen in a creative conflict management or negotiation? Absolutely! I don't want to suggest that other people will always play fair or with sympathy. What I do know, however, is that it is difficult to formulate sustainable agreements if we are unwilling to reveal our underlying needs.

What happens instead is that one party wins and the other feels cheated, plotting revenge against the winner at some future point during the implementation of the agreement through foot dragging, sabotage, or other forms of passive/aggressive behavior. If we don't stop to understand the real needs of the parties, the solution may not be the best or most creative for all over the long haul. In addition, we may not be considering the needs of the customers, clients, co-workers, or shareholders that the parties represent, which could lead to a fatal flaw in any suggested solution.

The other reason to reveal our own needs and interests is because people at work usually know how we feel even if we don't tell them.

Certainly, we don't need to reveal everything at work or in any negotiation; that's never smart. Yet, if we can be the first to open the door and be just a little bit vulnerable, we will witness miracles in our negotiations.

In contrast, if we stay stuck on arguing for our positions, the conflict may never be managed creatively. The classic story used to illustrate this difference is about two sisters and an orange. Two sisters lived in an isolated house, far from any convenience store. They had only one orange in the house, and they both believed they needed and wanted the orange. If they stay stuck on their *position*, "I want the orange," the conflict is unlikely to be managed creatively.

They may decide to compromise—an idea that's considered enlightened by many in our society. If they compromise in this situation, they might decide to cut the orange in half. Compromise frequently results in a very interesting situation: both parties end up with half of what they thought they wanted!

In contrast, if the sisters are willing to reveal their underlying *needs* and *interests*, they may be able to find a creative way to meet all of them. For example, why might someone need an orange? They might need one for cooking, juggling, making a pompadour, painting a still life of fruit, or for one of many other reasons.

In this situation, if one sister wants the juice of an orange to bake a cake and the other wants to use the peel (the zest of the orange) to bake a muffin, they are both able to receive what they want—if they're willing to be vulnerable enough to say *why* they want it.

Revealing our underlying needs frequently sparks creative solutions. If we're concealing our true interests, it's hard to fuel an innovative solution. In addition to being unwilling to be vulnerable, we may also fail to reveal our needs and interests because we fall in love with our solution; we become attached to our conclusion as the best or only way. Sometimes we even choose our friends based on our solutions. We only favor those who agree with us.

Here are some additional examples of *positions* and *needs and interests* that may help you understand the difference.

Position	Need or Interest
I must have a raise or I'll leave.	I need to have more recognition of my work.
You need to transfer to a different department.	We need to find a better way to match your skills with the needs of this department.
I'm quitting to work some place closer to home.	I need to find a way to spend more time with my children.
We have to ship this new product before July 4.	We need to find a way to show headquarters we've been productive and are making progress.

What if the other party stonewalls and refuses to reveal *his* or *her* interests? What if the other party's only real interest is to win? Then you need to ask some skillful questions. The following probes may help you find the underlying cause of stonewalling or a "winner takes all" attitude.

Questions That Reveal Needs and Interests:

- What's important to you about this issue?
- What's most important to you about this issue?
- What's least important to you about this issue?
- I'm wondering about why you want _____ (the proposed solution).
- I'm puzzled about why you want _____ (the proposed solution).
- I'm curious about your reasons for proposing _____ (the proposed solution).
- Explain to me how this solution might work for both of us.
- Well, that's an interesting idea. What other ideas do you have that might work for both of us?
- What do you think will happen if we don't find a creative solution that meets both our needs and interests?

- What would you suggest I tell my team (group, organization, etc.) if we don't create a solution that meets all of our needs and interests?
- What standards do you think we should use to resolve this issue?
- What might be an innovative idea that would allow us all to get what we want?

Identifying the other parties' needs and interests when they're trying to stonewall or win at all costs requires that you engage in detective work. What's most important is that you listen and try to understand the other person's story.

When we're in conflict, we always have a story—usually one that justifies our proposed solution. If we focus on listening and ask open-ended questions, eventually the other person or parties will reveal a clue that will lead us to their underlying need or interest. For a "winner," for example, we may discover they need a way to save face. They may need to take a "time out" to consider their real options. You may be able to find a small point or give them an unimportant win that will help them save face.

Some parties are so stubborn about revealing their needs and interests that they may even refuse to sit down at the table to talk. Yet persistence and detective work can eventually pay off. Armand Hammer, for example, the late oil magnate, well known for his wheeling and dealing in Russia and other countries, recalled that he had considerable difficulty in negotiating with Muammar Qaddafi of Libya on oil production contracts. Yet he kept talking and kept trying to find out what Libya really wanted. Then one day, Hammer arrived in Libya and met with Prime Minister Abdussalam Jalloud, who sat him down on a sofa. Jalloud unbuckled his gun belt and laid it on the table in front of him with the barrel of the .45 in full view. "I knew then," Hammer said, "that Qaddafi was ready to negotiate."

Most of us don't face a loaded gun when we're trying to manage workplace conflicts. Yet trying to unravel the motivations of a stubborn stonewaller can sometimes feel just as threatening. We may need to emulate the persistence of Columbo in order to uncover what the other parties are concealing.

4. Tackle the Problem, Not the Person

Try to focus on identifying the problem and persuading the other party to join you in solving the problem. If you can make the *problem* your common enemy rather than blaming the other person for causing the problem, creative solutions may arise.

Research clearly shows that destructive conflict is mired in personality clashes. To harness the creative power of conflict, we need to nurture conflict about ideas, but discourage conflicts from becoming personal. Part of what drives conflict into negative spirals of personal attacks is not assuming leadership and stepping in early enough to manage the conflict.

If the other person insists on blaming you for the problem, keep reframing. One way of reframing is to restate general complaints into specific requests. If they say, for example: "We wouldn't have this project disaster if you could get your part of the job finished on time." You could respond: "It sounds as if you're concerned about deadlines. Perhaps we could discuss how to establish reasonable timetables that work for everyone and allow us to succeed on this project."

Continue to reframe and to ask for their innovative ideas about transforming your *joint* problem rather than blaming each other for causing the problem.

Personality Clashes

Creatively working through a conflict requires the individuals involved to share a high degree of trust in each other as well as in the process of conflict management. If there are interpersonal issues as well as substantive issues, you must sort out the interpersonal issues first. This may require the use of an unbiased mediator. If used skillfully, people can trust the process until they are able to trust each other. Whether working directly with someone or with a mediator, it's important to acknowledge the relationship issue up front and then work through it systematically.

How do you know if it's a relationship issue? If most problems you're trying to solve degenerate into personal attacks, name-calling, a slugfest, or walk out, the underlying issue may be personal.

First, try going through an analysis of the conflict styles in Part II. This step alone sometimes helps people sort through relationship issues by helping them realize that people approach conflicts differently because their brain and personality are "hardwired" uniquely, not because they're trying to annoy the other party.

If this step fails to work, try charting the relationship history. Often people who did work well together experience an event that changes their relationship. They may perceive this event differently, or one party may not even be aware that the other party felt so strongly about the issue.

For example, I was mediating a dispute between Jerry, a CEO, and Joanne, one of his vice presidents. They had reached the point in the *negative spiral of conflict* where almost everything they did irritated each other.

I led them back to the beginning of their relationship. Both of their facial expressions softened, and smiles and grins emerged as they described the early days of building the company together. As we traveled through their joint history, however, things changed radically when they spoke of a sexual harassment case that had dramatically altered their relationship. Joanne still felt that Jerry had handled the entire incident incorrectly, something she had argued at the time. Jerry had responded then, and repeated in our session, that he was just following the advice of their attorney. Joanne thought they were both wrong, and they were off and running again on the substantive argument.

This sexual harassment case had happened *three years before*, but Joanne had never released her personal anger about the situation. Nothing about their relationship had been the same since.

Jerry—a very busy CEO with a host of other vice presidents under his management—had not realized this was when the relationship had unraveled. We were finally able to clear the air over this issue, go on to manage current conflicts, and agree on how they would work together in the future.

A tool I have used effectively in this process is to ask the participants to individually fill out the following relationship chart before we meet.

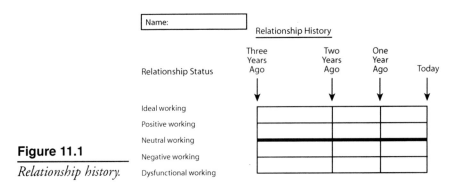

Figure 11.1

Relationship history.

Adapted with permission from John Wiley and Sons, Inc. (Landau, Sy, Barbara Landau, and Daryl Landau. From Conflict to Creativity. San Francisco: John Wiley and Sons, Inc., 2001).

When the parties come together, I invite them to share their results. This analysis frequently allows them to step back and become more objective about their feelings and understand the role played by their own personal perceptions and approaches.

Once the parties understand how the other party may have misinterpreted their behavior, they are usually able to make commitments to reduce the negative fall-out.

If the parties are still stuck, a helpful process I have used at this stage is to have the participants fill out another chart as a pair or group. It is especially useful if everyone is blaming someone else for the problem. This chart tracks all the ways the participants must change in order to make the relationships work.

Using this technique in a meeting with all the blamers, draw a large chart with all their names across the top and along the side in the same order. Tell the group that each column represents that person's opinions, and each row represents changes the group would like to see in one person's behavior. Ask each participant to fill in each of his or her squares.

	Anne says:	Bob says:	Carl says:	Doug says:
Anne change:	?	stop seeing Bob as enemy	stop being paranoid	cut out power struggle with Doug
Bob change:	end male chauvinism, end animosity toward Anne, move his office	?		end animosity toward Anne
Carl change:	end male chauvinism, take more initiative		?	wake up and look beyond organization chart
Doug change:	end male chauvinism		stop usurping authority	cut out power struggle with Doug

Figure 11.2

Who changes what?

Reprinted with permission from Kaye, Kenneth, *Workplace Wars and How to End Them.* New York, Amacom, 1994.

It is common for each party to leave one significant space blank: the one indicating what *they* must change in order to make the relationships work. After the group fills out all of the other squares, I often engage in a bit of creative manipulation, saying something like, "Oh well, it looks like I can't help resolve this then because you've left the most important space blank. I guess there's no hope and we might as well close." I sigh deeply, cross my arms, and sit silently. One party usually comes to his or her senses when I say this, fills in their missing square, and we break the deadlock.

When we believe a problem is a personality conflict, we need to focus on specific behavior, not personality. Sometimes people annoy us for no rational reason: the proverbial oil and water. Sometimes it's chemistry, sometimes it's something from our past that we can't release. The best solution is to focus on the future and the specific.

What exact behavior do we want from the other person? This approach is particularly useful in relationship conflicts that continue despite other attempts to resolve the conflict.

Treating People with Respect

In my experience in trying to resolve workplace conflicts, people frequently focus on vague personality characteristics rather than on what they specifically want. Someone might insist, for example, that the other person is a rude jerk who shouldn't be allowed to walk the planet and doesn't respect him or her.

The problem with words like "respect" is that we all have different ideas about what we mean by respect. If I'm a person who just likes to come in, do my work as quickly and quietly as possible, and leave the office early, for example, I might not even notice if my co-workers acknowledge my presence in the hallway. For some people, however, acknowledging their presence and making polite conversation is an essential part of their ability to work with other members of the team and to trust them. If you fail, on a regular basis, to say hello in the hall, they may see that as a deliberate snub.

A few years ago, I worked with a team with exactly this problem. A group of male utility construction workers kept clashing with their new manager, Rudy. When I asked them what they wanted, they said that Rudy didn't like them. When I forced them to be specific, all they could come up with was that he never said "hello" to them in the halls and that he was "stuck up." When I brought him their request, he was floored! "That's it?" Rudy couldn't believe it. "What is this," he fumed, "high school?"

You might as well assume that it is. As one of the characters—an elderly priest—in one of Graham Greene's novels responded when he was asked what he had learned from a lifetime of hearing confessions, "I've learned that there are no real grown ups."

So, rather than making vague statements such as "I want you to respect me," you need to make a specific request. You should ask for exactly the *behavior* that you want. Say, for example, "I want you to talk with me in a normal tone of voice, and I don't want you to use obscenities when you talk to me," or "I want you to focus on creatively solving our problems instead of constantly telling me why my ideas *won't* work."

When we're focusing on behavior, we talk about things we can objectively see or hear rather than our conclusions, assumptions, or biases. These examples may help you understand:

Personality   *Behavior*

You're not a good listener.	I need you to stop talking and listen.
You lack leadership ability.	I need you to make decisions faster.
You're not a good choice for the job because you're an introvert.	If you want to be considered for this position, you need to spend more time talking to the team members and getting to know them.
You're lazy.	I need you to meet deadlines.
Your ideas are stupid.	Let's brainstorm some ways we can create more innovation in our department.

If the *other* person insists on using vague terms, telling you, for example, that "you need to change your attitude," ask them to explain exactly what they want. Ask what they mean by attitude. You might say: "When I hear people use the word 'attitude,' I know they mean many different things. When you say that I need to have a different attitude, can you give me an example of what specific behavior would indicate to you that I have a different attitude?" My experience is that this kind of dialogue leads to creative conflict management.

5. Play Within the Bounds

Standards can lift you out of an intractable conflict. If the other party remains difficult, start talking more about standards and procedures than about the problem. This can help you creatively manage a conflict that seems like an unmovable object.

For example, if you want to take every Friday off to be with your children and you're willing to make up the time on other days, but your boss insists everyone work the same hours, ask your boss what standards he or she is using to solve the problem. Does he or she believe that retaining good people is a priority? Does he or she believe that people who are more relaxed make better workers? Or does your boss think that everyone has to be treated the same in all situations? If so, how does that work with his or her other standards? Is he or she interested in getting the work done or in "face time"? Also, review the material on conflict mapping in Chapter 12. Intractable conflicts are sometimes caused by process problems rather than substantive issues.

6. Stir Up a Storm

Brainstorming is vital to successful conflict management and a step many miss. Make sure all sides, as a part of their preparation, discuss many possible solutions, not just one. We need to understand that the best resolution for all concerned may not be the one we had previously discussed. Many of us fall in love with our solutions and decide that our idea is the only possibility.

Brainstorming was invented by Alex Osborn in 1938 for his advertising firm. He believed that of all the requirements for imaginative thinking, "the most important is to guard against being both critical and creative at one and the same time."

To achieve this goal, a facilitator, participant, or leader needs to enforce a few basic rules such as:

- No discussion of the ideas until after the brainstorming process.
- Generate as many ideas as possible.
- All ideas are welcome.
- Separate the process of generating ideas from the process of

evaluating ideas.

In order to discuss more creative possibilities, use *brainstorming*—have everyone list possible solutions as quickly as possible—no criticism or cynicism allowed. Welcome all suggestions to get the brainpower flowing. After that, you can spend more time sorting suggestions and determining which ones merit further study.

This is a good way to move people off their positions.

In order to make brainstorming effective—especially in a group setting—you'll need to establish both the process and the purpose. Unless skillfully managed, brainstorms can merely promote the illusion that the group is being creative. Laboratory research actually shows that people generate more and better ideas working alone if you don't carefully attend to process and purpose.

People fear appearing stupid in a group. Therefore, it's useful to submit the issues ahead of time, and ask people to come with several ideas. Alternatively, during the session you can have individuals generate their ideas on separate note pages. The facilitator or mediator can then collect the notes and arrange them according to some theme or let the group develop the arrangements. The group can then expound on them using the same brainstorming rules.

A newer and sometimes useful variant on traditional brainstorming designed to eliminate idea blocking is electronic brainstorming. Participants type their ideas while the ideas of other members appear in a separate window on the screen. The virtual brainstormers are encouraged to read others' contributions and elaborate on them. Evidence suggests that because people are free to focus on their own idea production, more ideas are generated than in traditional brainstorming.

Depending on their style, some people need to think through both the problem and the solution before they offer any of their own thoughts. Others are stimulated by the group and prefer to work with others.

If people are clear about the process and the purpose, however, brainstorming in groups can work well. At IDEO, for example, one of the top design and engineering firms in the country, almost every project includes some brainstorming. A "brainstorm" gathers staff members with diverse skills—people skills, mechanical engineering, industrial design, and sometimes even a client—to generate product ideas. A facilitator runs the meeting. Although everyone knows the rules, they are also stenciled around the top of the walls in the room used for the brainstorm. They are: defer judgment; build on the ideas of others; one conversation at a time; stay focused on the topic; encourage wild ideas. Because many of the attendees can draw, the sessions are more visual than other groups. In addition to the words on white board, there are sketches on the table where participants sit.

I have also used visual brainstorming with groups to break entrenched conflicts. When a group is stuck, for example, I'll frequently give them large pieces of paper and crayons and have them work on the floor. After dividing them into small teams, I'll ask them to come up with a visual image of how they want things to be, kind of a thematic purpose they then use to steer the group toward a creative solution. Although most people groan at first and may suggest firing the facilitator, they usually sink into the task and the resulting creative and colorful work can spur a breakthrough. I've also brought in an artist to quickly sketch the ideas of various blocked parties. Sometimes a visual representation of a solution to a conflict can move people beyond their positions into new ground.

Role-plays and skits can also help break through a deadlock with a group if used skillfully. Either the facilitator can put something together or ask separate groups to generate ideas and then act them out.

I've also placed various toys placed around the room and on the tables to help the group come up with creative solutions during a conflict. Modeling clay, Silly Putty™, Tinker Toys™, or Legos™, all help people move through the session with a more creative and playful spirit, and may even help them actually "construct" a solution they had never before imagined.

It's especially important during the brainstorming process for the leader or an enlightened participant to model a non-commitment to a point of view and urge others to do the same. This may be challenging for most of us since in our society, non-commitment to a point of view is considered an equivocation, a point of weakness.

Hirshberg points out that one way to decide if any real creative options are being generated in these sessions is to look at the quality of the *questions* being asked. If they are open and unguarded, the possibility of new ideas is there. Most people, however, don't ask real questions in these session, but make speeches instead, shutting down true inquiry and creative problem solving.

7. Take a Time Out

Classic advocates of creative conflict management have used this move. Martin Luther King, Jr., for example, suggested that we "go to the mountain" during conflict to gain the higher ground and a better perspective on the problem. Gandhi retreated to meditation and fasting during the most intense periods of his struggle to free the Indian people.

Jerry Hirshberg suggests a more modern solution: going to the movies. During the height of creative problem solving when his staff is tense, quarrelsome, and tapped out of creative solutions, he shuts down the entire design center and treats everyone to the movies. After watching a thriller and munching popcorn, the group returns in a better mood and with renewed creative juice:

> In my own mediation and conflict management practice, I've developed a keen awareness of when individual combatants or groups need a "time out" from the process. If you're feeling overwhelmed and stuck, or if you can't seem to prod the other side into thinking creatively rather than only of their own positions, it's time for a break. Sometimes, it's best to allow people their own time away from the process, but at other times, it's my sense that forcing them to take a break together—going out for ice cream or coffee—with no talking about the issues allowed, can forge a breakthrough.

In my experience, intimidation works equally poorly as a motivator when groups stall. Instead, consider taking a time out!

8. Talk Until You Drop

The truth is, most of us do not allow enough time for creative conflict management. William Ury in his book, *Getting to Peace*, studied conflict resolution techniques from around the world. As he spent time with the Bushmen of Africa—who have an extremely sophisticated conflict resolution system—he learned why their methods are so successful. First, they spend 40% of their time visiting with other community members building strong ties so they have a deep foundation when a conflict does break out.

Then, when two members of the community do fight, the entire community drops everything and sits with them until they come up with a solution that serves the community as well as the individuals. If it takes hours, they sit. If it takes all night, they sit. If it takes days, they sit. The community stands ready to serve as what Ury calls the "third side" in the conflict.

In our modern world, where we scream at the microwave because it's too slow, where we expect everything to come to us through a drive-through, and where instant gratification takes too long, we believe that we just don't have time for this.

Yet look at the costs of unproductive conflict: simmering resentments, lack of innovation, passive/aggressive behavior, open warfare, delay, and sabotage. If we don't creatively and thoroughly manage problems as they arise, the long-term costs are far greater than the short-term conflict management time.

I'm not advocating that you use this technique for every conflict. One thing I hope you will learn through studying the methods outlined in this book is that some conflicts truly are not worth our time and energy. We need to be much more discerning about what is and what isn't a conflict.

Yet when we do realize we have an issue, we need to make sure we allow sufficient time for management. My own experience is that it usually takes longer than we think to produce good fights instead of bad ones.

9. Circle the Wagons

When you reach an agreement or a creative solution, you need to go through some sort of closure process. Perhaps you need to arrange to meet some time in the future to review how the agreed upon solution is working. Also agree upon an action plan to accomplish the goals of an agreement. Decide who does what, when, and where.

In this step, an agreement is also more likely to be sustainable by closing with a review to learn from the conflict. The intention is to provide closure and to improve your conflict management skills for the future as well as to strengthen your relationships. Try to discourage discussion; just ask each party to speak and listen.

Option One (for close colleagues or partners):

- What worked during the conflict management session?
- What didn't work?
- Who do we need to forgive and for what?
- Who do we need to thank and for what?

- What do we need to say to feel complete?
- In the future, how could we use this conflict or one like it to be more creative, innovative, or productive?

Option Two (other workplace situations):

- What was effective about the way we managed this conflict?
- What was ineffective?
- What can we say by way of compassion for others' shortcomings or incompetence?
- What can we say by way of respect for the others, their competence, their conduct in this situation, and their commitment to resolving this case?
- Assuming we might not speak again about this matter, what else do we need to say?
- In the future, how could we use this conflict or one like it to be more creative, innovative, or productive?

"Circling the wagons" by paying attention to closing the conflict, can help people learn to value the conflict and be more creative in the future.

10. Write to Avoid New Fights

As an attorney and former litigator, I have scant faith in the ability of written contracts to protect our individual rights. If you have to sue to enforce an agreement, all parties have lost since lawsuits take too long and cost too much. Even if you win you lose.

I do have great faith, however, in the ability of written contracts to facilitate the possibility of creative conflict management. If you write down what you think you've agreed upon at various stages, the process helps clarify your own thinking as well as the agreement. We all tend to assume the meaning we ascribe to a certain word or discussion is the same for everyone. This causes more conflict. In fact, we all use words differently.

As Lewis Carroll said in *Alice and Wonderland*, "A word means just exactly what I say it means, no more, no less."

If you find some words or phrases are controversial, you may even need to include a "definitions section" in your written document.

Welcome the process of clarifying your agreement by committing the details to writing. That act will save you a world of hurt down the road.

Using the Ten Steps

The ten steps can provide a roadmap to lead you skillfully through using the conflict to generate creativity. While you may not need to use all ten for every situation, it's useful to review them before you try to resolve any specific issue. If you do, you'll be able to see where you're stuck and what step needs more emphasis. For complex disputes, working your way through all ten steps with all the parties will serve you well.

Chapter 12
Preparing for Conflict: How to Move from Despairing to Preparing

---

Suffering is a part of our reality, a natural fact of our existence. It is something that we have to undergo, whether we like it or not. We might as well adopt an attitude that enables us to tolerate it so that we are not so intensely affected by it mentally.

—The Dalai Lama

Scott Fitzpatrick is a rising star at a high-tech company in Boulder, Colorado and was just promoted to director and head of a new group. While he was surprised they didn't offer him the vice president's title for the new job, he chalked it up to the fact that he's so young—and pretty new at managing a large team. The last thing Scott does before he calls it a day is flip open his Palm Pilot® and review his schedule for the next day. He prides himself on being prepared. He's got an important meeting tomorrow so he decides to wear his new suit. He's also got an impossible schedule with competing priorities so he writes a "to do" list. The justification for his budget is due in four days so he stays late to plot a strategy and draft some talking points. Last, he's scheduled to talk with a staff member who's not performing well. He's certain the conversation will be difficult. He sighs and shuts down his computer— he'll cross that bridge tomorrow.

The one thing that stands in the way of Scott's meteoric rise to greatness is his reluctance to deal with conflict. It doesn't have to be that hard. The steps to successful management of a conflict begin with preparation. Conflict is a predictable and valuable part of everyday life, and there are numerous ways to pave the way for innovative success instead of frustration. Yet, most of us, including Scott, spend more time organizing our "to do lists" than doing the legwork essential to managing a conflict.

Every conflict has two elements: the content—the facts of the disagreement and the process—and the pattern and style of dealing with the disagreement. Working with both is what facilitates creative conflict management. Great diplomats, negotiators, and famous military strategists aren't noted for their luck; they are revered for their strategies and tactics. It's their fastidious preparation undertaken to understand the terrain and their parties—their viewpoints, priorities, passions, unspoken issues, points of compromise, strengths, weaknesses—and the cultural and political landscape. Preparation leads to good fights that harness the power of conflict. But, you're asking, don't most senior managers already know how to deal with conflict? Isn't this something they've been trained in? Something they have had to be good at in order to succeed? Surprisingly, no. Many senior managers rise from within the company avoiding conflict as they go. Many have found mechanisms for avoiding conflict like hiring strong pit bull number twos who can run interference. And others have moved so quickly through the ranks that they left behind any problems without fully resolving anything with anyone.

Regardless of the reason, many executives find they lack the most basic skills for effectively dealing with conflict. By learning some basic techniques and preparing for conflict, they can begin to identify and resolve people issues that may be holding back their projects, teams, and even careers. In addition, while some executives may instinctively handle conflict creatively, they lack the strategies and skills to pass these ideals on to their team.

Process versus Content

First on your preparation list should be to consider whether you're dealing with a process problem or a content problem. For example, a CEO and his chief financial officer came to me complaining about their long-running battles. The CFO—younger and female—liked to debate the finer points of every financial statement and quarrel about how things should be reported. She relished arguments and details. The CEO often reacted quickly and intensely to her. He didn't have time for all those details, he told me. He just wanted *her* to handle their problems.

She carped that he didn't take her seriously. They both whined that the other drove him/her nuts. The CEO said the CFO never gave up and always had to be right. "She tells me what to do," he complained. The CFO said the CEO treated her as if she had nothing valid to say. "He won't listen to me and avoids our meetings," was her rebuttal.

I got the picture and while I was used to hearing about the standard CEO/ CFO tensions, this conflict was all about process and style—the way they handled issues. I worked out a plan with the two of them: they agreed to specific times and time limits during which they would discuss the company's financial matters and came up with a specific agenda about what the CEO did and did not want to discuss.

When they came back for a follow-up session with me, they agreed that they had a much more peaceful month. In the car coming to my office, however, an argument had erupted.

The CEO had been musing about a recent meeting they'd had with the board of directors and some things he felt he hadn't done as well as he should have. He just wanted to ventilate and have a sympathetic ear. The CFO jumped at the chance to critique his performance and inform him of all the ways she believed he hadn't presented her numbers as well as he could have and all the details they should have included. They were off to the races and the conflict spiraled downward from there.

Of course, the argument started all over again in my office. I let them fuss for a while so I could observe their process. I finally stopped them and reminded them they had agreed to work on not always thinking it's the other's fault—our project for the week.

"What were you each doing wrong in the argument?" I asked them, shifting our attention from an argument over the facts to a discussion about process.

After I persisted for a while, the CEO admitted he had overreacted, yelled, and been too caught up in countering the CFO's argumentative points. The CFO admitted that she was telling him what to do rather than asking what, if any, feedback he wanted, and that she had been judging him as well as been overly critical. Then she added, "And I have another point to make …," and she started up again about how he had misrepresented her numbers at the board meeting.

This was a great chance for me to point out that their respective views of the CEO presentation was the content (a fleeing, resolvable topic), and we were not trying to resolve the content or we would have to convene every day for every new issue. I was not a judge charged with determining right and wrong, fault or blame. We'd agreed to work on what was really bothering the executive team: *the habitual dysfunctional process.*

Once the two finally began to consider what they were doing wrong, they did a pretty good job of self-criticizing. The lesson didn't take hold immediately, but over time they learned and improved.

Distinguishing between *process* and *content* is similar to determining, "What are you really angry about?" Many times what really drives a conflict is a process issue—not content, and the process becomes the real substantive "what."

All organizations have a process for managing conflict—some are healthy, creative, and skillful processes and some are not. The process may not be formal but most seasoned people in any organization understand, as one of the "unwritten rules" of the organization, how conflict is approached or avoided. Ironically, for new employees or for some employees who read social cues poorly, they may be unable to understand the prevailing model in the group. These differences in styles and strategies can lead to even more unhealthy conflict. Your job in planning and assuming leadership in conflict management is to see and reveal the process behind the current feud and to model and teach the best way. In order to use the conflict as fuel for creative energy, you must be able to reflect upon process and to make that process transparent for others in your organization.

Pick Your Time, Place, and Mood

Timing is everything in creative conflict management. Whether you're leading the discussion between two bickering employees or confronting someone yourself, you won't be likely to manage a conflict if you or the person with whom you're entangled is hungry, angry, tired, or distracted.

In order to successfully manage conflict, we need to calm ourselves down and warm up the person with whom we're in conflict in whatever way works for them. Both our moods and the other's need to be considered. If we're too light, silly, tentative, nonchalant, or pleading, the other person(s) may not take us seriously or may not feel we take the conflict or their problem seriously. On the other hand, if we're stern, stubbornly authoritative, intense, or irritable, we're also not likely to successfully manage the conflict. And we're probably likely to provoke more resistance and resentment than cooperation and creativity. Be prepared to be upbeat and positive. We're probably not ready to manage the conflict if what comes to mind to say first is, "I'm sick of this problem with your temper, and you're going to learn this way to fix it." We need to soften our "tee-up" to the problem.

We're more likely to succeed if we genuinely feel like saying, "Wouldn't it be productive if we learned a new way . . . ." Our mood leads to our tone. Our tone—the aura we create around us as we step up to assume leadership in conflict resolution—largely determines whether the other person will be defensive or not.

Understanding the Circle of Conflict

The classic Circle of Conflict below outlines some of the major sources of conflict, whether interpersonal, intra- or inter-organizational, communal, or societal, and regardless of setting. As explained by C. Moore, in *The Mediation Process: Practical Strategies for Resolving Conflict*, there are five central causes of conflict:

- Relationship conflicts: problems with the people's relationships
- Data conflicts: problems with data
- Interest conflicts: perceived or actual incompatible interests
- Structural conflicts: structural forces
- Value conflicts: differing values

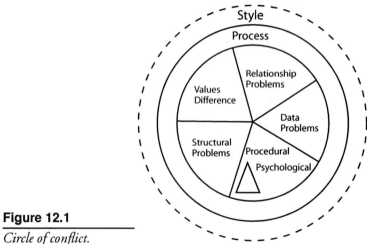

Figure 12.1

Circle of conflict.

Adapted with permission from C. Moore, The Mediation Process, (San Francisco: Jossey Bass, 1996).

I would also add the issue of style (see Chapter 4) to Moore's model as well as the issue of process as described above. Both of these issues are over-arching concerns in any conflict.

Relationship Conflicts

Relationship conflicts happen when we carry baggage from our past interactions forward into our current relationships. We may be holding onto strong negative emotions, stereotypes, previous miscommunications or misperceptions about someone, or we believe they engage in destructive behaviors or they are against us. When we do this, the result is unnecessary conflict since we may have relationship conflicts even when other reasons for conflict such as limited resources or different goals or values are not an issue. Relationship problems often fuel disputes and lead to the negative spiral of destructive conflict. When we're stuck in a relationship conflict at work, we're unable to separate the person from the problem. Creative conflicts are not fueled by relationship problems. As suggested in the last chapter, if we find we're mired in a relationship problem, we need to resolve it first.

Data Conflicts

Data conflicts happen when we lack accurate information to make an informed decision, or when different people or groups advocate conflicting information or interpret the same data differently. Poor communication can also drive data conflict. Other data conflicts may be genuine because the way people collect or view the information is frequently different.

Interest Conflicts

Interest conflicts involve competition between perceived or actual needs and interests. If we believe that in order to satisfy our own needs and interests, the other party must give up his or hers, we have an interest conflict. We can carry these over substantive issues, such as money or space, as well as procedural issues, such as the way the dispute is resolved. We can also create interest conflicts over psychological issues, such as perceptions of trust or fairness. In order to creatively manage a true conflict of interest, all parties must find a way to have a significant number of their interests acknowledged or met (psychological, procedural, and substantive) on issues.

The Satisfaction Triangle below shows the relationship of these three kinds of needs. A creative conflict management is not *sustainable* (meaning it will not last) until all three sides of the triangle are complete. For example, even if you satisfy the parties' substantive needs, if you don't address their procedural and psychological satisfaction, you will not produce a lasting agreement.

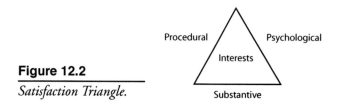

Figure 12.2

Satisfaction Triangle.

Often, conflict is caused when one or more of the parties insists only one solution will meet their needs. Usually, if the parties work hard enough to solve the problem, there's a variety of creative ways to meet everyone's needs. The key is to urge everyone involved to bring all of their creative potential to the table to brainstorm the best solutions for all concerned. Bringing these underlying needs to the table fuels creativity and productivity.

Structural Conflicts

Structural conflicts result from organizational issues. The organization may have limited resources, space, time, poor role definition, or conflicting agendas. These structural issues may cause conflicts and be beyond the control of the involved parties. Simply identifying a structural conflict, however, can help the parties begin to see what parts are within their control.

Some structural conflicts are utterly predictable in most organizations, such as sales versus marketing or HR versus finance. If you can bring these out into the open and problem solve without blame, these structural conflicts can be managed creatively.

Value Conflicts

Value conflicts are created when perceived or actual belief systems clash. We use values to explain what we believe is good or bad, right or wrong, just or unjust. Values often cause conflict yet need not. People can work together with strikingly different value systems as long as they accept their differences and do not try to force their own values on anyone else. It's also helpful if the organization itself has clear values and goals. You may need to remind the parties of these organizational priorities when they're in the midst of a conflict.

Using the Circle of Conflict and Conflict Mapping

To prepare for conflict, and use the conflict to create value and assume leadership in creative conflict management, use the circle of conflict and conflict mapping. These tools can help you gain perspective on the dispute, detach from the emotions involved, and reveal the root cause of the conflict behavior. If we examine the dispute according to the five categories—relationship, data, interest, structural, and value—and if we consider the over-arching issues of style and process, we can begin to determine what the primary and secondary causes of the dispute are (there may be more than one) and determine if the cause is a genuine incompatibility of interests or some other issue. If we stop to do this analysis before jumping in to resolve the dispute, our chances of success will be much greater. We will be better able to harness the conflict to drive innovation and productivity.

For example, I recently worked with a financial institution that wanted to revamp its process for loan approval. Committees met for months without success, trying to understand why the process took so long, engendered so many disagreements, and created so much customer dissatisfaction. After interviewing several members of the team individually to determine what they thought the problem might be, I brought the group together to work on the issue. One of the first steps was to ask them to map the various conflicts that had emerged. This activity helped de-personalize the issues and helped everyone see what was contributing to their inability to work through the issues. Hidden structural and values conflicts quickly emerged when they were able to step back from the problem and see the problem diagrammed in this way.

When we prepare for conflict by gaining this broader perspective, we're more able to use the other skills outlined in the chapters that follow, including the next chapter about skillful confrontation. Diagramming the conflict helps us harness the contention to use it for productivity and creativity. Launching into an attack *without preparation*—a common practice—can lead to many bad fights.

Chapter 13
Grace Under Fire:
How to Skillfully Confront Others

Facts do not cease to exist because they are ignored.

—Aldous Huxley

Denise Everhardt is an operations manager for a large insurance carrier. An endless stream of email from the VP who is her boss dogs her. He chooses to communicate exclusively electronically. He gives her all her assignments, holds virtual discussions, and even does her performance appraisal via email—despite the fact that their offices are next door to one another. Denise finally has enough; she slaps her boss with a complaint for harassment for his relentless electronic feedback. Whose fault is this? Both of them, of course, but the VP more than Denise. He needs to learn how to skillfully confront Denise about her strengths and weaknesses, instead of avoiding difficult confrontations by hiding behind email. As a leader, he needs to model constructive confrontation for his employees.

Of all the situations a manager has to prepare for, giving constructive feedback to an employee can be one of the hardest. Managers from supervisor to CEO have to prepare to skillfully deliver feedback in a variety of situations—from performance reviews to input on projects. For managers who don't know how to skillfully handle the confrontation, a situation can all too quickly turn into an unproductive confrontation or conflict. While you would think that most leaders would have acquired this skill, my experience proves that many, if not most of them, lack this crucial ability.

According to Webster's, feedback is "the return of information about the results of a process." It sounds pretty innocuous. Yet, it is the bane of many a manager's existence. Feedback, by definition, is not meant to be personal. Yet, often the way it's given and received causes people to take such umbrage that they feel assaulted, maligned, misunderstood, or personally criticized. Constructive feedback and skillful confrontation is an elemental part of almost anyone's job in these days of interdependent teams.

Good managers must frequently evaluate the performance of others. If you want productivity, profits, and goal achievement to increase, then individual performance improvement is a must. Logically, then, that entails finding ways to improve processes. It means using tact and motivation to assist co-workers in garnering new skills, being more creative, and seeking "personal bests" on the job. It means skillful confrontation and feedback. You also have the responsibility, as a leader in your organization, to model this skill for others.

An essential skill, then, is to learn when and how to raise conflict, especially how to skillfully confront and criticize someone else's behaviors. Yet, sometimes, in working in today's diverse workforce, we become so confused or paranoid about making mistakes that we withhold positive or negative criticism or fail to confront someone about their performance or behavior.

Our withholding denies the person the opportunity to grow and fails to fulfill our duty and the organization's responsibility to give employees feedback on their performance. In addition, leaders and managers have a legal—not to mention ethical and moral—obligation to intervene when they see or hear behavior in the workplace that is harassing, discriminating, unproductive, non-inclusive, or disrespectful. Many of us, however, feel uncomfortable addressing these issues and don't know how to constructively confront someone. With awareness and practice, skillful confrontation is possible.

When we provide constructive feedback with the motive of giving support and encouraging growth, learning begins. If we're afraid to confront someone, we also won't be able to use the conflict to drive creativity, innovation, or productivity.

Why We Have Trouble Giving Good Feedback

Why don't we talk more directly to people about our conflicts? Why do we have such problem giving good feedback to our employees? We may be concerned about one or more of the following:

- We lack the skills to handle the confrontation and fear, making the situation worse.
- We've had a history of negative experience with conflict or come from a family with violence, alcoholism, abuse, or other serious dysfunctions.

- We fear they will bring up our shortcomings and confront us back.
- We fear losing an otherwise good employee, client, and/or friend.
- We fear retaliation in some way.
- We fear making the other person angry and the loss of their respect or approval.

We've all seen these things happen, so our fears are not totally groundless. Most of these problems can be avoided by following the tips outlined in this chapter. Failure to act doesn't lead to the kind of positive learning environment most of us want to create in our workplace.

Positive Criticism and Confrontation

When we avoid talking to someone because we fear creating conflict, we don't avoid the underlying problem, and we may create even worse issues by waiting. We also miss opportunities to use the conflict creatively.

In order to skillfully confront someone, follow these guidelines:

- Just do it! Intervene early and often. The biggest mistake leaders, managers, and co-workers make is looking the other way when they see poor performance or inappropriate behavior. We are not doing co-workers or our companies any favors by taking a passive stance.
- Be prepared. Be clear about what it is that concerns you—have specific examples and know how you want the other person to change. You may need to prepare by first role-playing the interaction with someone else.
- Talk privately to the co-worker, unless there's a specific need to stop an entire group from engaging in inappropriate behavior.
- Come to the point quickly; don't keep the other person guessing.
- Talk about specific performance or behavior—not the person, their personality, or attitude. Describe the details of what you *saw* and *heard*. Don't speculate on their motivation. You want them to *behave* differently.
- Make "I" statements; own the conflict as yours or the company's. Let the other person know how his or her behavior affects you. "When you're late for our meetings, we can't get our work done." "When you called Susan a sexpot, it violated our company policy on harassment." "When we were brainstorming in that meeting, you dismissed all my ideas." Focus on the *results* and *impact* of the person's behavior, not your opinions about it.

- Listen to the other person's story. Conflicts are frequently the result of poor communication and/or misunderstandings.
- Once you're clear there is no misunderstanding or miscommunication, be specific about the behavior change you seek. Explain what was wrong with the behavior: that it doesn't contribute to creative conflict management, that it violates the company policy, affects the ability of the team or you to do your work, is inconsistent with the team's goals and objectives, is uncreative, unproductive, harassing, disrespectful, discriminatory, or non-inclusive. Clarify any confusion your co-worker has about what behavior is unacceptable.
- Directly ask the co-worker to stop engaging in the behavior and obtain a commitment to stop. If you're their manager or leader, let them know you expect compliance as a part of the requirements of the job.
- If the situation is serious, or this is something you've talked with them about before, be specific about the consequences if the behavior continues, and then follow through. For example: "If you continue to miss deadlines, I will need to put a letter in your file or bring it up with your boss."
- Monitor the workplace to make sure the behavior stops and/or improves.

When giving feedback, make sure you include positive statements. Many organizations value only negative criticism. These organizations expect excellence and assume that people will do their jobs well, so they don't even mention when things proceed in the way they expect. Leaders in these types of institutions have no idea how hungry those they lead are for positive interactions with them. It's often easy to find things that are wrong, yet it seems unimportant or difficult to identify positive aspects. Your co-workers will respond much more positively to your confrontation or criticism if you also regularly include positive comments. Reinforcing creative or innovative behavior also leads to more of the same. People need to know exactly what they have done well. Identify specific behaviors, what the person said and did. For example, to say, "Bob, you did a nice job," or "Mary, I feel good about your work" is not as useful as saying, "Mary, when we were trying to generate new ideas and you told Bob you wanted him to listen to Jim and stop interrupting him, the communication really started working well." This kind of information lets people know what tools, skills, and behaviors work effectively. It also helps drive more creative and productive interactions.

Negative Criticism and Confrontation

Negative criticism shouldn't be used as a *weapon*, for example, for *revenge* when someone criticizes your work or to *hurt* someone because they did an ineffective job.

Example of unhelpful feedback: "Jane, your report was bad. How could you do such terrible work?"

This criticism doesn't help the co-worker learn because it doesn't specifically describe what Jane did wrong, nor does it identify what behavior would be acceptable, creatively manage conflicts, or foster long-term relationships. This type of criticism leaves the receiver feeling badly and doesn't foster learning or correction. Ask yourself why you would offer such a critique. If you're not allowing someone to change his or her behavior or skills so the work can improve, why are you saying it?

Example of helpful feedback: "John, I noticed when you typed this report you didn't use the margins I specified. We need to stay within a certain page count to fit the form. Also, when you answered the phone just now, you didn't ask how you could help the caller. Please do that in the future."

This criticism improves the learner because it lets John know what he did, when, and how the other party was affected.

Here's a list of techniques that contribute to unskillful confrontation:

- Leaders sometimes fail to come to the point; instead they talk around the issue, leaving people unsure of their point.
- If you wait to confront someone, your anger may be out of control and you may explode, which can damage the relationship.
- Many managers give feedback only at yearly performance reviews instead of more frequently. People need feedback early and often.
- Sometimes leaders talk to third parties instead of the person directly involved. Most workplaces foster gossip. Your job should be to discourage such talk, not to encourage indirect communications.
- Be specific. The more examples you use, the more likely that people will be able to improve.

Curiosity or Confrontation

When you feel the need to confront someone about an issue, consider changing your own attitude before you talk to the person. Can you find a way to be *curious* about the other person's behavior? If you come from a place of curiosity and wonder, the interaction will have a much better chance of succeeding. Consider *reframing* your confrontation to use the following statements:

- I'm *puzzled* by "x" behavior. Can you explain to me how it would help our team meet our goals?
- I was *curious* about why you did "y." Can you explain it to me?
- I'm *confused* by the statement you made yesterday about "z." Can you explain to me how you believe it will help us finish this job?

There are, of course, some personality types who value direct confrontations: pit bulls being a notorious example. These people may want you to tell them straight away what the problem is and what you want them to do differently. This "curiosity" technique works best when there's a big power differential between the speaker and the listener, or you know that you have a tendency to come on too strong and that people will not be able to hear what you say when you're that abrupt.

Land Mines to Avoid

Be prepared for defensiveness. Most of us feel defensive when we're receiving feedback or criticism, even when it's skillfully delivered. If we're speeding and the state patrol stops us, for example, most of us do not jump out of our car and declare: "Oh, thank you, officer! I'm so glad you stopped me! I could have hurt someone! Write me a ticket immediately!"

When we notice that our feedback frequently leads to defensiveness, another reason may be that we offer complaints without requests. As the popular psychologist Gay Hendricks points out:

> If every ounce of energy human beings use in complaining was dedicated to productive change, we could clear up many of the world's problems virtually overnight. It takes courage to turn a complaint into a request for effective action. It requires that you think about what needs to be done rather than about what wasn't done. It requires that you get outside the negative-thinking cycle of "What's wrong with me? What's wrong with you? What's wrong with the world?" and make a courageous leap of thought to "Forget what's wrong—let's focus on what needs to be done."

If we're generating a "flight or fight" mode in someone else (as discussed in Chapter 4), we may want to step back and examine whether we are expressing our emotions in the most skillful ways. If we rage at someone or alternatively, if we're holding our emotions in with a stony expression, we may trigger a fight or flight response in another. Most of us have not really thought about or practiced the appropriate expression of emotion, especially during feedback and conflict. What is the most effective way to *express* strong feelings without *dumping* them on someone?

Using Emotions for Successful Confrontations

The best way to communicate our own emotions while we're giving someone feedback is in a straightforward way. Think about it as a weather report: "It's raining and I'm angry." Our feelings change just as the weather does and when we can report on what we experience without blaming or judging another, the other person is better able to hear what we're saying. We don't need to dramatize or hide the weather; like our feelings, it just is what it is.

While describing the effect someone's behavior has on your work can be helpful, people are more likely to be able to hear you if you use "I" statements and stay neutral in your report, stating that "I'm angry," for example, instead of "You make me angry."

When we decide it's necessary, we can, before we state the problem and communicate our request, add a clear expression of feelings. Consider the following examples:

Jane, *I'm angry.* I just realized that you didn't finish the report on time. When our reports are late, it puts the entire production schedule behind our goals. From now on, I need you to turn them in on time or let me know well in advance that you can't do it so I can find someone else.

Harry, my stomach feels queasy and I just realized that *I'm afraid.* When you yell at me when you ask for corrections, I'm afraid you're going to fire me. I need you to stop yelling and give me your corrections in a normal tone of voice.

Expressing our emotions this clearly and without drama during a confrontation takes practice. Most of us have not thought about the idea of this kind of emotional practice. How many of us ever received good modeling or suggestions from our parents or took a class on appropriate emotional expression? Yet cleanly offered emotion can make our feedback to others clearer and more congruent. If we deliver bad news with a forced smile because we're struggling to contain our anger, for example, we trigger uncertainty about our message or worse in the other person. We all have built-in radar that can be highly attuned to the emotions of others. Conversely, if we're out of control with our anger, or if we yell and use profanity when we offer feedback, the other person may freeze, flee, or fight back. When we don't offer our own feelings in an appropriate way, something frequently feels scary, false, or confusing to the other party and makes our feedback less effective than it could be.

Sometimes the problem is that we become defensive ourselves when we're offering feedback to someone. When this happens we may want to examine whether we're speaking from what Hendricks calls "discovery" or from our own defensiveness.

For instance, when we're talking to someone we might notice that they start frowning and look away. Because we're sure we're correct in our assessment of them, we might be prompted to say: "I don't know why what I'm saying makes you angry, you're the one who messed up this project." In putting in this way, we've just revealed our own defensiveness, which will probably prompt them to respond in kind.

Instead, if we notice someone frowning and avoiding our gaze while we are giving feedback, we can offer something like: "I just noticed an expression on your face. I'm wondering what you're feeling about what I just said?" Although it might feel awkward using this discovery method at first, we can become more skilled at the practice. Eventually, if we use this method of communicating, we will reduce the amount of defensiveness we trigger in others during feedback.

Be Aware of Past Issues with Conflict

Another land mine to avoid is triggering memories in someone else of past criticism. Many times someone will explode over what you might think is relatively minor feedback. Most of us received plenty of negative and unhelpful feedback from parents and teachers as children, and workplace criticism tends to remind us of these past wounds. If someone reacts out of proportion to the event, this may be a part of the reason.

I once had an employee, for example, who was much older than me. She had been doing her work for a long time, and I'm sure that she felt that her competence exceeded mine. Because she was basically a good employee, I didn't need to give her much criticism but occasionally, I had to mention a small matter, and she would always bristle with indignation. In addition, she would usually engage in passive/aggressive behavior by not correcting what

I asked her to do. I finally had to sit down with her and talk frankly about how necessary it was for us both to be able to give each other feedback and suggestions in order for us to be able to work together. I assured her that I valued her work and loyalty. I gently asked her if she had any ideas about how I could give her feedback in a way that she could accept more easily.

She confessed that she had grown up with an extremely critical father whose approval she had never been able to gain. His constant attacks had driven her to be a perfectionist who always wanted to do everything right. Any suggestion that she was not doing her job made her quite upset.

It took several exchanges like this for us to work out a feedback system we could both use. I had to learn to approach her carefully and always remind her that her work was excellent but that we needed to work on some small issue. It took time, but eventually, we turned the situation around.

Stick to the issue and try not to react yourself. If you don't, the problem may never be managed creatively. Take a time-out if you find yourself losing control. Be sure, however, not to give up. You may need to schedule additional sessions before the conflict moves to a higher level.

Managing confrontation effectively is an essential tool in your arsenal of creative contention. Because giving and receiving feedback is such a necessary part of the workplace environment, it's not a skill we can afford to leave undeveloped. You also need to model and teach these skills for those you lead. In order to complete the feedback loop you need two other skills: the subject of the next chapter, Chapter 14, "Who's on First? How to Hear and be Heard," and the subject of Chapter 15, "Welcoming a Different Opinion: How to be Confrontable."

Chapter 14
Who's on First?
How to Hear and Be Heard

I'm not arguing. I'm just talking to myself.

—Nicolas Eisaguirre Evans, Age 4

Costello: . . . . Who's on first?
Abbott: Yes.
Costello: I mean the fellow's name.
Abbott: Who.
Costello: The guy on first.
Abbott: Who.
Costello: The first baseman.
Abbott: Who.
Costello: The guy playing . . .
Abbott: Who is on first!

Despite their efforts, the hilarious dialogue between Abbott & Costello never leads to agreement on the line-up. This classic verbal jousting provides a light-hearted look at the frustration and agitation created when one is not heard correctly. Clearly, one of the skills of creatively using conflict is the ability to listen carefully.

We may think we listen well, yet listening is an underrated skill. There are all kinds of background noises vying for our attention that have to be fended off when we're trying to listen. Your stomach growls, the phone rings, you've heard this before, you think you know what's coming next, you've got to be somewhere else in five minutes, the other person says something that makes you want to pounce so you don't hear the rest of the sentence—the list is endless. If we listen this poorly in ordinary conversation, what do you think happens in a conflict? Near-deafness sets in!

While many executives and other leaders think they listen well, those who've had to sit through 360 feedbacks know that their staff may have other opinions! Many leaders tend to have short attention spans—classic pit bulls—who are used to being the smartest person in the room and may have trouble waiting for someone who likes to think before talking. While frequently the leader may have the best idea—otherwise, he or she would not have risen through the ranks—today's global competitive environment demands that we seek the best ideas from all our people. If you're managing people from around the world, for example, you may be discovering that many other cultures do not value direct communication as much as Americans do. In order to make sure that they understand that you value their communication, you'll have to slow down, draw them out, and yes, listen well.

Preparing to Listen

When we're arguing during a conflict, most of us are not listening; we are, as my son says, "just talking to ourselves." Clearly, one of the most important creative conflict management skills is listening. In order to listen well, we need to prepare.

This problem tends to become more prevalent the higher we climb in most organizations. If we're a class pit bull, we may have surrounded ourselves with golden retrievers who tend to say what we want to hear. We'll have to work extra hard to make sure that they know we're prepared to listen to all their ideas.

Most of us understand the importance of preparing ourselves to speak, but few of us think about preparing to listen. We take for granted that we all know how to listen. We may also assume listening is a passive activity, yet it is actually difficult to do and we are rarely prepared to listen well. The Indian philosopher Krishnamurti put it this way:

> I do not know if you have ever examined how you listen, it doesn't matter to what, whether to a bird, to the wind in the leaves, to the rushing waters, or how you listen in a dialogue with yourselves, to your conversation in various relationships with your intimate friends, your wife or husband. If we try to listen, we find it extraordinarily difficult, because we are always projecting our opinions and ideas, our prejudices, our background, our inclinations, our impulses; when they dominate, we hardly listen to what is being said. In that state,

there is no value at all. One listens and therefore learns only in a state of attention, a state of silence in which this whole background is in abeyance, is quiet; then, it seems to me, it is possible to communicate.

Deep listening also allows more space for the possibility of creativity and innovation. In order to listen well, we have to quiet our minds, to silence what my friend, Caryle, calls "the rock band in our heads." Most of us have a habit of taking our constant mind chatter seriously. We never stop to think about whether that makes any sense for us. Emerson once joked that 95% of what goes on inside our minds is none of our business.

This doesn't mean that we have to retreat to a cave or spend our lives meditating; it means that we have to consciously create a space where listening can occur, especially during conflict.

Part of the problem is our lack of understanding about how our minds work and how the mind and our senses interact, especially what we hold in our mind as "truths." Our hearing is ever present. There is no switch to turn it off. We can close our eyes, but not our ears. We live in a culture where we're constantly bombarded by sounds; our sense of balance is tied to our hearing. It's no accident that so many of us feel constantly out of balance because of the bombardment of information from inside our minds as well as external sounds.

My grandmother, Viva, became hard of hearing as she aged. At 90, her doctor gave her a hearing test and pronounced her hearing excellent. Family members continued to complain, however, that she frequently did not hear what they said or that they had to repeat themselves. The doctor tested her again and declared: "She does not have a hearing problem, she has a listening problem."

And no wonder. Approaching 90, my grandmother had raised seven children on a limited income, buried three of them (including one suicide) as well as her spouse, and served as sole caretaker for my 60-something invalid aunt. She remained the interested matriarch of a large family that included dozens of grandchildren and several great grandchildren. Viva kept up on current events, still tended her own roses, did her own cooking and house cleaning, and supervised various grandchildren who mowed her lawn ("mow it horizontal one week, alternating diagonals the next").

Viva had heard enough. She had earned the right to be selective in what she took in and what she didn't. Most of us, however, have not earned that right. Most of us have never bothered to *really* hear anyone. We live in a culture that has forgotten how to cultivate the art of listening. Unlike my grandmother, who was born before television and spent most of her life telling and listening to stories around the kitchen table, we are dominated by sight. Thousands of images flash across our minds in an hour of television or the Internet. Bombarded by rapid visuals, we've come to expect our information instantly. But listening operates on a different tempo.

We see through light. Light moves at 186,000 miles per second as opposed to sound, which travels at 1,100 feet per second. To listen, then, we must slow down far below the speed of light, far below the flickering changing images of videos and computers.

Our impatience hinders our listening and our creative conflict management. We want the world and we want it now! Yet, if we have the patience to listen, we'll learn more. In his book, *Nada Brohmn: The World is Sound Music and the Landscape of Consciousness*, Joachim-Ernst Berendt points out that the ear is the only sense that fuses an ability to measure with an ability to judge.

We can discern different colors, but we can give a precise *number* to different sounds. Our eyes do not let us perceive with this kind of perception. Even an unmusical person can recognize an octave. Berendt points out that there are few "acoustical illusions"—something sounding like something that, in fact, is not—while there are many optical illusions. The ears do not lie. The sense of hearing gives us a remarkable connection with the invisible, underlying order of things. Through our ears we gain access to vibrations, which lie below everything around us. The sense of tone and music in another's voice gives us an enormous amount of information about that person, about his or her intentions and stance toward life.

In fact, if we want to resolve a conflict and improve our relationship with someone, we might focus on the definition of resonance. In sound, energy *resonance* is transferred between objects that vibrate at the same frequency. Slowing down enough to listen well helps us develop resonance with the person with whom we have a conflict.

For example, I can be flip and glib. If you just read my words in an email communication and don't hear my tone and emotion, you may think I'm seriously attacking you.

This is why it's so important to talk face to face when we're having a conflict or anticipate that we might have a conflict with someone. If we communicate via email or letter, we can't really listen and we miss the subtle nuances that we might otherwise hear that reveal someone's true intentions. We also miss, of course, the visual clues that might help us understand someone, their facial expression and intention. Clearly, the ideal during conflict is to meet face to face.

Psychiatrist Edward Hallowell, in his wonderful book, *Connect*, talks about the high-powered executives he treats in the Boston area. These men have everything they ever thought they wanted: great jobs, beautiful houses, lovely children, and trophy wives. Yet, they're so depressed, they're being treated with medication. This was a significant change in Hallowell's practice over the last ten years. He started to research the reasons for their depression. What he discovered was that they all talked about how their work had changed.

A typical patient would wax nostalgically about how he used to spend his time coaching people, mentoring young associates, and leading group discussions. Now, instead, he spends his days "staring at a screen," answering email.

Hallowell started researching this problem and found that all of the time we spend interfacing with technology is actually changing the biochemistry of our brains and leading to clinical depression. He found this to be true in studies of adults as well as studies of children and animals. Babies, for example, who are fed and kept warm, but not held or loved, will gradually weaken and expire. Literally, we connect with others or we die.

And, as we are dying in our modern workplaces where we often lack connections, we become depressed and irritable. These moods fuel unproductive conflict and make valuable conflict more difficult to manage creatively.

Another contributing factor to this problem, I've found, is the increased focus on productivity in most organizations. We're doing more with less and Wall Street demands instant, or at least quarterly, results. We stare at the screen all day because that's where we may hope to find the most objective data about productivity. Yet productivity over the long haul demands more. Taking the time to mentor other managers, grow their leadership skills, or discuss how to add wellness programs will not give you immediate bottom-line results. I have no doubt, however, that these projects will ultimately improve both productivity and financial health long term.

Clearly, we're not going to regress to a world without voice or email, but the more human connections you can create at work, the better you and your associates will feel, and the more skillfully you'll be able to listen and manage conflict. And, when you're actually in the middle of trying to manage a significant dispute, make sure you do whatever it takes to sit down and communicate face to face.

We can learn to listen. We need to start with recognition of how we're listening now. Generally, we don't bother to think about how we listen. In addition to listening well to others, we need to listen to our own feelings and ourselves in order to communicate effectively during conflict.

Sometimes listening well during a conflict *is* enough. Sometimes all we need to do to miraculously solve an issue is make someone feel truly heard.

Ghosts in the Room

If we thoughtfully focus on how we listen, especially to our own thoughts and feelings, we will begin to identify what I call "ghosts in the room," when we're in conflict with someone.

To understand what I mean, think about a person you care about. When you do, you'll notice a flood of emotions and memories. To listen well is to understand that much of our present experience doesn't come from our current experience; it comes from our memory. And frequently, it's not even a memory of the person we're talking to right now, but a memory of someone long ago. We're reacting from stored reactions, not fresh responses. These are the *filters* through which we all listen. We hear everyone through our own filter of memory, desire, perceptions, and predispositions.

These filters are limited, even unintelligent, in the sense that they cannot respond in a *new* way to what is happening. We are busy reacting to something in the distant past. This limits our ability to be creative and innovative.

We need to learn to listen as *witnesses*. This means to learn to listen to what is objectively there as opposed to our messy stew of memory and desire. This is not easy to do. We are often unaware of the extent to which we assume what we see is what is there. Yet, if we think of ourselves as listening as a witness, we listen better.

When I use the term "witness," I mean it in two senses: both as a witness in court—an objective, sworn witness for the truth, not for the plaintiff or the defendant—and to learn to listen as the Quakers use the term "witness." In a Quaker fellowship, they practice a way to be present for the other person and wait to speak until they hear what they call the *still, small voice inside.*

Listen For and Check Out Misunderstandings

Many times, conflicts escalate because of misunderstandings, especially about the meaning of language. For example, I was having dinner with several business colleagues and one woman's spouse. The two people in the couple were both retired Army majors who had been in charge of large facilities. They were talking about their experiences during Vietnam and someone asked me if my then husband had served during that war. I said my husband was a C.O. They asked me of what unit. In their language, that phrase meant *commanding officer*. In fact, my ex-husband, who was raised as a Quaker, was a conscientious objector during the war. We all had a good laugh about the different meaning we automatically ascribe to the term "C.O."

We need to take care to check our misunderstandings—indeed, to assume misunderstandings—before we assume that someone is directly attacking us or trying to escalate the conflict.

In order to do this, we have to listen as a witness. We need to distinguish between the inferences we make about an experience and the experience itself. One way to do this is called the ladder of inference, developed by Chris Argyris, a professor at Harvard. He suggests that we process and create inferences about our experience at lightning speed, without noticing we are doing so. We don't notice the difference between a direct experience and our assessment of it.

We draw conclusions like this all of the time. Our conclusions take the form of reasoning that "this is the way it is." Yet, our first impressions are rarely accurate, as we can see from the example above.

Because we're all bombarded with so much stimulation, distraction, and data, we learn early in life to focus selectively on some things and ignore others. We leap to conclusions. While such leaps are efficient and sometimes essential, our speed sometimes causes us to confuse inference with fact. Chris Argyris calls this the "Ladder of Inference."

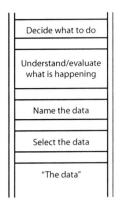

Figure 14.1

Inference ladder.

Based on the work of Chris Argyris in Reasoning, Learning, and Action: Individual and Organizational (San Francisco: Jossey-Bass, 1982).

Because we move so quickly from data to conclusions and opinions, we don't realize we have interpreted reality, screening out certain data along the way. During conflict, we can teach ourselves and the combatants to climb the ladder of inference openly and thoughtfully. If everyone understands such ladders exists and we climb them within seconds, usually suppressing all but the final step to a decision, then we can agree to be more explicit about how we reach conclusions. We can discuss whether others have different data or interpret data differently. We need to take ourselves through these steps:

- Objectively describe the behavior, what was said, or done or observed.
- Describe what each person heard, saw or observed in each person's own words.
- Determine what generalizations were made from the selected data.
- Describe how each person named the data, or labeled or categorized it.
- Determine what evaluation or conclusion was drawn.
- Describe how each person decided to act based on the evaluation or conclusion.

For example, consider a typical workplace conflict over schedule changes. One person, for example, hears there is a going to be a schedule change and she will now have to work weekends. She uses this data to pick a fight with her supervisor, sure that he picked on her because of a previous conflict. The argument escalates before he has a chance to explain he didn't order the change or develop the schedule. She moved at lightning speed from the data—the change itself—to a conclusion that their previous conflict was to blame and decides to engage in an angry confrontation. The supervisor, feeling defensive, fights back without taking the time to examine the cause of the conflict.

If the parties are "backed up" by going down the ladder of inference through the previous steps, it becomes clear why each reached the decision to act as he or she did. More important, when the rationale underlying the decision is laid bare, people can readily see where their inferences differ and can debate on those interpretations and logic rather than just on the final decision.

Conclusions, Facts, and More Ghosts

We form conclusions and then do not check them out, treating our initial conclusions as fact. We fail to investigate the roots of our own thinking. And even more damaging in the heat of conflict, we invest ourselves in an opinion and seek evidence that we are right and avoid evidence that we are wrong. This sends us into the *negative spiral of conflict*. We progress from our conclusions about subjects to assumptions that we invent about them and finally to belief. These beliefs tend to become dogma and resistant to change. We then see the world through the filter of our beliefs and, in fact, seek evidence that supports our opinions. This habit limits our creativity and productivity.

We can learn to listen in a way that challenges our automatic formation of beliefs that differentiates between the stories we make up about a set of facts from the facts themselves.

Listening well helps us creatively manage conflict. Yet, slowing down our thinking and listening in this way is not easy because the landscape is not neutral. Our memories and the resultant *ghosts in the room* can be quite painful. If I say something to you that you don't like, e.g., *you're stupid*, you may flash on a memory of an old teacher or parent who said the same thing. It will be difficult for you not to react emotionally, to respond from the present moment rather than from the pain of your memories. This is what we mean when we say that someone "pushes our buttons."

These ghosts from our past memory tend to cloud our listening. We listen mostly for evidence that our view of the world is right and others are wrong.

There is another way. We can listen instead at a deeper level for the *source* of the difficulty—whether it is in others or ourselves.

We can be *passionate* in our listening. We can learn to listen with as much energy and enthusiasm as we talk. Instead of listening for evidence that confirms our point of view, we can listen for the creative energy in the conflict—both in ourselves and in others. We listen for what challenges our view to begin to see how others see the world. This way of listening is not easy, yet it can create extraordinary creativity in managing conflict.

Then we can take the final and hardest step: we can begin to listen for disconnects, especially disconnect between what we say and what we do. None of us are 100% consistent. Most of us intend to do what we say we want to do, but few of us manage to do so. Frequently, if we listen hard enough to the rock bands in our own minds, we'll be surprised to realize that we're guilty of something similar to what we're accusing the other person of doing.

To grow in our own ability to listen, we need to be still, to listen to our own minds. We need to know when our own ghosts are in the room. If we do this long enough by ourselves, we'll find we're capable of really hearing others. We will have created a clear stream in which to be present for them.

To summarize, in order to listen well, follow these guidelines:

1. *Remember filters.* We all hear what is said through our own filters. Filters can include our assumptions, biases, our own history, experience, etc.

2. *Listen as a witness.* Ask, "how would I listen to this person if I knew I were going to be called as an objective witness in court?" "How can I listen well enough to hear the still, small voice inside of me?"

3. *Clarify.* Before you speak, make sure you understand what the other person is saying. Ask open-ended (non-leading) questions until you do.

4. *Restate.* Ask "I think you said ' . . . .' Is that accurate?" Continue restating until your partner agrees that you heard him or her accurately.

5. *Pause before you speak.* Ask yourself which conflict style you're using and why. Is it the style that will serve you best over the long term of this relationship? Is the response you're considering likely to lead to more creativity and productivity? What response would be most likely to lead to those results?

6. *At the end of a communication, summarize the conversation and clarify the original reason for the communication.* Did the speaker want your advice, feedback, a sympathetic ear, action, or a solution to a problem? Be sure you know *why* you were asked to listen and what you're expected to do—if anything—about the communication. Many of us jump in too quickly to give advice or fix a problem before even bothering to ask if the speaker wants advice.

7. *Assume 100% of the responsibility for the communication.* Assume leadership in your communication. Assume it is your responsibility to listen until you understand and to speak in a way others can understand.

8. *Check out misunderstandings.* Assume miscommunication before you assume someone is trying to undermine your efforts. Back yourself and the other parties up by going over the ladder of influence.

Conflict and Culture Clash

Sometimes a conflict is actually a clash of cultures. We need to realize different cultures have very different approaches to conflict and communication. As we previously learned, diverse work groups produce more creative results, but they also require more sophisticated communication skills. If you're trying to creatively manage conflicts, you need to recognize when this happens. Communication will stall, and we won't be able to hear and be heard if there's a culture clash and you're not aware it's happening.

For example, the dominant culture in this country values a conflict resolution model that is rather confrontational. We see ourselves in the John Wayne mode: we talk straight and we shoot straight. Yet this model is different from that used in many cultures where direct confrontation is considered rude. Instead, those cultures value the use of *mediators*. Conflict management is accomplished through a third party—a trusted family friend, priest, or advisor.

One way to find out if a conflict is culture related is to ask the following:

- Have several attempts at creatively managing this conflict failed?
- Is the present conflict one of a series?
- Does the conflict seem emotional beyond what you would predict based upon the immediate problem?
- Are the people involved in the conflict from different cultures? Are there obvious differences in race, gender, education, age, or work groups?

In addition to the creative conflict management tools we've already discussed, the following can help resolve a cultural clash.

Gain Agreement

Work with those involved to help them understand:

- There is a conflict.
- We share a common goal to creatively manage it.
- What we've tried so far hasn't worked.

Identify Hot Buttons

Say something like: "There seems to be something that 'x' says or that I say that always sets you off. What is it?"

Clarify back to the person: "It seems that what sets you off is . . . ."

Look for a Cultural Source

Ask something like: "With your background, is that an important concern?" or "With your background, how would you expect someone to act in this situation?"

Caution: Do not say: "With your background as an African American, woman, generation Xer, etc., is this an important concern?" There are many different aspects of our background that create our culture. Allow the co-worker (if he or she chooses) to bring up exactly what factors in his or her background drive the reaction.

Summarize the Conflict as a Cultural Difference

In your own words, emphasize to the other people involved: "Where you come from, you expect . . . ."

Negotiate a Creative Dialogue

Say something like: "We all agreed we want to creatively manage this conflict. We've begun to understand what the conflict is about. Because we have to work together, what do you suggest we do now to creatively use this conflict to help you work together more productively?"

- Keep asking until both of you can focus on specific behaviors—words and actions—that you need from the other person to work together.
- Get a commitment from each side to live up to or reject the others' request. Agree to monitor the situation to make sure it is managed.

If you are the conflicted parties' boss and you're trying to mediate a solution, emphasize you need everyone to work together effectively as a team in support of the organization's goals. If they cannot learn to work together as a team, you will have to explore other options, including discipline. Work to make creative conflict management skills a part of *their* job requirements.

Cultural conflicts can be intense yet bring creative results. Jerry Hirshberg, for example, faced a daunting and complex task of conceiving automobile designs in California and seeing them manufactured in Japan. Yet through constant communication they were able to bridge the gap. The resulting cultural clashes required "reaching across seemingly impregnable barriers between foreign cultures." As he explained the challenge:

> We were dealing with a people for whom "saying it like it is," "going directly to the horse's mouth," and "looking them straight in the eyes" were not universally recognized codes of conduct. Nor was turning down someone's urgent request with a straightforward, honest "no" considered more

noble than avoiding the possibility of causing them a "loss of face." Indeed, all these behaviors were considered highly unappealing and even untrustworthy by the Japanese.

While Hirshberg notes that standard "paperbacks" about doing business in Japan cautioned against directly discussing cultural issues, he walked a different path.

The solution, he found, was to struggle to remain open, learn to read the shadings of different cultures and, most importantly, risk talking openly about differences in culture: "While such discussions can at times be unsettling and possibly even threatening, they can also become trip wires for fresh takes on old assumptions. In other words, they are opportunities for new ideas."

Communication and Power

Most leaders agree that good communication is essential to creative conflict and a productive workplace. As the workplace becomes more diverse, good communication is even more important. What many leaders miss, however, is an understanding that our perceptions of the amount of power we have in any interaction influences our communication style.

Linguists tell us that if we perceive we have less power than the person or group that we're communicating with, we will engage in what linguist Deborah Tannen calls *rapport talk*. This is talk designed to improve and build relationships. It is conciliatory, polite, and friendly. When using rapport talk, we say things such as, "You might be unaware that . . . " before delivering a negative message. We may also say things such as, "I'm not sure if this is right, but maybe we should . . . ." We ask permission before we do things: "Would you mind if I . . .?" We tend to ask for the other person's advice and approval.

If we believe that we have more or equal power with the person we're talking to, we tend to use what Tannen calls *report talk*. This is communication that focuses on delivering information and accomplishing tasks. This talk tends to sound like orders. When we use this talk we tend to start our sentences with "I (or we) need to do 'x'." "I want or need 'x'."

Some linguists, such as Tannen in her book, *You Just Don't Understand*, believe that women tend to use more *rapport talk* and men tend to use more *report talk*. Others point to the difference in power as the key. Because women have tended to have less power in most workplaces, they tend to use more *rapport talk*. Studies have found that other groups that historically have had less power, such as African Americans, also use more *rapport talk*. Significantly, a person may use one kind of talk in the workplace and another kind of talk at home where they may believe they have more power.

The importance for diversity and conflict in the workplace is that the group that tends to use *report talk* may view other groups as weak or ineffectual or wasting time because they use so much *rapport talk*. Conversely, the group that tends to use communication to develop rapport, may view the group that uses *report talk* as brusque, cold, angry, rude, etc. Many conflicts result from this difference of perception.

Ask yourself the following questions:

- Which of the two styles do you see yourself using at work?
- With whom do you use a different style?
- What is the primary style you observe people in power using at work?
- What would the benefits be to you of using a different style?
- What benefits to the organization would there be if you used different styles as appropriate for different situations?

Is your style the one most likely to use conflict to drive creativity, productivity, and innovation?

There is no right or wrong style in all situations. The key to creative conflict management is to stop and think before you speak in order to determine which communication style is most appropriate in any given situation. As a leader, you will also need to be aware of your responsibility to mentor others in your organization so that they can gain these strategies. In addition, listening well and deeply will also help you slow down and welcome others' opinions, the subject of the next chapter.

Chapter 15
Welcoming a Different Opinion: How to Be Confrontable

People who don't mind telling the truth have mixed feelings about hearing the truth.

—Jerry Hirshberg, President,
Nissan Design International, Inc.

A vice president in a regional health care system is charged with merging the home care and hospice functions of two separate hospital systems. The staff of one system is furious their leader hadn't been put in charge. They complain. They sling mud. They are uncooperative. They even send anonymous, slanderous letters to the CEO. The vice president perseveres. She meets individually with every manager and supervisor to hear their concerns and deal directly with their anger. She spends an entire year building a dynamic team that would have the courage and strength to sit around a conference table and work out their disagreements to creatively solve problems. Eighteen months later, they lead the entire hospital system in bottom-line performance, customer satisfaction, and Gallup leadership results. This eagle vice president recognizes the signs that can signal big problems lurking ahead, and she sets a tenor that welcomes divergent opinions and disagreement.

When a leader creates an atmosphere that makes it safe to disagree, he or she is actually creating a much more productive and creative workplace. It minimizes down time and loss of focus and distractions that interfere with daily operations. There are numerous strategies you can use to value conflict and to make the environment safer for creative conflict management: an open door policy, using *rapport talk*, and maintaining confidentiality, as well as others. It goes without saying that the people who have the most difficulty with making these adjustments are those who are aggressive and intimidating—the pit bulls of the organization. In this chapter, old dogs will learn some new tricks.

133

Are You Confrontable?

Are you safe to confront? When I'm asked to coach executives who've been accused of not welcoming new ideas, abuse, harassment, discrimination, poor conflict management skills, or general "poor people management" skills, they frequently lament: "But I didn't know he or she objected to my behavior. Why didn't they tell me?"

To this popular excuse I always respond: "What have *you* done to make it safe for them to come to you and challenge your ideas or complain about your behavior?"

This question is usually followed by silence. The executive views *confrontaphobia* as the other person's problem. But if you feast on conflict like a pit bull *and* if you're viewed as a person who has power in the organization (these two frequently go hand-in-hand), then you're probably difficult for others to confront. You'll need to take specific steps to make it safer for people to confront you.

One of the best ways to overcome your previous reputation is to be honest about your style. At the next staff meeting, mention that your own awareness has been raised about this issue and you've realized you may not have been the easiest person to approach with a new idea or conflict. Announce that you've changed your attitude and ask for suggestions about what would make it easier for people to come to you. You might try something like this:

> I'm becoming increasingly aware of how much I need the feedback of each and every one of you to make this organization a success. I want us to be more innovative and productive. But because I've had a reputation in the past as a pit bull who approaches every conflict or new idea as a personal attack or as an opportunity to debate, I'm realizing that some of you may not have found me approachable. What could I do to make it easier for each of you to come to me with conflicts, feedback, or suggestions?

Be prepared for resounding silence.

Your reputation as a pit bull will not be easy to overcome. As one high-powered attorney I coached complained about the associates in his firm: "*They won't talk to me; they think I'm the prince of f----- darkness.*"

If you continue to ask for suggestions about your approachability, however, hints will eventually arrive at your doorstep.

You may ask, "Why do I care?" Many people with an abrasive style have been successful and even gained power in the workplace. As Vick, one VP of Finance complained when I gave him feedback about his brutal style that had generated a score of employee complaints, "In other organizations, my style would be viewed as an advantage. In fact, I used to receive compliments here for being a tough boss and a hard charger. People today are just too sensitive."

The reality is, the workplace *has* changed. An abrasive style may have been successful yesterday; it will not be successful in the future.

The intrusion of the law into people management in the workplace is one obvious reason for the change. The likelihood of an employee charging you with harassment, discrimination, or a violation of the Americans' With Disabilities Act (which now may cover psychological as well as physical disabilities) skyrockets if you have a pit bull reputation. You may protest you're not discriminating against any particular person, you treat everyone this way. In my experience, that argument won't fly with courts or juries. They assume that if you're abusive to everyone, you're even more abusive to people who have less power in the organization, usually women and people of color. Even if you do succeed, you will be stuck with the embarrassing defense of presenting a parade of witnesses to attest to how abusive you were to *them* also.

And these groups will make up more of the workplace as our labor force becomes more diverse. According to the Hudson Institute in their *Workforce 2000 Report,* by the year 2000, only 15% of new workers will be white males. In their updated version, *Workforce 2020,* the 21st century will bring a huge increase in older workers, adding new diversity management issues. A recent survey reports that almost two-thirds of these workers will have elder care responsibilities. The U.S. Census Bureau predicts that the U.S. population will swell from its current 288 million to over 400 million in the next 50 years. The majority of new immigrants will be non-English speakers. The addition of young people—the so-called generation Y—who have been raised in a world of technology with different values than their managers, requires new skills. Most experts find that these young workers need closer ties to their immediate supervisors, a high degree of stimulation, and also need to understand why they're being asked to perform any task in order to stay motivated and engaged. In addition, many executives today manage teams flung throughout the globe: a call center in India, a team of developers in France, or an army of telecommuters. These diverse workforces require entirely new skills and a high degree of awareness about cultural differences and mores.

The second reason is that with the change in the economy, the unpredictable labor market, and the interdependent way most organizations are managed, no one can succeed alone. You'll need the suggestions, dedication, and brainpower of all your people in order to prosper in the future. To elicit the best ideas from your troops, you need to encourage honest feedback.

Many organizations now evaluate both leaders and co-workers based upon how well they address issues such as diversity, consensus, and team building. You can't survive in most organizations without these kinds of skills.

If you're the boss, after announcing at your next meeting your change in your own *modus operandi*, I'd also suggest you start having weekly 15-minute one-on-one meetings with your direct reports. In those meetings, there should be one item on your agenda—keep asking the questions: *What do you need from me or others to be successful here? What behaviors do I or others engage in that limit your success?*

Again, when you first ask these questions, be prepared for silence. If you continue to ask these questions week after week, month after month, however, eventually your colleagues will tell you what they need from you. They'll be more willing to bring you new ideas. More importantly, you will start to see patterns in how others in the organization perceive you and what you must do to change.

You need to keep asking these kinds of questions—not because you're automatically going to change your behavior to suit others—but because you need to be able to skillfully manage their expectations about your behavior. Once you know how they want you to treat them, you can begin to have an honest dialogue about what you can both do differently in the future to make your relationship succeed.

If you're a leader in your organization, consider the model Robert Rodin, President and CEO of Marshall Industries, uses:

> The more you insist on hearing the truth, and the more often you act on what you've heard, the more often people will give it to you. But most leaders do precisely the opposite. Their companies systematically distort the truth—by design . . . . It's human nature to avoid conflict . . . . If you want to hear criticism, you have to invite it. At least once a month, I convene a forum called "Marshall Live." I gather people at one of our sites: no managers are allowed. I start every meeting by saying something like "This is your company. Tell me what's wrong with it." I get amazing feedback. And

then I promise to deal with the feedback in two weeks or less. We don't always do what people want: Companies aren't democracies. But people know that we haven't just heard their criticisms—we've dealt with them.

If someone does summon the nerve to complain directly to you about your behavior: stop. Do not immediately respond. Listen to the suggestion of Jerry Hirshberg:

> Even people who don't mind telling the truth have mixed feelings about hearing the truth. It's like a chemical reaction: Your face goes red, your temperature rises, you want to strike back. Those are signs of the "two D's": defending and debating. Try to fight back with the "two L's:" listening and learning . . . . So the next time you feel yourself defending and debating, stop—and start listening and learning instead. You'll be amazed by what you hear.

A Step-by-Step Approach

When someone comes to you with a conflict, a new idea, or a criticism about your behavior, follow these steps:

1. *Stop what you're doing and listen.* Give the person your complete attention. If you cannot do that, schedule an appointment as soon as possible.

2. *Do not get defensive.* First restate what the person said to make sure you understood. Say, for example, "Let me make sure I understand what you said. I heard you say you don't want me to yell at you when I give you feedback. Is that correct?" or "It sounds as if you have a new idea about how to speed up our production schedule."

3. *Apologize if appropriate.* If you're convinced you did nothing wrong, at least say you're sorry your behavior offended them. A good boss or co-worker should be sorry someone else is upset even if they're convinced the other person over-reacted. If you really did do something very wrong, grovel.

4. *Ask what specific behavior the person needs from you in order to work effectively with you in the future or what their specific idea or request is.* Be certain you focus on *behavior*, not *attitudes* or their *feelings*. You can change your own behavior, but you may never be able to change

how they feel. Also try to get them to focus on what their specific idea or request is rather than complaints.

5. *Thank them for bringing the matter to your attention and for their courage and honesty.* Let them know you respect and appreciate them for talking with you directly. Unless it's impossible or outrageous, tell them you'll consider their new idea or suggestion.

6. *Follow-up.* Make sure you schedule another meeting with them to see if your change in behavior or your response to their idea has met their needs.

7. *Keep talking and keep meeting until your working relationship improves.* If the two of you cannot make it work together, seek an experienced mediator to help you manage your differences.

Does this all sound like too much effort? Unfortunately, there's no quick and easy way to change a pit bull's reputation. You do it by changing your own behavior—inch-by-inch, day-by-day. You also do it by assuming leadership in conflict management in your organization and by encouraging feedback as learning.

How to Manage Your Own Anger

The biggest challenge for most pit bulls in becoming *confrontable* may be managing their own anger. *Understanding* your anger is the first step.

The practical, popular psychologist Dr. Joyce Brothers, in an interview, summarized the current research about anger management. Understand, she stressed, that your own anger is all about fear, especially the fear of exposing something about yourself and the fear of losing control.

When you feel anger, before exploding, ask yourself of what or whom you are afraid. What might you lose in the encounter? How might you be hurt? Knowing the real, underlying reason may help you control your anger.

Next, suggests Dr. Brothers, don't ignore your anger, but don't express rage inappropriately. There was a time when people thought it healthy to immediately express their anger. More recent research, however, suggests that constant ventilating actually makes us more angry rather than less. The most accepted theory is to assume a middle ground between exploding and suppressing anger. Follow these tips, Dr. Brothers suggests:

- Don't ignore your anger, but don't immediately blow up.
- Count to ten.
- Direct your anger at the proper person.

- Deal with the issue at hand; don't bring up old issues.
- Confront the person in private.
- Stay calm; act calm.
- Don't smile—smiling can be viewed as mocking and can increase anger.
- Use "I" statements, i.e., "I don't want you to throw away my papers without asking," rather than "You have no respect for my things."
- Wait for their explanation.
- Offer understanding (let them save face).

If counting to 10 doesn't work, Dr. Brothers suggests you count to 100!

If you can manage your anger so that you're *confrontable*, and if you encourage skillful confrontation in your own organization, you can move from defending and debating to listening and learning. You can evolve from debate to dialogue. You will have taken another giant step on the road to unleashing the power of a good fight.

Learning to Value the Confrontable Organization

It may be helpful to you and others in your organization as you do the hard work of learning to welcome a different opinion if you understand just how critical this essential skill is for the future of your organization. Sally Helgesen, author of *The Web of Inclusion: A New Architecture for Building Great Organizations* found in her study that the ability to create open communication where people felt comfortable giving and receiving feedback at all levels of the organization was one of the key predictors of organizational success.

One of my clients, Jane, started her own successful telecommunications company based on this very premise. A long-distance service "re-seller," Jane's company was one of a score of such companies that made their business on the idea of buying long-distance services from the larger telecommunications companies, bundling them in unique ways, and reselling them to individuals. Both Jane and her staff came from various members of the old Bell system.

Accustomed to large, hierarchical organizations, Jane and her staff wanted a change. "We wanted to look like the telecommunications network we were selling. We devised a complex web—like a matrix, really—of interlocking people and departments. We wanted everyone to have access to anyone they needed in the organization. We wanted everyone's thoughts and ideas so that we would up with the best solutions to our problems."

One of Jane's first problems was how to design the offices. Breaking with years of Bell tradition, she put her own office out in the open with the other staffers. She toiled at a desk, no walls or even a cube to separate her from her employees. Anyone could talk to her anytime about any concerns. Jane had no secretary and no set schedule. Although this sometimes resulted in a line surrounding her desk, she welcomed the open atmosphere the design created.

"Spontaneous meetings erupted around my desk," Jane told me. "We finally put a couch next to it so that people could participate without fainting from fatigue."

The informal system had another benefit: rumors were nipped in the bud because anyone who wanted to participate in the initial discussion could. There were no secret meetings behind closed doors. Jane's power as a leader came from the extraordinary openness she was able to demonstrate. Creative solutions flowed out of the chaos surrounding Jane's desk.

Jane also instituted an electronic bulletin board where anyone could post questions about what the company was doing and why. No queries were off limits. Postings ranged from "Why don't we have a better brand of coffee?" to "Why is our stock down this morning?" Jane, or one of her assistants, answered these queries within forty-eight hours or let the questioner know when the information would be available.

Perhaps most important, Jane shaped her successful company by listening and asking the right questions. When anyone would come to her with an issue, her response was always, "What do you think we should do?" Or, "What are your team's ideas for solving that problem?" No one doubted that Jane was anxious to seek out their opinion or to be confronted about any issue.

In part, because of the depth of inclusion and confrontability Jane was able to create, her company survived the recent telecommunications shake down that plunged many other companies into bankruptcy. When the market tightened, Jane simply solicited the best ideas of all of her employees. Instead of the lay-offs other companies had to stomach, Jane asked her people what they should do. When someone suggested offering voluntary three-month sabbaticals to those who wanted them, Jane agreed. Around 15% of her employees took advantage of her offer over the next two years; enough to get the company over its financial hump.

Similarly, Southwest Airlines has always created an inclusive culture where everyone from a vice president to a baggage handler knew they could offer suggestions and feedback. Everyone refers to president, chairman, and CEO Herb Kelleher as "Herb," and he seems to know all the employees by their first names. Once, after I gave a speech to their executives, I attempted to walk across the crowded hall with Herb to the buffet table. He stopped so often to ask how someone's divorce was going or to inquire after a new baby, that I gave up in starvation and fetched lunch by myself. The new head of Southwest, Coleen Barrett, is well known for her own encyclopedic knowledge of employee birthdays, anniversaries, and work preferences.

When new employees start at Southwest, they're given a list of one hundred questions to answer about the company. Everyone's door—right up to Herb's—is open to these new questioners. From an employee's first moment at Southwest, they know that they can approach anyone with questions or concerns.

What is the benefit of such extraordinary access? When other airlines were forced to lay off employees after the September 11 attacks on the World Trade Center and the United States Pentagon, Southwest instead assured employees that they would stand firm and asked employees to suggest any cost saving ideas they might have. The strategy worked and Southwest flew through the storm.

Another one of my clients, a manufacturing company, has always avoided unions in an industry that's largely unionized. "How do they manage this feat?", I once asked the vice president of employee relations. "If you don't want a union," he responded, "act as if you already have one."

Indeed, the company recently fought off an attempted organizing effort by stepping up its normally frenetic schedule of town meetings, management/labor baseball games, and CEO informal lunches with employees, emphasizing access, access, access. The would-be union lost again, gaining only 10% of the workers' votes. In addition, profits were up for the third year in a row, running against the industry norm.

Likewise, a large school district in our state was fraught with dissention from teacher unrest, parent unhappiness, and student agitation. When the new superintendent took over, she announced that she was delegating most of her day-to-day duties to one of her deputies. Instead, she would spend her first year "listening and learning." She got an earful.

Teachers wanted more pay and more support. Students wanted open campuses and smoking lounges; parents wanted higher educational standards; and voters wanted better administration accountability. She realized that there was only one way to achieve everyone's objectives: a new bond issue to raise money. The only problem? The past three bond issues had failed miserably.

Continuing to listen to the suggestions from the various stakeholders, she told the voters that she had adopted one citizens group's gutsy idea: the district would receive new money from voters only if they managed to achieve specific educational objectives. No gains, no money. The bond issue passed.

Creating a confrontable organization doesn't happen overnight, and the process can challenge some of our most cherished assumptions about the way things should be. Yet, as these examples illustrate, welcoming a different opinion can lead to good fights as well as increased success. Because the change itself can create conflict, in the next chapter we'll focus on another aspect of creative contention: dealing with change.

Chapter 16
Making Changes Makes Waves: How to Swim, Not Sink

All things must change to something new, to
something strange.

—Henry Wadsworth Longfellow

A large financial institution reorganizes its Human Resources department with the goal of overhauling employee training and development. Senior management thinks that employee skills are lagging. They bring in several new players to bring fresh energy and more capacity to the department. Maria, the new VP of HR, previously worked in a hierarchical company with a command and control structure. She roars into the fray with classic pit bull tactics: barking orders and charging into change without listening to the needs of the current team. Her hand-picked director, Michael, listens to everyone's ideas and then snipes behind their backs about how stupid he thinks they all are. Frustrated, the old team—accustomed to a consensus style management—agrees to changes in public meetings and then engages in foot-dragging and delaying tactics behind the scenes. The result is a huge culture clash between the new and old employees that paralyzes the department.

When an organization makes changes, conflict increases. The upheaval creates uncertainty that can degenerate into turf wars, resentments, sabotage, and multiple negative behaviors. Underlying many of these behaviors are issues of culture, grief, loss, or fear of loss. These are major organizational issues that determine whether a merger will succeed or whether the employees will work to make it fail. On a smaller scale, substantial change within a single department or in reporting relationships, can create crippling conflicts if not handled with foresight, thoughtfulness, and respect. Coping with change is probably one of the single-most important skills in today's business arena.

143

Never before has so much change taken place so quickly. In the past 40 years there has been more technological advancement than in all of recorded history, and it has altered the way people, communities, and entire countries interact, work, and live. In order to use conflict creatively, we must understand the impact of change in our organizations and on our own lives.

Many times intractable conflicts are really about our resistance to change whether organizational, personal, or practical. Skillful conflict management requires an understanding of this dynamic at the strategic and employee level. While senior managers are worried about changes in leadership style, teams of employees may be upset about simple but small changes such as a change in the coffee or discontinued free sodas. It's hard for executives to often look at both the large and small reactions to change and focus on the essence. When we find ourselves resistant to a new idea, it's usually because we're resistant to *change*. Even if we don't like the way we're currently working or behaving, it's familiar. Sometimes we create unnecessary conflicts in the workplace because we refuse to recognize or admit this. If we continue to resist the change, we're unlikely to creatively harness the power of conflict.

I've worked with many groups who had conflicts between old leaders and employees and new leaders and employees. Many times, for example, when I'm facilitating a diversity workshop, the most conflicted groups will be those who represent the old versus the new as a result of mergers or acquisitions, not those who represent different ethnic backgrounds or genders.

In one such instance, I was brought in to help a larger HR department manage a simmering dispute between old and new members. The old managers saw themselves as serving the more traditional role of *employee advocates*. The old VP, Joe, came from an employer relations background and emphasized representing employee needs. The newer members of the department aligned with Ron, a new high-powered vice president of HR, and saw themselves as strategic *business partners* who needed to serve the highest-ranking manager of whatever business unit they were assigned to.

After much discussion, we came up with a creative definition of their role that embraced both ideas. The reason it took them so long and required a facilitator was not so much the substantive conflict itself as it was the whole issue of *change*. The old managers were literally struggling with the grieving process as they moved into a new and uncertain future. The new VP and the new managers were also struggling with the change process. Even though the move to new jobs was something they had all sought, they had to learn that even positive changes take us through the predictable stages of loss and grief. If we don't acknowledge and move through each stage, we will flounder. Frequently, because we're not conscious of why we feel upset, we will project our anxiety outside ourselves onto our co-workers. Conflicts naturally follow.

Once the group had an opportunity to talk honestly about the changes they were all experiencing and were able to express the common feelings they shared, the underlying issues were much easier to creatively explore.

The Stages of Grief

Most of us feel comforted by the familiar. Whenever we have to learn or do something new, we go through classic and predictable stages of leaving the old ways. These stages are those of the grief process, first identified by Elizabeth Kubler-Ross in her work with the dying. Conflicts almost always involve underlying issues of grief, loss, or the fear of loss. These stages are:

Denial—we deny the event or action is occurring. Sometimes we engage in bargaining at this stage.

Anger—we're angry the event or action has occurred; it's common at this stage to be unaware of the real source of our anger. We may lash out at other people or events instead.

Depression—we realize that bargaining won't work and we feel a deep sadness, usually disguised as depression, over this realization.

Acceptance—we accept that the change will occur, adjust our lives accordingly, and start planning for the future.

Be aware that most of us do not travel through these stages on a straight line. We may proceed with one step forward, two steps backward. Yet, if we're aware of the grief process and if we chart our progress, we generally move in an upward spiral to resolution and acceptance.

When we're faced with a new idea or change, it's important to take stock of where we are in the change process and work through our feelings. The only way around these feelings is through them. If we deny they exist, we block the energy that we could use more successfully for the future. If we sink too deeply into any stage, that also leaves us paralyzed. Some people remain stuck at one stage for months, years, or even a lifetime.

An awareness of the process and an active attempt to experience and move through your emotions will propel you to the future. Talking with someone—

a trusted friend, minister, or counselor—who is educated about the grieving process, can be helpful. Be careful to select someone who understands grieving and who will not just urge you to move on and ignore your feelings.

Expressing your emotions creatively through writing, dance, art, or singing can also be helpful. The trick is to do *something*—not just to sit back passively and assume that your emotions will take care of themselves. Taking care of our emotions responsibly, through one of these methods, is just as essential as taking care of our bodies through diet, exercise, and visits to a health care practitioner.

Managing Change or Managing Your Future?

Once you have started a regular process to deal with your emotions around change and how you personally handle transitions, try to expand your thinking about "change management" to "managing your future." Many organizations, speakers, and books these days emphasize change management, but I caution you about these programs. If we're only managing change, we're probably in a reactive or catch-up mode. I try to help people anticipate and plan for the future instead. Now the future is all about change, but language is so important that I avoid the words "managing change." Managing the future goes hand-in-hand with learning how to assume leadership in conflict and use it creatively.

Organizational change management programs make people focus on something that's being done to them rather than their own active participation. "Change management" programs also sometimes create the illusion this change will be the last and allows the ostriches among us to hunker down and wait it out—an "I'm going to hide until things calm down" attitude. Most organizations today are trying to encourage employees to feel "empowered" (another fuzzy word). The whole idea of change management runs counter to that goal.

As John Scully, one of the founders of Apple, emphasizes: "The best way to be ready for the future is to invent it." I agree with author William Bridges' prediction in *Jobshift: How to Prosper in the New Economy*, that in the future we will all be contingent workers without traditional tidy job descriptions. Learning how to manage work in the "dejobbed" workplace of the future will require skills far beyond "change management." All of these workplace changes tend to create more conflict.

You will need to acquire creative conflict management skills in order to stay happily working. Successful people stay ahead of change and anticipate the future. As Andy Grove, founder of Intel, emphasizes in his book, *Only The Paranoid Survive*, we need to learn the power of positive paranoia. In a future without jobs, we need to learn how to forecast the future, and then imagine and place ourselves in new work rather than just learning how to manage the present chaos. Future forecasting and planning is a way you can create power in the present moment.

A provocative ad I saw asked: "The World Wide Web is the Future. Do you want to be the spider or the fly?" To which I would add the twist, "Do you want to spin your own future work or just be caught in the web of change?"

To do this you will need an additional element—a *querencia*. Querencia is a term from bullfighting, which is not a bad metaphor for how you may feel as you evolve into future workers.

In bullfighting, matadors swear every bull has a place in the ring where he feels safe, untouchable, and where—no matter how much skill the bullfighter has—the bull remains unreachable as long as he is in this space—his *querencia*. If the bull can reach this spot, he stops running and gathers his strength. From the matador's point of view, the bull is a powerful opponent in this space. A matador must know where the sanctuary lies for each bull and make sure the animal cannot reach his own refuge.

In a future with so much constant change and the resulting conflict, you will need to create your own individual *querencia*. I would recommend an actual physical space—not just a psychological metaphor. Some suggestions: a house you love that's paid for or with low mortgage payments, a supportive social, spiritual, or neighborhood community, or a trade or professional association. What cannot be your *querencia* in the future is a traditional job because most organizations will continue to evolve, reorganize, and change. Unfortunately, in recent history, too many of us relied upon our jobs to serve as our security and refuge.

When I coach executives and other professionals who are dealing with change and the resulting conflict, that's the first thing I ask: where is your *querencia*? Once you have a sanctuary in the ring, the stress of feeling as if you're a constant target subsides. Yet, for most of us in our mobile, transient society, we haven't stopped whirling through change long enough to create a safe place. If you fit that profile, before you attempt to do anything else related to "change management" or an intense conflict: stop. Do whatever it takes to find, create, and nurture your own *querencia*. Without it, you will not be able to harness the creative power of conflict.

In times of organization change and transition, conflicts increase. In order to increase your skills in managing conflict, you need to understand the relationship between change and transition.

Transition Management

Author William Bridges, Ph.D., has been fundamental in introducing the concept of *transition management* as opposed to *change management*. Change management focuses on designing the desired change and using persuasion to move a group toward change.

Transition management acknowledges that even if the change is beneficial and desirable, most people have trouble moving through the stages of change and their resistance creates conflicts. While the traditional grieving process described earlier tends to show up for individuals, groups also need to look at transition management. Frequently, it's not the outcome that people are resisting; it's the sometimes painful, disruptive, and scary movement through the transition process. Failure to acknowledge that fact and design systems to assist with the movement toward change frequently results in a failed change effort. Bridges identifies three stages of transition management:

1. *Endings*. The old way is ending and must be acknowledged. Groups often design ceremonies, parties, or other ways of marking this stage. Some groups even have fun with this stage by presenting elaborate mock "funerals" for the ending.

2. *The Neutral Zone*. What I like to call the "no man's land," or "chaos zone." The old way is ending, but the new is not yet visible. In this stage, a great many people problems, productivity problems, and conflicts arise.

3. *The New Beginning*. When the new is finally in place and visible, and people are actually implementing the new system or idea. Beginnings also require acknowledgment through a ceremony, party, or other visible sign.

For example, one of my clients began a large-scale reorganization effort designed to change their command-and-control environment to a more inclusive one. The CEO expected employees to love the changes, since they would have more input into decision-making. Much to his surprise, however, workers balked. They questioned the changes, carped that the proposal was too complex, and generally stalled on implementing new processes and procedures.

At first the executive team assumed that the employees were resisting the change itself, so they started a series of focus groups to better inform people of why they were installing the new methods and procedures. What the groups revealed, however, was that workers didn't object to the goal, what they were resisting was the transition process through the change itself. Their number one question? "What resources are going to be available to help me do my job during this transition?" Without knowing *how* they personally could get through the change, the workers wanted no part in understanding the *whys* behind the change.

Start to consider how many of your own conflicts or the conflicts you observe around you at work are actually issues around change and transition. Once you recognize your own or another's reaction to change, the conflict will become easier to manage. If you can educate your co-workers about the normal and predictable stages of change, grieving, and transition, you can help use the conflict to fuel the creative edge you'll need in the future.

CHAPTER 17

The Dogfight Referees: How to Mediate, Facilitate, and Survive

---

Blessed are the peacemakers.

—The Bible

Richard, the CFO, and Helen, the Vice President of Human Resources are at each other's throats over employee schedules, leave, overtime, and health insurance budgets. He wants to keep the costs down and cut the most expensive insurance option, also the most popular with employees. He would replace it with a less expensive option. Helen has done nothing but complain about how it will affect her ability to hire good people and cause high turnover. Richard is frustrated because she just can't see the bottom-line financial issue. Their disagreement has escalated into unreturned emails, hang-ups on the phone, and communication through their assistants. Their boss, the CEO, doesn't know how to stop the fighting so he's thrown up his hands and hired an outside mediator. She starts the mediation process by sorting the issues into three categories: historical problems, current issues, and "beyond" issues—those things that are beyond Richard's and Helen's ability to resolve.

To their amazement, most of their issues end up in the "beyond" category. The mediator was then able to present their joint list to the CEO for him to make a decision. She was also able to give him some useful feedback about his own role in the conflict. A classic conflict-avoider and roadrunner, the CEO had unknowingly fueled the dispute by refusing to decide critical issues that affected the working relationship of his two executives.

Tired of refereeing dogfights in the office without knowing the rules? Most managers and leaders spend at least one-fourth of their time resolving disputes, yet little, if any, time honing their mediator or facilitation skills. In fact, 81% of workers think they have "lousy bosses," up from 63% just two years ago, according to a survey of 700 workers by author Gordon Miller. While every executive can become better at handling the day-to-day conflicts, sometimes larger issues or institutional tensions rise up causing unresolvable arguments. Unlike in lower-level groups, firing executives and rehiring new ones isn't always a feasible option. Additionally, in many companies executives—at the director level and above—have risen through the management ranks and have often avoided conflict. Some of these managers have risen with other teams or mentors and may not have acquired needed conflict management tools in order to tackle tough situations.

Clearly, most bosses need some kind of mediation and facilitation skills, but CEOs and other executive leaders sometimes need to use other tools—namely professional mediators or facilitators. Studying a few basics about the process can help leaders navigate the war zones and come out alive.

Mediation Basics

Mediation is a complex subject—one many experts and professionals have spent years studying and practicing to refine their skills. Even basic workplace training for mediators can take two to five days. Yet, many of us end up mediating in the workplace whether we're prepared or not. A leader—and many employees—face daily conflicting interests that require mediation.

The basics of direct conflict resolution will serve you well in mediating workplace disputes. As a mediator, you are going to facilitate a negotiation. Perhaps the most important skill is understanding the difference between positions and interests and following the ten steps outlined in Chapter 11. You also need to map the conflict and decide what kind of conflict you're resolving as described in Chapter 12. Positional bargaining starts with the answer. Your job is to move the parties away from positional bargaining to discover the answer that best meets the needs and interests of everyone involved.

The Mediator's Role

Your job as a mediator is to use questions that will help the parties elicit their underlying needs and interests rather than staying stuck upon whatever solution they favor.

First, make sure you are the appropriate person to mediate the dispute. If both sides cannot see you as neutral, you may not be. Additionally, know when you need to bring in a professional. Sometimes, outside mediation that can officially resolve disputes with legal implications is a better option at the executive level. Mediation may not be the best use of your time. Skillful resolution can take days or weeks. An experienced mediator can also give you good coaching on the underlying issues: problems you may have missed because you're too immersed in the situation as well as too busy.

In addition, keep in mind the following basics whenever you find yourself mediating workplace disputes:

- Remember *who* owns the problem. As a mediator, your job is not to solve the problem; you must help the parties discover the solution to the problem: *the solution is in their hands.* If you find yourself frustrated as a mediator, this is frequently where you've made a mistake.
- Studies have shown that small things, such as where people sit during mediation, can make a big difference. If the parties to the conflict sit across from each other, for example, the problem will escalate. If they sit beside each other, they can look at each other or not, as they choose, and may develop that necessary feeling that they are on the same team in attacking the problem, not the person.
- Understand that your first goal as a mediator should be to help the parties agree on a definition of the problem. Don't hurry on this step. Many misunderstandings result from a failure to agree about what the parties are fighting about.

Preparing the Parties

Before the mediation, you need to individually prepare the parties. Talk to each party separately (preferably in person) in order to find out what their issues are and decide whether the problem is medial. Start planting the suggestion that conflicts are normal and can be valuable, and that creative solutions can help foster productivity and innovation. Suggest that conflict is an opportunity to change what's not working and acknowledge them for being willing to face the issues. Veteran mediator Judy Mares-Dixon of the Boulder-based Center For Dispute Resolution recommends asking the following questions:

1. What are the issues you want resolved?
2. What is your sense of the issues the other party wants resolved?
3. What ideas do you have for resolving the problem? (Start planting the suggestion that there are *multiple* solutions to the problem.)
4. What do you need to resolve this? What does the other party need to resolve this?
5. How will you convince the other party of the reasonableness of your proposal?
6. Give both parties an overview of mediation. If they've had a bad experience with previous mediators, ask what happened. (This will tell you what was important to them.)

The Mediation Session

When you actually start the session, be sure you've scheduled enough time and privacy. Tell the parties you may need time-outs, caucuses (individual sessions when you confer separately with each side), or breaks. Let them know you want to make as much progress as possible in this session, but that you understand either side may need to break.

If possible, hold the session off site. Begin at the start of the day when most people can focus best. Require everyone to turn off their cell phones, pagers, beeping watches, Blackberries, and other electronic devices. Assure them that you will have breaks when they can reconnect to their lifelines. I like to joke with groups I work with that if any of these devices go off or make an appearance in my sessions, I'll confiscate them and give them to my twelve-year-old twins, who are dying for cell phones! I add that we will have an interesting experiment by seeing how many minutes they can rack up in a week. Joking aside, emphasize the importance of the process, how much you value their willingness to participate, and how you hope that they will take this as an opportunity learn better conflict management skills and develop creative solutions as well as resolving the current issue.

Then, explain the purpose of the mediation. Make sure you do so in a way that doesn't allow one person or another to fight what you're saying. In addition, as a part of your introductory session, inform the parties that you will *not* decide who is right and who is wrong (unless you are their boss and have announced that you will decide the issue by a certain time if they are unable to resolve the dispute). Your role as a mediator is to help the parties resolve the issue. Explain that you understand managing conflicts can be difficult and that the parties are going to have to work hard to creatively manage the issues, otherwise they would have been able to resolve the problem by themselves.

Explain any ground rules for the sessions. In most workplaces, people want ground rules such as no insulting, put downs, or interruptions. In more formal sessions or one conducted by an outside mediator, explain that normal workplace policies regarding harassment, ethics, codes of conduct, threats, and violence will apply. Ask them if they need any special rules in order to concentrate and be able to stay in the room and do the work.

Some ground rules can actually *inhibit* resolution. For example, some people just can't talk about issues they feel passionate about without speaking loudly. Ask if this is an issue for anyone and obtain agreement about what rules will best fit everyone's needs.

Explain, if applicable, any rules about confidentiality that the organization or any court has required. Be careful not to promise confidentiality. If the mediation ends up subject to internal review, administrative hearings, or court proceedings, you (or the parties) may need to disclose your discussion.

If you're using an experienced, professional mediator, keep in mind that many will not mediate without a signed, written agreement outlining the ground rules, confidentiality agreements, and consequences if the mediation fails. While this may be ideal, written agreements may not be practical for mediating day-to-day workplace disputes and may sometimes intimidate unsophisticated disputants and make them reluctant or unwilling to mediate.

Also, be aware ground rules themselves can spark a conflict. I once had a woman walk out of a mediation and refuse to return because her manager started talking (in what she felt, justifiably, was a condescending way) about the rules he wanted *her* to follow! One of the ways to establish ground rules is to ask the participants to think about what didn't work when they tried to discuss the issues before.

After your introduction, ask each side to give you an overview of the problems and issues. Your job at this point is to try to reveal the needs and interests of the parties, to understand what is important to them before you ask for solutions. Ask each of them to contribute to a list of the issues and confirm that the list is correct, then pick one issue (it's good to start with one you think may be easiest to creatively manage) and brainstorm as many ways as possible to resolve the issue. Keep encouraging the parties to move into the *future* in this step rather than repeating what has occurred between them in the past. As a mediator, consistently try to use the suggestions about reframing and listening outlined in this book.

Also, remind them of any purpose you know they share. Ask them what they value that will be served by resolving the dispute through mediation; for example, a better working relationship, a more successful project, less personal stress, or alignment with the organization's values.

Try to keep to a pace that's fast enough so both sides believe they are making progress, yet slow enough to allow each party to carefully consider what they need and what agreements will meet their interests.

If the parties seem stuck or unable to come up with any solutions, encourage them to talk about how and why they feel stuck, and acknowledge their hard work. Perhaps taking a break will help, although make sure they do not use this as an excuse to avoid mediation. If they're still stuck, ask any or all of the following questions:

- If we don't come up with a creative solution in this session, what do think will happen? How will you meet your needs and interests? How will the other side meet his or her needs and interests?
- If both of you could be content with a solution, what would it be?
- What could the two of you propose that would really work for both of you?
- Talk about similar situations you have mediated and the solutions the parties found.
- Ask one party to give advice to the other about what would really work for them.
- Ask each party to give you advice about what would work for each of them.
- Ask each party to restate the other party's issues, needs, and interests as well as what they think would work best for the other party.
- Try to find successes wherever possible: focus on breaking down the issues and finding solutions for some part of the problem.

Caucus

A caucus is when you, as a mediator, talk individually with each of the parties outside the mediating room. If you decide to caucus with each side, first ask if there's something in the caucus they need you to keep confidential. Ask them what they need to have this work for them. In the meeting, you can ask them to role-play with you, to play with options, and to try out solutions with you. Make certain you spend an equal amount of time with each side to make sure you do not undermine your neutrality.

Finalizing a Proposal

Once you have reached a proposal that seems to meet everyone's needs, consider committing it to writing to make sure both sides understand the solution. Also, remember to test the proposal. Testing involves asking each side questions such as: tell me how you believe this proposal will meet your needs.

Throughout the session and at the end, acknowledge and praise the parties for their effort. Consider some sort of small celebration, such as going out for coffee or ice cream, a picnic in a nearby park, a field trip to the movies, or an unexpected afternoon off. These kinds of rewards can reinforce the idea that creative conflict management is a valued part of your goals as an organization and that you, as a mediator or leader, appreciate their ability to resolve the difficulties.

Facilitation Basics

Facilitation is the task of leading a group through a decision-making process, whereas mediation usually involves working with two or more parties in a specific conflict. While leaders can also serve as facilitators, it's frequently useful to use someone objective and removed from the issue.

What makes a good facilitator? The best practitioners demonstrate the ability to structure a discussion, synthesize comments, capture ideas in text and informal graphics, encourage diverse comments, and remain neutral. Objectivity, patience, listening ability, and the ability to probe and question assumptions should be added to the list. Many leaders favor quick decisions and may not be the best facilitators.

People who have backgrounds in more than one discipline make good natural facilitators among diverse groups, those with both a marketing and finance background, for example, who can speak both languages.

Some of the mediation techniques we've considered in this chapter—such as sorting the issues—are also helpful in facilitation. Other techniques are sprinkled throughout this book, especially the next two chapters. Although more detailed facilitation techniques are beyond the scope of this book, several excellent sources are listed in the bibliography.

Why Unproductive Conflict Continues

As most leaders know, many pairs or groups, left to themselves, maintain destructive conflict. If you need to repeatedly mediate or facilitate bad fights with the same group, you may be frustrated by their behavior. Given how costly, painful, and uncreative such conflict is, why do they do this? As psychologist Kenneth Kaye writes in his book *Workplace Wars and How to End Them: Turning Personal Conflicts into Productive Teamwork:*

> The best answer psychologists have been able to discover is that members of a group *are* working together when they engage in repetitive, predictable dispute cycles. They are *collaborating to avoid something worse.*

One of my client companies, for example, is a construction company that has experienced phenomenal growth over the past five years, starting with a gross in the low six figures and expecting in the current year a gross of $6 million. Don, their young leader, had worked hard to build an effective team, reward good work, and involve everyone in major decision-making. With the slowdown in the economy, however, the business started to experience cash flow problems. New accounts still flocked to Don's company because of their excellent reputation, but clients paid slower and fought more over seemingly insignificant mistakes.

While Don struggled to borrow money to manage the cash flow, he found himself increasingly drawn into mediating clashes among his team and responding to their complaints. His staff began to fight constantly, usually over some petty matter such as who failed to record something, lost an estimate, forgot to pass along a message, or allowed a member of the crew to leave early. Don would mediate the current quarrel and a temporary cease-fire would ensue. Yet within a few days, another battle erupted over new and trivial issues.

In desperation, Don brought me in to diagnose the problem. He couldn't understand why his formerly compatible staff seemed to love destructive fights. When I met individually with the parties, the answer quickly came to me.

Why does a temporary peace frequently lead to conflict? Psychologist Kaye finds it happens for two reasons:

1. Peace isn't really peace. The true conflict hasn't been discussed, or perhaps even acknowledged and everyone knows it—at least at some level. The combatants keep fighting about trivia in hopes of getting to the real issues but when it gets too dangerous they "agree" to back away.

2. Alternatively, the peace itself makes them uncomfortable. With the resolution of some issues, the peace itself raises new questions the collaborators aren't ready to face, such as, if we're working this well together, does that mean one of us isn't needed? Which one?

With Don's company, everyone was fighting to avoid the real issue: they were terrified because of the company's cash flow problems and the resulting change in Don's behavior. Their formerly available and nurturing leader had become distracted and distant. Did that mean that the business was going under? Would they lose their jobs? Was there an even greater problem he was hiding from them?

When you find the group or pair you're mediating mired in a cycle of sustained conflict, you may break the cycle by asking some radical questions: "What are you fighting together to avoid?" Or ask them, "What would you do with all this creative energy if you weren't stuck in a destructive dispute?" Or, "What do you think might happen if you did something different in that situation?"

Planting the suggestion that a group is actually *working together* to achieve a common goal frequently shocks the participants out of their trance of denial. When you ask these questions, the real energy behind the conflict usually emerges. It could be anything from "she'd walk all over me" to "we'd have to face the possibility of failure" or "we wouldn't have any more excuses for our poor performance."

Most constant combatants are aware of these underlying forces, but are not aware that they've been fighting to keep the entire group from having to deal with the issue. In many cases, they're actually protecting the noncombatants.

With Don's construction business, for example, the distracting disputes saved him from facing his deepest fears about losing the business he'd worked so hard to build, and also helped him save face by relieving him from talking to his team about the extent of the business's financial problems. What he didn't realize was his staff suffered from a fear of the unknown that was more debilitating than facing the true numbers. Oddly, the solution to the continuing conflict wasn't to help the disputants work better together, but involved instead a series of frank discussions with the entire team to let them know the current financial status and the various options. Once Don was willing to let go of his "big daddy with everything under control" facade and involve his staff in the difficult problems he needed to face, they surprised him with their own creative solutions to the current crises.

Long-standing conflicts sometimes have the unspoken agreement: "Let's you and me fight." The mutually destructive pattern of fighting will continue until someone gives the parties a more direct way to deal with the issues they've been successfully avoiding through the continual disputes.

Kaye recommends four steps to interrupt the process:

1. *Identify the individual fears and shared apprehensions* that trigger conflict and alienation.

2. Help the parties themselves *learn to recognize* and even anticipate that those apprehensions will lead to another round of "here we go again," unless they consciously choose to respond more constructively.

3. Help them *learn to interrupt the process* of mutual button pushing that typically escalates their conflict.

4. *Help members continue to use their existing ways* of making peace (already in their repertoires), reinforcing them to use those behaviors sooner.

Identifying the shared fears involves forcing the group to answer the questions designed to elicit the real reasons for the conflict. In order to help the parties recognize the warning signs, the facilitator assembles a list of gestures and feelings that frequently lead to trouble. I call this list "hot buttons," and a simple technique is to share these lists and respond with an "ouch" if someone hits them. Helping them learn to interrupt the process means to make sure someone keeps track of the traditional cycle of battles and learns to point out the repetition to the group whenever they're stuck. Finally, the leader or facilitator needs to reinforce the productive and creative skills the group has learned.

Surviving as a Referee—Keeping the Faith

Mediation or facilitation takes skill and patience, yet can lead to valuable and creative results. Perhaps the most important skill you need to develop is your own patience with the process and your own listening ability. As a mediator or facilitator, you need to serve as a sort of "cheerleader," constantly assuring the parties that if they stay on task, a solution that meets everyone's needs will emerge. Work to develop your skills to referee good fights, and your reputation as a leader will flourish.

Need inspiration? Consider the experience of mediation veteran Susan Podziba, a faculty associate with the Program on Negotiation at Harvard Law School, who has facilitated dialogue between Israelis and Palestinians, between environmentalists and fishermen, and between pro-choice and pro-life activists.

She proceeds from the assumption that the combatants hold the key to resolving their own conflicts. "Life isn't fair," she says. "The reality is that people everywhere have hard choices to make. My job is to challenge people to see the complexity of a situation and to encourage them to take an active part in making those hard choices."

If you think that resolving your own workplace's disputes is difficult, consider Podziba's efforts to facilitate a conversation between pro-life and pro-choice activists. She undertook this sensitive facilitation after a man shot and killed a receptionist and wounded three other people in one Planned Parenthood clinic in Massachusetts and then drove to another and killed another receptionist and injured two more people.

Podziba admits she was frightened. "What if the wrong person found that I was facilitating those meetings?"

Podziba helped both groups tone down the rhetoric. They realized that "If abortion doctors are called 'murderers,' then people on the fringes of society feel there's a justification for violence . . . . Neither side wanted that."

She facilitated meetings between the two sides for three years. They came up with the innovative idea of a hot line, modeling after the Cold War–era connection between the United States and the Soviet Union. The line helped stop violence when pro-life advocates used it to warn of a threat. The mediation process sparked a transformation among the participants. As Podziba put it:

> The mediation process was life-changing for all of us . . .
> the level of relationships built among people who had been
> "enemies" was just mysterious.

While most of us will never be called upon to mediate life-or-death disputes, we can draw inspiration from both Podziba's practice and her results.

Consider also, as a model, the experience of Vancouver Island. The community clashed in a destructive conflict between loggers who wanted to continue their traditional clear cutting and environmentalists who insisted that they stop to protect the fragile island ecology. Other community members believed that the logging industry was essential to the economy of the island. After nearly ten years of dialogue with the assistance of various mediators, the groups finally agreed upon a creative resolution to the conflict. Logging continued, but with a new company that practices sustainable logging. These innovative loggers don't strip the forest for huge roads because they lift all the logs out by helicopter! They selectively cut so that large sections of the forest surround any cleared sections. Although community members agree that the long battle was divisive and expensive, they are pleased with the ultimate creative solution, one that honors their special environment while protecting the local economy. None of this would have been possible if the participants hadn't been willing to embrace the conflict and keep working toward an innovative solution.

Looking to other successful mediation projects can help us develop our own skills as facilitators and lead our organizations to more good fights and more innovative solutions to our deepest problems.

Chapter 18
Avoid the Recount: How to Articulate a Clear Decision-Making Process

---

The idea of a charismatic leader, someone who gets his one idea realized by sheer force of his personality, is a myth!

—Professor Paul C. Putt

On November 7, 2000, chaos tumbled out of Florida voting booths and into communities across the country as a storm of controversy erupted over the presidential election. Did George W. Bush or Al Gore win Florida's electoral vote? Counties ordered hand counts of voters' punchcards, introducing Americans to new terms such as "chad"—which is the small piece of paper that should detach from a punchcard. Those doing the counting had to learn a whole new procedure and new standards overnight. Should a "dimpled" chad count? What about a "hanging" chad? And what in the world is a "pregnant" chad? On November 6, 2000, the decision process seemed clear: registered voters cast their ballots, they get counted, and the winner takes all Electoral College votes for that state. We've all learned it isn't nearly that simple. At the heart of the matter was the question: What exactly is the decision process?

Internal conflicts can explode within your organization when decisions are made in the absence of an articulated process and a strategic communication plan. Does the popular vote within the team rule the day, or does a corporate Electoral College really cast the ballots? More importantly, does everyone know the decision-making method beforehand? There are countless ways to reach a decision—circumstances call upon all of us to use a variety of strategies daily. You might take a poll about where to grab a bite of lunch with several colleagues, seek consensus about hiring a new person to join your management team, and

162

decide alone whether to approve overtime. Each decision-making model has a role, and a good leader is flexible, using this array of techniques as appropriate. Determining the right model is a key factor in creating good fights.

Decisions! Decisions!

Trying to help groups come to a decision about issues is complex. One mistake most groups make is to fail to talk about *how* the decision will be made. There are pros and cons to any decision process you may decide to use. The following example explains different group options.

Eight people want to go out to dinner together and are trying to decide on a restaurant.

Decision Process	Description
Unanimity	Everyone's first choice happens to be a Mexican restaurant.
Convincing Argument	One person likes a French restaurant. After presenting advantages, everyone is convinced this option is better than their original preference.
Follow a Popular Leader	One person wants to go to a German restaurant; everyone else wants to do whatever that person wants more than they want their own food preference, or they believe that person knows better what is best for the group than they do.
Compromise	Some want to go to a Thai restaurant, some want to go to the seafood restaurant, and some want to go to McDonald's; so they decide to go to a seafood restaurant this time, the Thai restaurant next time, and McDonald's after that. Or, they go to a different Thai restaurant that serves Thai dishes, seafood, and hamburgers, but none of the food is very good.
Intensity of Preferences	Maybe the five who want Thai food are mostly interested in eating ethnic food, the two who want seafood don't like spicy food, and the person who wants to go to McDonald's can afford to spend only $3. Here the people who don't like spicy food have a stronger reason not to go to a Thai restaurant than the people who like ethnic food have a reason to go so it takes precedence; but, the person who wants to go to McDonald's absolutely cannot go to the other, more expensive restaurants, whereas everyone else can go to McDonald's, so they decide to go to McDonald's.
Meeting Everyone's Needs; True Consensus	They decide to go to a Japanese restaurant (ethnic, but not spicy), and everyone chips in to cover the cost over $3 for the poor person.

Unanimity

Unanimity and consensus are often used interchangeably, but there are some important distinctions. Unanimity as a process usually occurs when everyone's first choice felicitously corresponds. Consensus is usually reached after a process of identifying everyone's needs and interests and looking for a creative solution that meets all of them. Consensus, then, is more often the *process* for reaching agreement whereas unanimity is the *result.*

The word "unanimous" comes from two Latin words: *unis,* meaning "one," and *animus,* meaning "spirit." In theory, a group that reaches unanimous agreement would proceed from one spirit. When a group commits to unanimity, they are agreeing everyone will converge and allow each person to have veto power. This means one person can delay the decision and prolong the decision-making process for hours, days, or even weeks. Conversely, some people may be reluctant to exercise this veto power and create delay. A group that decides to use unanimity is, in effect, committing to staying in dialogue until they reach an agreement that meets everyone's needs and interests.

The Latin root of "consensus" is *consentire,* which is a combination of two Latin words: *con,* meaning "with" or "together with" and *sentire,* meaning "to think and feel." *Consentire* means "to think and feel together."

Consensus is the participatory process through which a group thinks and feels together in order to reach a decision of unanimity. Unanimity is the point of closure for the group. Many groups say they use consensus even when they really use unanimity minus one, voting after a certain time has passed or 80% as an acceptable "consensus" point. In those groups, no one person has real veto power and yet a great effort is made to make sure all voices are heard. A true consensus would be 100% unanimity. Many business groups use a fallback consensus model where they agree to talk for a certain period of time and then if a consensus is not reached, the leader decides.

There is nothing wrong with deciding to use less than 100% consensus. What's important is to think carefully about the needs of the group, the particular decision involved, and then to make sure everyone in the group understands why that particular method was chosen.

Using consensus to reach unanimous agreement and obtain the best decision for all concerned may seem like a wonderful idea, but the reality of many groups struggling to do this may be quite different. One reason is a failure to assess when consensus should be appropriately used. A related reason may be a failure of understanding and training for the group in consensus decision-making. Some groups lack skilled leaders or facilitators who can guide them through the process. Another problem may arise when everyone says they "agree" to a certain proposal or solution yet they may mean different things— from enthusiastic support to "I just don't want to talk about this any more."

The veto power of unanimity can also create problems for an inexperienced group or facilitator. If there's no skill at encouraging everyone to speak up, someone may drag out the discussion for days without surfacing the underlying issue. Others may refuse to agree when what they really mean is they still have questions or concerns that need to be answered. In other groups, some people may be reluctant to invoke the veto power because they don't want to feel responsible for prolonging the discussion. They may say "I agree" when what they really mean is they don't want to take responsibility for holding the group back. Some solutions to these issues are presented in the next chapter.

The advantages to a unanimous decision reached through consensus is that everyone feels heard and the organization knows it has found a solution that is likely to be *sustainable*—one that will not have to be reversed and that meets everyone's needs and interests.

Convincing Argument

This solution favors the orators in the group and those who think and talk well on their feet. These people may or may not have the best solution for the individuals and the group. What they do have is a clear understanding of their own interests and a high level of ability to communicate their interests to the group.

The advantage of this method is that it tends to be quicker than consensus. Many people may feel reluctant to take on someone skilled in this kind of argument so they will quickly agree. Sometimes a group will get lucky and the most persuasive members will also be those who will happen upon the best solution for all concerned. Sometimes the issue is not important enough or so few people are affected that it's simply not worth a long discussion.

The problem is, if the issue is important to the group, this method of decision-making can create long-simmering resentments among those members who simply go along. They may dig in their heels or take a stand over seemingly unimportant issues. The leader or facilitator may find himself or herself quite confused as to why something seemingly trivial has erupted into a major dispute.

This method may also create problems for the group at the implementation stage. Some members may go along with the decision, but later indulge in delays, sabotage, forgetting, or other passive/aggressive techniques in order to interfere with implementation.

Following a Popular Leader

A strong and charismatic leader can often simplify decision-making by convincing a group to follow his or her lead. This works as long as the leader has a deep understanding of the different needs and interests of individuals and groups within the organization and an alignment with the best future for the organization. Obviously, this options only works if we have a truly enlightened leader, not a despot or dictator. Sadaam Hussein, for example, ruled by violence and intimidation, not because he had a deep understanding or interest in his followers. Winston Churchill, by contract, especially during the war, led decisively and effectively. Ideally, such a leader would be a classic Eagle style. This method works well during emergencies such as an all-out war, for example, when time for consensus building may be short. The obvious disadvantage is that the leader cannot know everything about a complex situation. He or she may make decisions that simply miss important issues.

Problems occur when a leader becomes removed from the individual needs of the group, especially when an organization grows. Then, no matter how enlightened the leader, he or she may make decisions that do not work well for all stakeholders. Then the group may experience the same kind of problems as those that result from one person using convincing argument.

Compromise

Compromise is a process where everyone agrees to give up part of what they want in order to reach something that everyone can follow. What's interesting about this method is that many people view it as quite enlightened. Yet the reality is it means everyone is settling for less than what they really want. This may mean no one is really happy since no one gets what he or she wants most.

Congress generally operates on this method when most bills are passed. There is much "horse trading" among the various factions. The advantage is that issues do get resolved. The disadvantage is that many laws invoke the classic statement about committees: they are what designed camels. No one receives what they really wanted and the courts end up sorting out the vagaries for years to come.

The advantage is that there is less a sense of winners and losers since everyone gives something in order to come up with a solution. Another advantage is that it can be a faster method than true consensus. Sometimes it's simply not worth taking the long road to reaching a resolution that meets everyone's true needs.

Implicit Majority or Voting

This method means that majority rules. The advantage is that it's frequently quicker than the other methods, and the result is that people become less frustrated with the decision-making process.

The disadvantages are that some people, departments, and groups are left out of the process and their needs and interests are not met. In addition, the group may not make the best decisions since the process doesn't seek to utilize all of the ideas, suggestions, and minds of the group. The whole idea of consensus decision-making is that the process requires everyone to think deeply about the problem, resulting in better quality decisions. As the Quakers say, everyone has a *piece* of the truth. Putting the pieces together helps the group come up with a more creative, and ultimately more satisfying and sustainable decision, than the organization would have otherwise. If a group continually uses voting, the people who know that they will end up in the minority may simply give up and opt-out of the entire process. These members will feel less passion for their work and most likely will eventually leave the organization.

Intensity of Preferences

This decision-making method may be best when only a few people really care about a decision and the issue is relatively minor. There are some things in which many people simply have no stake. If this is the case for a particular issue, allowing the needs of these few to dominate may be a good solution. A leader or facilitator needs to be very skilled, however, to make sure the needs and interests of those who do not participate in the process are really minor and they don't care. In addition, for important issues, this method doesn't give the group everyone's best thinking to come up with the highest, most creative, and best decision. Also, some conflict styles seem to have so much passion—such as pit bulls—that they purport to care about everything. Their object may be to win and argue, rather than assist the group in arriving at the best decision.

Using the Best Process

Before making a decision, a leader or group needs to step back from the process and ask which method is the most appropriate for any particular decision. Make a list of the pros and cons of any particular method. You can then make an informed and thoughtful decision about which process best meets the needs of the group.

Paul C. Nutt, a professor of management at Ohio State University's Fisher College of Business, has been studying for more than 20 years the question of why smart companies make dumb decisions. Nutt's research focuses on how executives make decisions and whether those decisions succeed or fail. After examining strategic decisions at 356 companies, he found that half such decisions were abandoned, partially implemented, or never adopted. He offers three ideas for making sure decisions will translate into action:

1. *Manage your ego.* When executives impose their ideas on the organizations, they frequently do so because they believe they're acting like "take-charge" leaders. Only 42% of the decisions that used this approach were actually adopted, Nutt found. When executives conferred with colleagues and rethought long-term priorities, they had a 96% success rate for decisions. "People like to impose their ideas on others or look for a scapegoat because these techniques eliminate ambiguity," says Nutt. "Real visionaries see that they need to reconsider the norm."

2. *Keep examining options.* Everyone likes a decisive leader, yet the business world is now so complex, being decisive can lead to leading blindly. When executives failed to investigate alternatives once they'd made a decision, 60% of those decisions were dropped or never adopted at all. Leaders need to constantly broaden their scope, Nutt advises.

3. *We all have a piece of the truth.* Only one-fifth of the leaders Nutt interviewed consulted staffers when making decisions. Most ramrod their decisions through by persuasion (41%) or by edict (40%). Each approach usually failed. Persuasion failed in 53% of the cases; edict in 65%. Nutt stresses the problem isn't just that decisions lack merit, it's that staffers resent the railroading and thus undermine their leaders. "If you involve people in at least some of the steps of the process, they will become missionaries for you," found Nutt. "The idea of a charismatic leader, someone who gets his one idea realized by sheer force of personality, is a myth."

Resisting a Premature Urge to Merge

To be creative and make the best decision, a group must first generate lots of options. Many factors, however, sometimes prevent this. A leader or facilitator may need to help the group resist the urge to decide too quickly. If the group's leader is overly directive, the group resists hearing outside opinions, the group experiences time pressures, or the group has a norm that defeats divergent thinking, the group may reach a decision before it's really explored all the relevant issues. When a financial department, for example, is up against quarter close deadlines, the harried group may just decide to book certain items in the way that their leaders suggests, even though some members have lurking doubts about the accounting. With more time and a leader who invites dissent, the group may reach a more accurate view. Many of the Enron debacles, as we now know, resulted from the leaders squashing disagreements with their methods.

Deadlines, if they're real, can concentrate the mind and help a group stay on task, but an artificial deadline can kill creativity and lead to bad decisions.

The tragic end for the U.S. space shuttle *Challenger*, for example, where six astronauts and the "teacher in space," were killed, may be partly due to time pressures in the decision-making process. Delayed once, the window for another launch was closing. The leaders of the decision team were concerned about public and congressional perceptions of the entire space shuttle program and its continued funding. Today, the decision makers wished they had taken more time to make the decision to launch and had listened to a few vocal dissenters. Documents show that the same problem may have occurred with the explosion on re-entry of the space shuttle Columbia. Engineers were discussing possible problems incurred during launch while there was time to repair the damage, but were encouraged to be team players.

An overly directive leadership style can also close off the pursuit of creative options, especially if a leader signals how he or she wants the group to converge at the outset. Group members may not want to risk their status with the leader by disagreeing. Most organizational histories contain at least one story about someone who disagreed and suffered the consequences.

When William Niskanen was chief economist at Ford Motor Co. in 1980, for example, his free-trader views came into conflict with his superiors' new protectionism in the face of increasing Japanese competition. Niskanen was fired. CFO Will Caldwell explained to him, "In this company, Bill . . ., the people who do well wait until they hear their superiors express their views.

Then they add something in support of those views." While times may have changed toward encouraging more diverse thinking, many groups still carry this unspoken message.

The leadership problem is compounded by the tendency of many leaders to favor quick thinking and quick decision-making. Creative group decisions, as we've discussed, take time. Effective decision-making requires a balance between exploration and speed.

Making a Pact with the Devil's Advocate

The perils of *groupthink* can be avoided by appointing a devil's advocate. President Kennedy, for example, took this tack by appointing his brother, Attorney General Bobby Kennedy, to serve in that role during critical policy decisions after the Bay of Pigs fiasco.

In the Roman Catholic tradition, a devil's advocate is an official of the Congregation of Rites whose duty is to point out defects in the evidence upon which the case for beatification or canonization rests. While its a good practice to favor encouraging everyone to act as a critical thinker, challenging premature convergence, sometimes assigning a formal devil's advocate role is useful.

To be most effective, the devil's advocate must have the absolute support of the group leader rather than being a token. He or she should also be clear what the actual contrary decision is and should be able to act as if they totally believe in it. Finally, the role should rotate among group members to prevent the advocate from being a mere token and also to prevent the group from confusing the advocate with the devil himself!

In one study of team decision-making, for example, several groups of managers were formed to solve a complex problem. Told that their performance would be judged by a panel of experts in terms of the quantity and quality of the solutions generated, the groups were identical in size and composition, with the exception that half of them included a "confederate." The researcher instructed this person to play the role of devil's advocate. This manager was to challenge the group's conclusions, forcing the others to critically examine their assumptions and the logic of their arguments. At the end of the problem-solving period, the experts compared the recommendations made by both groups.

Significantly, the groups with the devil's advocates had performed significantly better on the tasks. They generated more alternatives and their proposals were judged as superior.

After a short break, the groups reassembled and were told they would perform a similar task during the next session. Before they started discussing the next problem, however, the researchers gave them permission to eliminate one member. In every group containing the confederate, he or she was asked to leave. The fact that every high-performance group expelled their unique competitive advantage because that member made others feel uncomfortable speaks volumes about most managers' reactions to conflict, as one participant stated: "I know it has positive outcomes for the performance of the organization as a whole, but I don't like how it makes me feel personally."

While this study was an experiment, the decision to expel the "devil" of an organization for being a "trouble maker" happens in real life. In 1984 Ross Perot sold Electronic Data Systems (EDS) to General Motors (GM) for $2.5 billion and immediately became GM's largest stockholder and a member of the board of directors. GM desperately needed EDS's expertise to update and coordinate its massive information system. Roger Smith, GM's chairman, thought that Perot's fiery "the crazy aunt in the attic" spirit would reinvigorate GM's stogy bureaucracy. Perot leapt into the fray and immediately started criticizing GM policy and practice. He squawked that it took longer for GM to produce a car than it took the country to win the Second World War. He lashed out at GM's bureaucracy, claiming it fostered conformity at the expense of results. By December of 1986, Roger Smith was fed up with Perot's "reinvigoration." GM paid dearly to exorcise its devil, paying Perot nearly twice the market value of his stock ($740 million) to silence him and extract him from the board.

Other CEOs have been more receptive to the concept of playing or receiving a devil's advocate. Such leaders establish norms that make spirited debate the rule rather than the exception. They also realize that making decisions is a process, not an event.

Chuck Knight, for example, for 27 years the CEO of Emerson Electric, accomplished this by relentlessly cross-examining managers during planning reviews, no matter what he actually believed about the proposal under review. He asked aggressive questions and expected intelligent responses. Knight dubbed the process the "logic of illogic" because of his willingness to test even thoughtful arguments by raising unexpected, and occasionally trivial, concerns. Yet his reign produced a steady stream of smart investment decisions and quarterly increases in income.

Bob Galvin, CEO of Motorola in the 1980s, took a different tack. He constantly asked surprising hypothetical questions that stimulated innovative thinking. Subsequently, as chairman of the board of overseers for the Malcolm Baldridge National Quality Program, Galvin startled his fellow board members when, in response to a question about broadening the criteria for the award, he suggested narrowing them instead. After a lively discussion, the board did in fact broaden the criteria, but his unexpected suggestion sparked a creative and productive conflict.

Of course, the unrestricted use of such advocates can lead to new bedevilment problems, as pointed out by several recent authors, including Tom Kelley in *The Ten Faces of Innovation: IDEO's Strategies for Beating the Devil's Advocate and Driving Creativity Throughout Your Organization.* Kelley argues that some such advocates can end up killing all creativity and discouraging innovation. The key is to limit when they're used in the process. During early brainstorming on a project, for example, such a role is inappropriate. At that creative stage, all ideas should be welcomed and embraced. Similarly, if such advocates are used at a final presentation stage, after a team has spent months, or even years on a project, the dash of the Devil's cold water can permanently discourage the players from ever coming forward again. The best use is somewhere in the middle, with someone in that role who is skillful and optimistic enough to offer praise as well as pointing out overlooked flaws. Leaders need to avoid anointing an all-powerful devil's advocate who relishes the role of raining on others' parades for no useful reason.

In addition, some executive teams may be too small for the addition of such an advocate. In those situations, the leader needs to be willing to experiment in order to find out what works best for his or her group. The key again, is to make certain that the leader fosters an environment that welcomes unpopular views.

Fostering Good Fights That Lead to Good Decisions

Good fights are fueled by clear discussions of the decision-making process. Many bad decisions arise from using the wrong process. Leaders must also model the openness necessary to convince participants that they haven't already made up their minds. Leaders or facilitators must also resist the early urge to merge, perhaps even enlisting the devil or his advocates when appropriate.

Chapter 19
Getting to Yes Without Going to War: How to Build Consensus

In our present society the governing idea is that we can trust no one, and therefore, we must protect ourselves if we are to have any security in our decisions. The most we will be willing to do is compromise, and this leads to a very interesting way of viewing the outcome of working together. It means we are willing to settle for less than the very best—and that we will often have a sense of dissatisfaction with our decisions unless we can somehow outmaneuver others involved in the process.

—Caroline Estes

In 1954 the United States Supreme Court rendered a landmark decision in the case of Brown vs. Topeka Board of Education. In a historic 9 to 0 vote, the Supreme Court shattered the notion of "separate but equal" and began untangling the web of racial segregation. In the hope of finding common ground, Chief Justice Earl Warren spent the five months between arguments and the issuance of the opinion cultivating consensus, repeatedly gathering the Justices to discuss the many issues involved in the case. To come to agreement, he went to lunch 20 times with one particular Justice. Chief Justice Warren believed adamantly that the country would be best served if the Court could render a clear and unanimous opinion—and his remarkable leadership in garnering that decision changed the course of history.

Warren's masterful use of consensus illustrates how important it is for leaders to take the time and trouble to gain a true consensus before proceeding with key new projects. Corporate execs would be well advised to remember his model before charging ahead with new and important ventures without the full support of the troops.

Yet, achieving true consensus is an arduous task that is often misunderstood by leaders. Gaining consensus is a process by which members of a group gather and agree to keep talking until they reach a solution that addresses the needs of all the stakeholders. It can be a time-consuming process that requires skilled facilitation, but can add significant gains in creativity and innovation.

Many organizations today want to use consensus in order to fully utilize the ideas and talents of all of their people. As explored in Chapter 14, there are advantages and disadvantages to this approach.

In the strategic corporate realm, leaders need to seek consensus for important new projects if they want the enthusiastic buy-in from the troops. In addition, many failed mergers could have been avoided if the participants sought consensus from the merged cultures about important integration issues. Failing to use consensus when it's imperative can affect everything from corporate culture to stock price. On the other hand, a true consensus has its drawbacks in certain situations if not used skillfully.

Consider the following seven tools if your group thinks it wants to use consensus.

Step One: Decide If Consensus Is Really Required

Many leaders tell me they "manage by consensus." Just their terminology always makes me question whether this is truly their approach. Consensus is not something that can be "managed." Usually, when leaders says this, what they mean is that they already have in mind an approach, but want to give their group the idea they are interested in their input. They will convene some kind of an open forum in order to go through the appearance of listening to other ideas. This approach can backfire since, although people may be enthusiastic the first time this occurs, they will soon realize something else is going on.

One of my clients, for example, asked me to help them revamp their group brainstorming process. Although this large financial institution had effectively utilized this method to design creative financial packages in the past, as the company grew, the process stalled. Debates dragged on endlessly, participation waned, and people groaned when invited to participate in a meeting using their brainstorming methodology. When they brought me in, they thought the problem was that newer people didn't understand the system or the ground rules. After I interviewed the executive team and watched one of their meetings, however, the true problem emerged.

The CEO, Rich, oozed charisma and power. He'd started the company with little more than a few thousand dollars and a dream, and built it into a billion dollar deal shop. All eyes swiveled toward him whenever anyone made a comment or offered a suggestion. Although he declared he valued the process of group decision-making and the creativity inherent in working through the process, his face gave him away. Raised eyebrows or rolled eyes instantly signaled his lack of enthusiasm for what someone said. Most participants felt sure that Rich had made up his mind before the meeting, but wanted to create the illusion of participatory decision-making by leading them through the process. He fooled no one. Consequently, his employees saw no point in going through the motions.

Sometimes a leader is a bit more sincere in the process. He or she has a basic approach outlined, but will listen if someone comes up with an idea or objection that has not been considered. In either event, this is not a true consensus.

A true consensus means going in with an open mind in order to consider all the needs and interests of the entire group. The group agrees to keep talking until a solution that truly addresses all of the needs and interests of all stakeholders has been reached. This is a time-consuming process.

It also requires each member of the group take the responsibility of speaking up in order to make sure the group hears their concerns as well as truly listening to the issues of others. Consensus requires each member to give up their beloved positions and focus on underlying needs. Most groups need a fair amount of training, discussion, and practice in order to make this work successfully.

Step 2: Identify Needs and Interests

This step requires each member of the group to take seriously the difference between positions and those of needs and interests. Group members need to avoid positions, which are predetermined solutions to the problem, and focus instead on meeting the needs and interests of each person, department, or group. The process takes a lot of active listening and creativity.

Step 3: Use a Facilitator

Consider using a facilitator for contentious meetings so everyone is heard and all interested parties can participate. Everyone has a piece of the truth. Ideally, a facilitator is a disinterested party who has no stake in the outcome. Such a person can come from outside the organization or from another department or group. Their job is to focus on the group process—to make sure the group is focusing on solving the problem and not getting distracted on personality issues. A professional facilitator can also stay alert for process problems and solutions, which also frees the leader from the role of running the meeting so that he or she can join in the discussion and participate.

One tool that facilitators find useful is to have each member use laminated, color-coded strips of paper they hold up when they want to speak or express agreement or disagreement with another speaker. Especially with large groups, this helps the facilitator keep track of what's happening and quickly read the group. Similar strips can also be used to keep track of group process. One side of the strip can be used to express an opinion and the other side to raise process issues. Especially for members of the group who may have much to offer, but who do not feel comfortable speaking up in meetings, this process can help them contribute to the group in a non-threatening way.

Some strips I have used successfully with groups (the left side for decisions/ the right for expressing process concerns):

Green: I agree with the proposal/with what's being expressed.

Blue: I'm neutral about the proposal/I have a question or comment.

Orange: I have an individual (as opposed to a group) concern about the proposal/I have an individual question or comment.

Red: Veto; I believe the proposal harms the organization/Stop the process; there is something about the way we're discussing this issue that harms the organization.

Using these strips allows the facilitator to easily read where the group is on an issue. A facilitator can also use the strips to take straw polls on a particular issue and to keep track of who wants to speak.

Facilitating a successful meeting involves skill and art. An outside, experienced facilitator can bring many different process ideas to a group. This frees the group from process concerns to focus solely on creatively solving the problem.

For example, one exercise I use as a facilitator is to post various suggestions around the room after a brainstorming session. I then allow the participants to circulate around the room with colored markers, marking the ones they agree with and writing down questions or concerns. In addition to allowing the group to move around the room, which tends to increase creative thinking, this process helps those who have trouble speaking up.

Always remember when conducting meetings that the fear of public speaking is the number one fear of many people—second only to drowning! This fear manifests for many creative people in large and small group meetings. What this means is that you miss the creative energy of people who have that particular style of interaction.

Everyone has a piece of the truth is an old Quaker saying. The Quakers, who have perfected the art of consensus decisions, know that it takes many different perspectives in order to come up with the best solutions to any particular problem. They acknowledge and know the power of group wisdom to solve any problem and realize that no one person can do it alone. When the group is stuck or polarized in any creative problem-solving session, this is a good way to encourage the group to think differently.

Calcified positions are frequently the result of someone assuming their way is the only way. Sometimes just stopping the process and reminding the group of this issue is helpful.

Step 4: For Contentious Issues, Conduct a Written Survey

When you know an issue is likely to be contentious, consider first conducting a written survey. In the survey tool, ask for the parties' *thoughts* on the subject and about their individual, department or group *needs and interests*. Avoid asking for positions, decisions, or solutions at this stage. Avoid backing people into positions; allow for "wiggle room" and creative group solutions. Written surveys allow people to think carefully and individually rather than to take positions in a group meeting.

Again, this suggestion helps bring forth the creativity, thoughts, and ideas of each group member. Many people communicate better through the written word than in meetings. It's also true that many people do not think well on their feet.

Written surveys also encourage people to think before they speak. I was married for 20 years, and my husband tended to be a brilliant, absent-minded professor kind of introvert. I came to learn the value of thinking before talking. This was a revelation to me. I used to be the kind of person that if you asked me a question, I would answer it. I may or may not know the answer, but I always had an opinion and wouldn't hesitate to express my views. As an extrovert, I tend to feel left out of meetings if I'm not talking. But in the face of a room full of extroverts, many team members who have difficulty speaking up just won't. Many people have to feel comfortable giving their opinion, which means those of us who have no problem speaking up need to be sensitive to those who do.

Because of the work I do, and because of my research and understanding on the way personality style impacts conflict, I've learned to think before I talk (at least most of the time). Written surveys, through paper or email, force those of us who tend to speak first to slow down and think about the issue. It also allows the leader or facilitator to retrieve the valuable thoughts of those who are more comfortable expressing themselves in a written format.

Sometimes it is helpful to tabulate all or part of the survey and distribute it before the meeting. Sometimes you may not want to take that step. Tabulated written surveys offer the advantage of allowing everyone to see what others are thinking. The disadvantage is that tabulation may serve to deter people from expressing thoughts that are outside the mainstream when you actually have a meeting. There's no right or wrong answer to this issue other than to think carefully before you do—or do not—tabulate the results and distribute them.

In some cases, written surveys can also help you formulate, eliminate, or expand the issues that need to be discussed. Often, especially if an issue is controversial or emotional, you may need to limit the discussion to just a piece of the issue.

In mediation we call this *eating the elephant bite by bite*. Sometimes a group needs to experience success in coming to agreement upon a part of the issue before moving on to something larger. Sometimes the leader or a facilitator, after studying the written surveys, will realize a meeting is unnecessary. Sometimes a new issue or a different way of framing the question will emerge. In any event, formulating the problem successfully can make all the difference in the outcome of the discussion.

Step 5: Use Subgroups for Small Groups of Polarized Positions

If it appears that only some people in a meeting are polarized and positioned, ask them to form an ad hoc team or sub-group. This suggestion can be extremely successful for bringing together a polarized group. At the end of a meeting to discuss a particular problem, you may realize the group is hopelessly deadlocked. You may be able to identify certain people who seem to be the most intractable. Appointing these people to work together as an ad hoc team or sub-group can help.

Encourage the most polarized and opinionated members to go through a consensus-building process on their own and to make recommendations to the entire group. This gives the sub-group ownership of both the problem and the solution. It also forces them to work together. Make sure they understand the rules from this book or other resources you want them to follow. Also encourage them to first agree upon how they will agree. If the polarized parties can agree on a solution, the rest of the group will be likely to follow their recommendations.

Be prepared for some surprises. I have watched some groups go through this process and have seen interesting results. Sometimes the members of the polarized group have long-simmering conflicts. When forced to work together to present a solution to the group, they may form new alliances. The remainder of the group—somehow used to those members carrying all the various objections of the group—starts squabbling among themselves or sometimes even object to the ad hoc's groups proposed solution, surprising the leader who thought the formerly silent group members had little interest in the issue.

I have seen leaders inexperienced with true consensus give up at this point, convinced that "this consensus stuff doesn't work." The reality is the process is working beautifully. The leader has now forced everyone to play his or her true hand. Rather than allowing some members of the group to remain silent and forcing the more noisy members to raise all the issues, more people are taking responsibility for speaking up and voicing their own previously hidden needs and interests. Now the leader and the group can go on to craft a solution that truly meets everyone's needs, even though that process may take longer than expected.

Step 6: Allow Sufficient Time for Consensus Decision-Making

Building a true consensus takes extra time on the front end, but avoids time wasting and foot-dragging as well as many other negative consequences on the back end. As a leader or group trying to decide if true consensus is necessary or desirable, you need to constantly ask whether you can make the necessary time available. Failure to do so can contribute to the entire process going array.

Ultimately, when consensus is used for the right process, it saves time in the long run. If people have legitimate interests that are being ignored, the only way to make sure they are met is to force people to go through a true consensus process. Otherwise you are left guessing about their concerns. If they have substantive interests that are ignored in the final solution, these issues will rebound to haunt you. People will delay acting upon necessary implementation steps for the solution, they will raise procedural objections and éven sabotage the enactment of the proposal. Forcing everyone to consider the best solution for the organization and all concerned on the front end may ultimately save you time.

It can be hard to remember this when you're in the midst of the endless discussions frequently required to reach a true consensus. As a member of a co-housing community (a community built for neighborhood interaction) that makes all decisions by consensus, I've had many painful experiences around this issue. Patience is not my strong suit. I sometimes want to scream in frustration at my fellow community members. Since I frequently do not care about the underlying substance of the decision, I want to jump in and push for a decision, any decision, just to get it over with so we can stop talking about the issue. Yet, I have seen many creative and sustainable solutions come from this process.

For example, many of the parents in the community thought we should cover all the window wells in order to prevent injury to small children. Non-parents objected, citing the need for light and air in the basement rooms. The discussion dragged on for months. Sub-groups formed, fumed, and met. Finally, when we were all ready to throw up our hands and admit defeat, Bob, a skilled carpenter, designed a window covering out of strong plastic mesh. The covering protected wayward toddlers yet allowed in light and air. Problem solved.

Many of my business clients experience frustration with the slow process of consensus, which is why I also counsel them to consider whether a true consensus is really required or wise. Once they decide it is, I advise them to take a deep breath and wait out the process.

One book that has helped me increase my own patience with the process is *A Different Drum: Community Building and Peace*, by Scott Peck, in which he profiles many different types of business and community organizations that use consensus. He talks about one spiritual residential community of monks he followed over 20 years of successful group living. On one important issue, it took the community an entire year to reach consensus. He (and the community) viewed this as a successful solution.

In our modern world, we want decisions *now*. The Internet age has contributed to our impatience. In addition, many people feel businesses, in order to compete, need to be able to change directions quickly. Wall Street has added to the pressure by demanding quick quarterly gains.

I don't disagree with this assessment of the modern, global climate. Yet I still think there's much room for thought on many decisions. Many quickly made decisions have to later be reversed, resulting in huge losses of time and money. Taking the time to reach a true consensus on the front end can save you later on.

Step 7: Educate Your People about the Decision-Making Process

It's helpful to share the pros and cons of the decision-making process with your group. Many problems with so-called consensus decision-making could be avoided if people were educated in the true meaning of consensus, how and when to use a facilitator, group process, and the realistic time required for the process. When people do not understand basic concepts of consensus building such as *everyone has a piece of the truth* and the difference between needs and interests, they will simply continue to use their old tools in a new process. You can avoid this problem by educating them about consensus and sharing with them the theories and tools of this book.

What Do We Mean By Agreement?

Many times, a manager or leader will stress that he or she wants a "consensus," "everyone's agreement," or "everyone's buy-in" on an idea. Yet, many times those same leaders have left a meeting to discover that everyone's *agreement* was not what they thought.

Saying, "I agree" with the proposal may mean many things, including any of the following:

"This is great! I can't wait to get started."

"I'd agree to anything right now. I'm sick of discussing this issue."

"I'll go along to get along."

"It's better than the alternatives I've seen, but it doesn't really address my issues."

Similarly, saying, "I disagree" may also mean different things to different people. It may mean:

"Wait! I haven't had time to digest the idea and decide what I think."

"I'm angry with you. I'd disagree with any proposal you have at this point."

"This offends my core values."

"I like another proposal better."

"I would agree if we could change one minor part."

Groups create confusion when they don't take the time to sort out all of these variables that describe, "I agree" and "I disagree." This may result in stalemates or in groups agreeing to proposals that are never implemented or are actively sabotaged.

To avoid this problem, after you think you have agreement about a proposal, consider using a *variables of agreement scale*. This scale allows participants to rate their agreement with the proposal from enthusiastic endorsement through the middle ground of abstention to blocking the proposal.

Not all agreements require the enthusiastic support of the entire group. Such support is essential when the stakes are high, when the decision is not easily reversible, or when the issue has been difficult to solve. Groups may also want enthusiastic support of issues where there is a need for a stakeholder buy-in on the issue or if there's a need to empower group members because the members will be expected to use their own judgment and creativity to implement the decision. Such decisions require each member to understand the reasoning behind that decision.

Enthusiastic support is often necessary, for example, for major strategic initiatives, new business ventures, or major changes in the goals or direction of an organization.

A less important decision around day-to-day tactics or when fewer members of the group are involved in implementation would require less support. A way to determine how much "agreement" you really have about an issue is to have people assess their standing on the following scale.

Variables of Agreement

When you finally believe you have a true consensus, you need to test it against the variables of agreement scale.

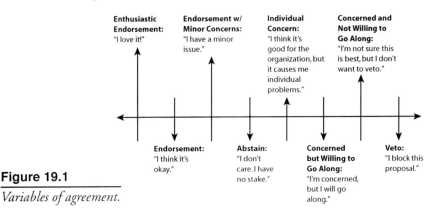

Figure 19.1

Variables of agreement.

"Variables of agreement. (Adapted with permission From Kaner, Sam. Facilitator's Guide to Participatory Decision-Making. Gabriola Island, BC: New Society Publishing, 1996)

A facilitator, either through polling the individuals, having them mark on a scale, or asking for a show of different-colored cards responding to the scale, can quickly see if the argument is solid and how sustainable the agreement is. By recording the results and presenting them to the group, this scale allows the group to see whether the agreement has the degree of support the group needs.

For example, I worked with a team of executives for a large corporation who were polarized over the direction of the company. While new business was strong, their initial under-capitalization had taken its toll over the years and they were short of cash. Some of the leaders wanted to continue to aggressively seek new markets, others wanted to pull back and wait. After going through a consensus process where the CEO pushed prematurely for a decision, we asked everyone to fill out the "Variables of Agreement" scale. It soon became apparent to the CEO that he had lukewarm support at best. He decided to go back to discussing options until he had a stronger agreement, realizing that such an important decision required a stronger consensus of the group. Although the decisions raged over several weeks, and were at times quite frustrating, they finally hammered out an acceptable plan.

When the stakes are high, when many players have "skin in the game," Eagle leaders know to slow down, step back, and fight for true agreement. When what's on the table is an important decision, nothing less will do than a good, sustainable agreement.

There may come a time, however, when you're faced with a truly intractable conflict, even after trying all the strategies in this and other chapters. What do you do when all your most skillful attempts to find a consensus fail? That thorny question is the subject of the next chapter.

Chapter 20
Surfing the Waves of Conflict: How to Manage When the Conflict Tide Refuses to Recede

---

I don't give them hell. I just tell them the truth
and they think it's hell.

—Harry S. Truman

Steve Miller gazes out the window of his new office with folded arms. A reformed roadrunner, he's not a man comfortable with conflict—but he's less comfortable with failure. He used to work around conflict, avoiding other art directors who were bickering over budgets, staff, and processes, even when it meant working harder. But after a performance review two years ago, his boss made it clear that his "work hard and avoid the issue style" was holding him back from running his own graphic design team. He decided to take action attending classes, mentoring with an executive, and learning to speak up and face conflict. Three months ago he was promoted but given a new department made up of designers and art directors from three different divisions of the company along with their baggage, old arguments, and culture differences. He's done everything the conflict resolution specialist they hired suggested: mediated with his team, listened endlessly to their concerns about the restructuring, even informed his team that they were facing discipline if they couldn't manage their differences. Nothing worked. All the talking and worrying feels like a waste of Steve's valuable time and effort and frankly, makes him want to run in the other direction.

"Surfing the waves of conflict" is a term I've borrowed from veteran community facilitator Rob Sandelin. As readers of this book may have guessed by now, I'm an optimist when it comes to managing conflict. I truly believe that we can meet the seemingly conflicting needs of most people most of the time if we're simply willing to put enough time and effort into the process.

Sadly, however, even I have to admit that some conflicts stay stuck despite our most valiant attempts. This may be because the other parties simply won't participate at the level we need in order to work our way through the issue or because our true needs and interests are ultimately incompatible. In that situation, what do you do?

Sandelin suggests an interesting alternative, "conflict surfing." He offers the idea that while some conflicts truly are not resolvable, you can "surf them with agility and understand the wave as you ride it."

Sandelin's suggestion points to intriguing solutions. While resolution may not provide the neat solution we'd hoped, we can both surf and understand the wave of the disagreement. Surfing skillfully can in itself lead to solutions, although not those we'd originally planned.

What Is a Solution?

Sometimes, the reason we can't resolve a conflict creatively is that we're sure we know what the solution *should* be. One way of surfing is to drop back from the waves into calmer seas while we consider whether our view of what "resolution" looks like is too narrow.

In my personal life, I've had this experience many times. As my then husband and I struggled to save our marriage, for example, we both thought that resolving the issues would lead to keeping our family together—a solution we both thought that we wanted. Yet the longer we wrestled with our unique and challenging situation, the more we came to the sad conclusion that we had no common ground for keeping the marriage together. We both adored our two children, however, and were passionately committed to their welfare.

We hashed out a plan that put their needs first. We would keep our house in the community where our kids felt safe and happy. John would move to a house in the neighborhood next door—about a block and one half away—and we would share time and duties equally with the children.

The children stayed put in the neighborhood and school. Little about their life changed, except that—most of the time—they no longer enjoy the company of both of us. The kids stay in my house the majority of the time, but they run freely back and forth and stay with John on some weekends and when I'm out of town. They know that we're both "on duty" as parents most of the time, and are available to them any hour of the day and night. Both houses are always open to them and their friends. Nicholas is a drummer in a rock band,

and they practice in a special band practice room in John's house, no matter which parent officially "has" the kids.

We also maintain a strict policy of not discussing our differences in front of the children or using them as cannon fodder in the war over our private feelings. We share dinner together as a "bi-nuclear family" a couple of times a week, John comes over to help with homework, and we hold regular family meetings where everyone has a chance to raise issues and share concerns. On holidays, everyone gathers at my house along with our extended family and we've even taken a couple of vacations together, with a "boy's" room and a "girl's" room.

While the situation involves complex logistics and continual negotiation, our children are responding well to what could have been a tragic outcome. Obviously, this solution would not work for every family. The arrangement succeeds because we're both flexible about trying to accommodate everyone's needs and interests, and we've maintained a level of caring and good will for each other even though we're divorced. When we decided that the marriage was hopeless, I insisted upon a purpose for our relationship going forward that involved treating each other and the kids with kindness and respect. Luckily, John agreed. We've also managed to continue to put our children first. As my daughter, Elizabeth, responded one day when I asked how she felt about the divorce, that "it doesn't hurt *my* feelings." Both kids shrug when anyone asks them about the divorce—it has become a non-event in their lives.

While I'm sure that someday they will be more in touch with the impact our divorce will ultimately have on her life, for now, we have managed to "surf the divorce wave" in a way that—while not resolving the marriage— did reorganize our family in a way that works for everyone (even though the original conflict was not resolvable in the traditional way).

Ask Last-Ditch Questions

Sometimes we can move a conflict that feels hopeless by asking what I call "last-ditch questions." These questions may help raise doubt in the minds of the parties about whether clinging to their own views is really in their best interest. Asking what mediators call "reality testing" questions can sometimes help bring parties back to the table, or at least help them surf the waves if they walk away. Doubt can be useful because by walking away, the parties are assuming that they have better options waiting. If we can raise the specter of doubt, we may help them see when that isn't true.

If you're mediating between warring factions, ask the questions alone with each party. If you're negotiating with someone else, try to raise these issues in a way that sounds truly open ended and curious. The most common reality testing questions are:

- What do you think I will do if we don't reach agreement?
- What do you think you will do if we don't reach agreement?
- What advice would you give me if we don't reach agreement?

Here are some additional queries mediation expert Christopher W. Moore recommends in his book, *The Mediation Process*:

- Do you think you can win in court (or other public setting such as before a commission or in the legislature)?
- How certain are you? 90 percent? 75 percent? 50 percent?
- What risk are you willing to take?
- What if you lose?
- What will your life be like then?
- What impact do you think your victory in court (or other arena) will have on your ongoing relationship with the other party?
- Will you ever be able to work together again?
- Who else might be affected?
- What would they think of your position?
- Would you be proud to publicly announce this stance?
- Would others whom you respect feel it is reasonable?
- If you were in the other party's place and this proposal were made to you, would you accept it?
- Could you accept it over the long run?

These questions help educate the other side about the reality of walking away. Lee Iacocca skillfully used these kinds of queries when Chrysler Corporation was facing bankruptcy in 1979. As he tried to negotiate with Congress for a loan guarantee of the bailout, most legislatures refused to even discuss the issue because they didn't believe that the government should rescue private businesses.

As the Congressional hearings progressed, Iacocca educated the legislators by examining what would happen if they refused his proposal. He asked, for example: "Would this country really be better off if Chrysler folded and the nation's unemployment rate went up another half of one percent overnight? Would free enterprise really be served if Chrysler failed and tens of thousands of jobs were lost abroad?"

Focusing on what it would cost the government in unemployment insurance and welfare payments if they laid everyone off, he said: "You guys have a choice. Do you want to pay the $2.7 billion dollars now, or do you want to guarantee half that amount with a good chance of getting it all back?"

Gradually, Congress realized how many people in their own districts depended upon Chrysler work. Iacocca walked away with his requested $1.5 billion dollar loan guarantee.

If we ask these kinds of questions with care and curiosity, we may be able to move someone to keep talking. At the least, I find, it will help us go forward with a better understanding of the other party or parties' issues and helps us surf the wave of an irresolvable situation.

As a part of the process, we also need to ask ourselves the same questions. This requires that we know our own "exit point," the point at which it makes more sense for us to walk away than to continue to expend energy in trying to creatively manage the conflict with the other parties. We can do a cost benefit analysis of staying or "voting with our feet." Yet we need to constantly test our exit strategy with these kinds of queries to make sure that leaving is the best option. Sometimes just reminding ourselves that we're not trapped can help us continue the work of creative conflict management.

Mobilize the Third Force

If you're sinking under the waves of conflict, consider mobilizing what negotiation expert William Ury calls "The Third Force." The third force may be team members who have an interest in the conflict, although not one as intense as the parties who have been striving to manage the situation. This is one time where triangulation may be appropriate. Try to find out if others can influence the parties to keep working toward a solution. Try to enlist them in opening up the minds of people who seem closed to creativity.

The third force can also be some external authority such as the party's boss, a judge, or arbitrator. Someone with power in the situation may be able to engage the parties in a way that you have not been able to do. Many times, for example, a judge will recognize that the parties have not reached a settlement and so will bring the parties together and either indicate a solution that favors one party, bringing the other back to the table, or hint at a solution that neither party finds favorable.

If you're mediating between workplace combatants, their boss may be able to remind them that creatively resolving conflict is in their job description.

On the world stage, there's been no better example of this strategy than the Dalai Lama. Forced to flee Tibet with his countrymen after the brutal Chinese take-over, and realizing that negotiation with the Chinese government would be futile, he has managed over the years to mobilize the press and many political supporters for the idea of restoring Tibet. While the Chinese have not yet relented, they have softened their stance on many issues. Clearly the Dalai Lama is able to do what many of us are not: take the long view. While he's frequently stated that he understands that a solution may not be imminent, perhaps not even in his lifetime, he's never given up hope that one may someday arrive.

The third force, then, can be the media or a political constituency that shares your interests. I once consulted with a group of women in a major corporation, for example, who were unhappy with the progress of women in the company. After many negotiations about the issues with upper management failed, they formed an ongoing "Women of 'ABC' Corp" group in order to continue to address their issues. They contacted the local paper and had a reporter attend their meetings. Stories started to filter out into other media. Eventually, the CEO asked to meet with representatives of the group and founded a successful women's initiative to speak to their concerns.

In using the third force, however, be sure that you've explored all your other options. Triangulating or going public with your concerns can sometimes back the other parties into a corner and thwart your ultimate goal of creatively managing the conflict. Yet used as a strategy when you've exhausted all other options, it can sometimes produce effective results. At a minimum, it will remind you that you always have the power to control your own options— including your own exit plot.

Consider Unilateral Action

If all of our attempts to convince, cajole, or persuade others to participate in a way that creatively manages the conflict fail, we can take the responsibility for dealing with our piece of the puzzle, even if no one else will play the game by our rules. But even managers and executives frequently have to persuade others at their own level, even if they are leading their own teams.

As a leader, you always retain the power to take unilateral action. Most of the strategies we've discussed so far in this book require a certain amount of willingness and cooperation on the part of employees and team members in order to change the organization. Sometimes, however, people may promise to change while dragging their heels on actually doing so. Even still, you have more power than you might expect as a single individual. You can still incubate positive change. By modeling for others the changes you would like to see in them, you can be effective in increasing your influence on the organization.

I worked with Bill, a young vice president of a pharmaceutical corporation. The company had recently merged with a much larger organization, creating layers of bureaucracy that both Bill and his group resisted. At some point, Bill realized that his team's own actions were undermining its effectiveness, and he decided to persuade his fellows to abandon their protest. His words fell on deaf ears. They didn't budge. He tried again. They dug their heels in further. He circled back for another round. They shunned him. Finally, he briefly flirted with the idea of firing the entire lot. The momentary respite of that fantasy gave him the will to try something else. Something more subtle. He stopped talking and just acted. Calmly, without a word, he just changed his own behavior and abandoned the notion of changing the group's approach.

Bill followed the rules the new ownership demanded. When appropriate, he continued to advise his team of his own decisions to "go with the flow." He dealt with his employees, as well as his superiors, in a fair and even-handed manner, avoiding the politics and passive/aggressive sabotage that some of his teammates delivered. He stopped lecturing his group on how they needed to follow his example and surrender to the enemy. He remained a calm and cheerful example of leadership.

Gradually, his employees adjusted and followed his lead. While they continued to insist that they liked the old regime better, they slowly adapted to the new ways. When they realized that their boss was no longer going to support the conflict, they began to realize they had to adapt. Many felt relief at having a clear direction—or at least a more conflict-free one. While they still had issues with the new culture, their resistance melted in droplets like the saying "the rock will wear away."

Today, Bill is an Executive Vice President and his team leads the world in sales for their global conglomerate. While people sometimes still talk about the "good old days," they don't actively resist the efforts and directives of headquarters. In five years it's likely that they'll end up referring to these times as the good old days too!

While one individual may not be able to change a whole system, you can always control your own behavior within the system and whether you continue to work for the organization. When you give up fighting with the other combatants without expecting that they change, you inspire by example, instead of convincing by argument.

As you take on the role of leading in this way, it helps to tell your co-workers what to expect and then to be sure that you act in step with those expectations. Make sure that you use "I" statements and talk only about your own behavior, instead of the behavior of others. Also outline the ways in which you will change, instead of asking for others to change or focusing on their past behavior.

For your own sanity, give up hoping that others will appreciate your efforts. They may someday, but in the meantime, if you're using unilateral action, you need to attend to our own business. If you do notice tiny changes in the direction you want others to move, appreciate their efforts, no matter how small. Last, but certainly not least, spend some time thinking about why the system seems so resistant to change and what kinds of healthier systems you could encourage.

One of my clients, Diana, an HR manager who has a long-running feud with John, a marketing director, used this technique. John had continually ignored and even sabotaged various HR policies that he considered a waste of his and his team's time and energy. Diana, however, had to deal with an indignant parade of employees who disliked John's management style. She tried to persuade John that he was violating good management practices, as well as company policy. No matter what approach she tried, he rebuffed her efforts.

After talking with me, she devised a new plan. Trapped in a no-win game, Diana caught John working late one night and informed him that she was no longer going to harangue him about the problems he was causing employees. She realized that he didn't want or seem to need her advice and so she would stop the campaign. Diana told him that she would inform employees that John would be handling his own HR problems from now on. She explained her new policy without anger and advised John that she was open to suggestions about how they could make their relationship work better.

For once, John was shocked into silence. While not willing to initially acknowledge her efforts, over time, as employee complaints started landing on his desk, he started to seek Diana out for advice and counsel. Today, while Diana still ruefully describes John as one of her "problem children," the unilateral truce seems to be working.

While such disarmament may appear to demonstrate weakness during the throes of battle, it can actually lead to a more lasting peace than continuing a futile fight.

There are many examples in history of unilateral action that has resulted in creative conflict management. In 1948, for example, after the end of World War II, Soviet leader Joseph Stalin blockaded West Berlin, insisting that Allied troops leave the city. The Western Allies considered blasting through the blockade with an armed convoy but feared starting World War III. Instead, they chose the unilateral action of mounting a huge airlift of food and supplies to the isolated Berliners. Frustrated, Stalin called off the blockade and agreed to negotiate.

Sometimes we can use skillful words to turn a stalled situation around. During the American Civil War, for example, President Lincoln spoke sympathetically about the Southern rebels in a public address. Fully aware that he would need to try to unite the country after the war, he started the process of healing with his own unilateral action. When a staunch Unionist lambasted him for speaking kindly of his enemies when he should be destroying them, Lincoln answered with his classic reply: "Why, madam, do I not destroy my enemies when I make them my friends?"

Unilateral disarmament can be preferable to a forced settlement. Many historians believe, for example, that forcing unacceptable terms on the Germans after World War I helped fuel World War II. One of the conditions the Axis insisted upon in the Treaty of Versailles was staggering reparations to pay for the costs of the war. The payments devastated the value of the German mark. Cartoonists during that time, for example, depicted German housewives using wheelbarrows of essentially worthless marks to buy a loaf of bread.

Most of the world had such revulsion to the idea of another war, that they pinned all their hopes for a future peace on the League of Nations, the predecessor of today's United Nations. Yet the forced—and many believe untenable—settlement of World War I allowed Hitler to gain power and helped spark World War II.

Sometimes the best unilateral action is to walk away. That's what schoolteacher Christine Pelton decided. After discovering that nearly a fifth of her biology students had plagiarized their semester projects from the Internet, the Piper, Kansas, teacher sought and received the backing of the district to fail the 28 sophomores. Yet after parents complained, the school board reversed the decision. Her integrity at stake, Pelton resigned when she couldn't convince the board to change their stance. "The students no longer listened to what I had to say," she said. "They knew if they didn't like anything in my classroom from here on out, they can just go to the school board and complain."

Pelton didn't feel that she could maintain her own honest standards if she stayed. In this case, the costs to her own personal integrity would have been too great. When conflict violates our own sense of self and what's most important to our identity, sometimes the best solution is to walk away.

When all your other frantic efforts at conflict management have simply whipped up the waves, consider grabbing your board and going surfing. Surfing can involve paddling away from the conflict forever, if necessary, as in quitting a job or firing an uncooperative employee. Surfing can also involve asking the last-ditch questions or considering unilateral actions. Sometimes surfing means hanging in the midst of conflict for longer than you anticipate, but still riding the waves as skillfully as the Dalai Lama, instead of expecting the waters to recede.

While you're contemplating your options, keep in mind the power of culture to incubate eagles, the subject we return to in the last chapter.

Chapter 21
Saving an Endangered Species: How to Incubate Eagles

It's okay to spend a lot of time arguing about which route to take to San Francisco when everyone wants to end up there, but a lot of time gets wasted in such arguments if one person wants to go to San Francisco and another secretly wants to go to San Diego.

—Steve Jobs, Apple Computers

Joe Dishman spent six years working endless hours as an associate in a major law firm. His track record and work ethic were impeccable; his personality was not. He was a notorious pit bull. Nonetheless, the other partners felt Joe's results spoke for themselves and they rewarded him by making him a partner. Joe's new position only made his bulldog personality worse. Associates quit because of his aggressive barking and partners avoided him. Finally, Joe became so miserable he sought help. Slowly, he began a metamorphosis by trying new communication tools in small interactions. Joe made the comeback of his career, becoming an eagle in his firm. Rifts with partners were healed. He became a mentor to young associates. He could disagree without it becoming a personal grudge. His influence, power, and happiness grew exponentially.

The workplace has undergone dramatic shifts in the last several decades, which require employees to embrace an inclusive culture. Successful, cutting-edge organizations are thinking out of the box, turning obstacles into opportunities and capitalizing on the strengths of a diverse workforce—they are creating eagles. If your organization wants to join the ranks of the "best practice"

195

companies, it is incumbent that staff members are skilled at creatively managing conflict and they engender a culture of inclusivity that is solution oriented. Creating a strong culture fosters a team environment that can give the organization tremendous synergy. However, without such a culture, the company can fall prey to unproductive conflicts that will reduce effectiveness, profits, and performance.

Leaders and the Power of Culture

A client—the CEO of a high-tech company—recently called me. For several years my company had provided consulting and training services to his company. He finally decided to fire Frank, his CFO—a technically brilliant man who was lacking in "people skills." Employees constantly carped about the CFO's abusive, abrupt, and intimidating manner.

When the CEO delivered the news that he could no longer defend his executive against the rising tide of employee complaints (and even one pending lawsuit), Frank's surprised response is typical of many I hear in today's workplace: "In some companies, my style would be considered an advantage! People around here are just too sensitive!"

Another client decided to upgrade the computer department in his company from data management to a true information technology department. On the advice of a headhunter, he hired someone from a large computer firm, an old-fashioned hierarchical company. The ensuing cultural wars shocked my CEO client. Long-time employees reacted with anger and tears to the dictatorial regime of the new manager. The CEO found he had no time to run his thriving and complex company. Instead, his days were spent trying to mediate disputes among the new manager, his team, and other departments.

A third client reorganized its large HR department and brought in several new players to invigorate the team. The result? Another culture clash! The old team insisted workers need HR representatives who are *employee advocates*. The new managers wanted to move up the ladder of corporate success. They were convinced the way to do that was to raise the visibility of HR and make HR representatives *business partners* with the leaders of their business units. When I came in to facilitate a session to creatively manage this dispute, some of the people were not even speaking to one another.

What is the common denominator in all of these situations? The leaders in these organizations had not spent enough time and energy thinking about *culture*—that invisible glue that holds organizations together and determines organizational effectiveness. Especially lacking was a failure to think about how they want the culture to address and creatively manage the inevitable conflicts each organization faces on a daily basis. A lack of agreement about a common culture frequently shows up as constant and unproductive conflicts.

I'm amazed that even the most successful organizations have spent so little time thinking about what kind of culture they want to create and what kind of employees will assist them in building that culture as well as how to shape, deliver, and reinforce that message. I'm also amazed at how little thought business executives give to the culture that certain business philosophies will create. All overreaching cultures at the top trickle down to the bottom whether the company engages in a clear communication policy or not. When I use the term "culture" I'm talking about the entire collection of ideals and values that make an organization unique, including philosophies on outsourcing instead of hiring, creating groups in other countries instead of in the United States, whether conflict is approached directly or in more subtle ways, and whether the organization is focused on long-term growth or short-term gain. At the strategic level, cultural clashes are usually deeply tied to business decisions or business philosophies.

A clear culture can become an organization's brand: a powerful tool in attracting and retaining top talent. The executive team may have spent a few hours working on a superficial and platitudinous mission statement they then proceeded to plaster on the walls of employee lunch rooms and inserted into the employee manual, but the kind of culture I'm talking about will only result from two things: 1) top leaders walking the talk and 2) constantly engaging employees in ongoing discussions about culture.

When organizations take the time to do this kind of work, the culture they want to create becomes what Margaret Wheatley, in her book, *Leadership and the New Science*, calls a "field of vision"—a powerful structuring field where certain types of individual behavior and events are guaranteed. Such a structuring field is especially important in communicating how you want people to manage conflict. Jim Collins, in his classic book, *Built to Last*, identifies culture as one of the most important factors in creating a healthy, long-lasting company.

In order to shape the future, leaders need to be aware of how the decisions they make will affect culture and encourage other leaders and serve as models to create energy fields that shape organizational culture, especially how they model and value conflict management. Wheatley sees leaders as "broadcasters, talk radio beacons of information, pulsing out messages everywhere . . . stating, clarifying, discussing, modeling, filling all of the space with the messages we care about."

Leading in the future will require even the best executives to acquire new skills. The old order in the workplace is clearly crumbling, but the new has not yet emerged. In between, a great many misunderstandings occur. If not skillfully managed, these misunderstandings escalate into productive conflicts.

For example, I was asked to conduct a diversity project for a major law firm. They had gone through a number of steps of the project over a series of months, but kept putting off the one key phase: having a series of focus groups with partners and associates to help us determine the issues we'd need to address in diversity trainings. When I finally met with the Executive Committee to find out why they kept dragging their feet on scheduling those meetings, the chairman blurted out:

> But we don't want some of our partners meeting with associates. They're idiots. They'll say all the wrong things! They'll make the associates want to leave! They just don't understand these issues. In fact, I don't even like them. I haven't talked to some of them in years.

Now this is an interesting way to run a law firm, but it doesn't lead to productivity, teamwork, and profitability. It's impossible to forever keep toxic partners, managers, or supposed leaders away from lower-level employees. If the firm doesn't have leaders who will "walk the talk," reinforcing the culture they want to create, there's no way it will ultimately accomplish its goal.

The reality is that today's new workforce trends call for new leadership attitudes. Organizations now face historic shortages of skilled employees to fill many positions, making it essential to retain productive employees and attract the best new employees. Worker loyalty is at an all-time low, with people changing jobs so frequently that leaders have no time to build cohesive teams. Those workers who are available are much more diverse and have a different work ethic, creating the need to lead differently. Increased employee litigation and unproductive conflict distracts leaders from their mission. Setting aside the time to create, discuss, and shape organizational culture is one part of the solution to these problems. Leaders must force ongoing conversations at every level about the power of culture in an organization, especially about how to creatively manage the inevitable and increasing conflicts.

As discussed in Part I, one of the best ways to address the issue of purpose and culture is to strive to make community building a part of your own purpose. Many successful business leaders now see community building as a pragmatic business decision.

Larry Weber, for example, is founder of Weber Shandwick International, part of the Interpublic Group of Companies, a $7 billion advertising and marketing conglomerate. He believes new leaders succeed because they've abandoned the military management style and instead are what Weber calls the "provocateurs." Provocateurs, he emphasized in a recent interview, "see themselves as community builders, with the customer at the center. These days most customers are nomads who are looking for places to camp out. The more engaging, useful, or attractive provocateurs can make their communities, the better their chances are of attracting and keeping customers."

Weber cites Rick Wagoner, CEO of General Motors, as a new-style provocateur inside an old-style company:

> Every day, he has to deal with a dozen or more constituencies that he can't control, from customers to employees, strategic allies, business partners, legislators, and labor unions. Wagnor sees it as his job to get those constituencies to work together for the benefit of the GM community. If he can strengthen the GM community, then GM will succeed.

Weber believes that provocateurs understand that a CEO must see his or her primary job as "to engage in deep, constant dialogue with all the company's constituencies." Weber exhorts leaders to "build a community, not a company," noting that "the strength of a business is measured by the strength of its relationships."

Organizations and Purpose

Most organizations now have some kind of mission statement. If thoughtfully crafted, these statements can help organizations achieve their goals and create a powerful culture. Consider including one as a part of your organization's mission.

For example, I helped one of my clients, a large transportation district, craft the following addition about conflict to their general mission statement. You can see it also intersects well with the organization's union contract:

Goals Statement for Conflict Resolution

The Transportation District, as an organization, recognizes that conflict is a normal and predictable part of working together. Therefore, we adopt the following goals relating to conflict resolution:

1. We are committed to increasing our skills in resolving conflict.

2. At all levels of the organization, we strive to resolve conflicts in a productive and creative way, without threats, harassment or violence.

3. Nothing in this goal statement is meant to conflict with the RTD/AT Collective Bargaining Agreement or other RTD policies.

Section I: Management-Union Relations

The Employer agrees to meet in good faith with the duly elected representatives of the Union and attempt to resolve all questions arising between them. The Union fully agrees that within its ability each of its members shall render faithful service in their respective positions as outlined in the clauses of this Agreement and will cooperate with the management of the Employer in the efficient operation of the system in accordance with the rules, regulations, and operating conditions as announced by the Employer, and will cooperate and assist in fostering cordial relations between the Employer and the public.

As you can see, we combined elements with their usual mission statement with the mission statement on conflict. We then included a statement about their goals for labor/management relations since they were a unionized organization. You can see the parallels between the two mission statements. Reprinting these two together helped the organization come together around the issue of conflict with the union.

What is the mission of your organization? What are its goals? How would it help your organization reach its goals if you included your mission for conflict resolution?

One of the most powerful statements, in my experience, is to emphasize you recognize, as a group, that conflict is a part of life, can be valuable, and that it's your goal to skillfully manage conflict. This can serve as a revelation to those in your organization who are constantly frustrated by the very existence of conflict. They need to know their leaders understand conflict is normal and healthy. Yet, leaders also need to make it clear that *skillful* and creative conflict management is something they consider a part of everyone's job description. Just making these statements and serving as role models for their enactment can help to resolve many problems around conflict.

Fostering a Creative Culture

What other organizational characteristics most encourage a creative culture? A group of creativity researchers used the Department of Labor's classification of the characteristics of U.S. organizations to determine what organizational values led to innovation and identified four factors: (1) people orientation, such as collaboration, supportiveness and team orientation; (2) risk taking, such as a willingness to experiment and aggressiveness; (3) attention to detail, such as precision and results orientation; and (4) stability, such as security of employment. These results suggest an organizational culture that supports risk taking, collaboration, quality, and security is likely to be innovative and "high performance." They also found using teams and information sharing led to higher levels of group interaction and fostered creative decision-making. Organizations with these characteristics in their culture will be most able to generate good fights and the resulting innovation.

Perhaps one of the most critical components of fostering a creative culture is encouraging risk taking. How do you encourage reasonable risk? Dick Liebhaber, executive vice president of MCI, has observed: "We do not shoot people who make mistakes. We shoot people who do not take risks."

Organizational norms, top management walking the talk, and managers encouraging risk help encourage creative risk taking. Without encouraging risks, it's difficult for anything creative to emerge. Researcher Amy Edmonson, for example, studied the effects of "psychological safety" in a large number of teams in an office furniture manufacturing company. Psychological safety "is characterized by a shared belief that well-intentioned action will not lead to punishment or rejection." She measured safety with a survey instrument that included statements such as "it is safe to take a risk on this team." Edmonson found the level of psychological safety felt by team members affected learning behavior and led to higher team performance. She also found that team leadership needed to create the climate for risk taking that led to enhanced performance. Leaders must be careful how they respond to failure in order to encourage risks. A superintendent at Chaparral Steel, for example, championed a $1.5 million arch saw for trimming finished steel beams. When he brought the saw back to the site, it totally failed. After a year of unsuccessful tinkering, the saw was replaced. The superintendent was promoted to vice president of operations, surprising outsiders who "can't believe you can make a mistake like that and not get crucified."

Leaders can learn to deliver honest feedback in a way that encourages creativity and risk taking. Alan Horn, for example, chairman and CEO of Castle Rock Entertainment, is careful when first presented with creative ideas such as screenplays or ideas for marketing. He tries to cultivate a "heartfelt, internalized respect for what these people do." When they present a new idea,

> I want to remember that they are *completely* vulnerable at that moment. My job is not to kill them but to find the bright, creative, special parts of their proposal and focus on those first, to ease their anxiety, make them feel less vulnerable. Then I have to find a graceful way into the parts of what they've brought that need improving.

Feedback delivered in this way helps create a culture that welcomes risk taking and innovation.

Connectivity

Nurturing connectivity is critical to fostering a culture of creative conflict. At Hewlett-Packard Laboratories, for example, senior researchers, dubbed "Friends of Joel" Birnbaum, wander the halls of the labs on his behalf to identify potential research projects or small pockets of creativity or a potential product.

Leaders can foster connectivity through the Internet. At Unilever, for example, with food processing plants scattered around the world, "knowledge networks" are connected electronically, and members meet periodically so they can share problems and creative solutions. The company's tomato experts, for example, form a community of practice around that fruit, wherever they work around the world, holding workshops at different sites to create a complete knowledge map of what Unilever knows about tomatoes—from seeds to consumer sauce preferences.

Additional Organizational Tactics

The research on conflict confirms how a strong culture organized around a clear purpose helps lead to conflict-skilled organizations. In addition, researchers Kathleen Eisenhardt, Jean Kahwajy, and L. J. Bourgaeois, III, reporting on their findings in the *Harvard Business Review*, identified five other cultural tactics that helped companies skillfully manage conflict. The successful teams were able to separate substantive issues from those based on personalities, disagree over questions of strategic significance, and still get along with one another. The tactics were:

- They worked with more, rather than less, information and debated on the facts,
- They developed multiple solutions to raise the level of debate,
- They injected humor into the decision process,
- They maintained a balanced power structure, and
- They resolved issues without forcing consequences.

Let's look at how successful teams used all of these factors.

Focus on the Facts

The researchers found more information is better because it encourages people to focus on issues, not personalities. Companies who managed conflict skillfully claimed to "measure everything," including facts about the external environment. As one CEO explained his process, "we over-M.B.A. it." Otherwise, teams waste time in pointless debate over opinions and biases. Without timely and accurate information, people rather than issues become the focus, creating interpersonal conflict. Managers with high degrees of interpersonal conflict rely more on "hunches and guesses" than on current information.

The researchers found "a direct link between reliance on facts and low levels of interpersonal conflict." With facts, people moved swiftly to the central issues. In the absence of facts, people instead suspect others' motives. "Building decisions on facts creates a culture that emphasizes issues instead of personalities."

Multiple Alternatives

Sometimes leaders assume they reduce conflict by focusing on only one or two alternatives in order to minimize the possible disagreements. Yet the researchers found that teams with low interpersonal conflict do just the opposite. They purposefully float multiple alternatives, sometimes even suggesting options with which they disagree, just to promote debate.

Considering multiple alternatives lowers unhealthy conflicts because it diffuses conflict, choices become less black and white, and people can shift positions more easily. More creative options emerge, sometimes taking part of several different solutions. The process itself becomes more creative and enjoyable. The result is substantive conflict management instead of interpersonal.

The Power of Humor

The researchers found teams that handle conflict well make explicit and often contrived attempts to relieve tension and promote collaboration. They find competition exciting. In the teams with unhealthy interpersonal conflict, humor was absent.

The successful teams used humor as a healthy defense mechanism to protect people from the stress that arises in the course of making strategic decisions. The humor also put people in a more positive mood. Many researchers have found that people in a positive mood tend to be not only more optimistic, but also more forgiving of others and more creative.

Balanced Power Structures

Organizations with autocratic leaders as well as extremely weak leaders both generated high levels of unhealthy interpersonal conflict. The lowest level of destructive conflict comes from teams with balanced power structures in which the CEO is the most powerful, but the other members of management wield substantial power in their own areas of responsibility.

Qualified Consensus

The most successful teams didn't seek true consensus all the time. Instead, they used a kind of *fall back* or *qualified* consensus. The group talked and tried to reach consensus. If they couldn't within a relevant period of time, the most senior leader made the decision. Remarkably, the teams that insisted on resolving substantive conflict by forcing consensus displayed the unhealthiest interpersonal conflict. Insisting on consensus in all issues leads to "endless haggling."

As one V.P. of engineering put it: "Consensus means that everyone had veto power. Our products were too late and they were too expensive." What the researchers found was that people wanted to be heard; they wanted their opinions and ideas treated with respect, but that people were willing to accept outcomes they disagreed with if they believed that the process used to come to a decision was fair.

These five tactics, in addition to emphasizing common goals, lead not to less conflict, but to more healthy and productive conflict. What these researchers affirmed is that if there is little conflict over issues, there's also likely to be poor decision-making. Conflict over issues, not personalities, is valuable. The successful teams avoided "groupthink," which has been a primary cause of failure in both public and private sectors. The researchers found "the alternative to conflict is usually not agreement, but apathy and disengagement."

Organizational Conflict Management

Once you establish a mission statement around conflict for your organization and learn skills such as storytelling and facilitating, you'll want to consider structures that support conflict management. A successful model for the conflict-skilled organization involves the following:

- A creative conflict management mission statement.
- Leaders who model skillful conflict resolution through walking the talk and storytelling.

- Skilled mediators to resolve conflicts that people cannot resolve directly.
- Skilled coaches to advise people in the midst of conflict.
- Conflict management skills training specifically tailored for leaders, mediators, coaches and all employees.
- Accountability.

Along with the first element of this program—a mission statement, the other elements also require careful consideration.

Basic Conflict Management Skills Training

An organization that wants to successfully and creatively manage conflict should consider basic conflict management training for all employees. These trainings should be four to six hours in length and cover the organization's overall mission, policies, and procedures around conflict as well as the basic conflict management skills employees need. The sessions should be designed to be practical, hands-on, and experiential. Participants should experience a successful conflict resolution exercise as well as gain an understanding of the theories and steps involved. The session should emphasize the power of attitude about conflict to encourage employees to value and embrace conflict in order to drive innovation.

The most successful organizations will make such trainings mandatory for all employees. Ideally, these courses should be part of an organization's standard management training program. If an organization has a skilled training or organizational development department, these sessions can be developed internally. If not, there are outside firms like Workplaces That Work that develop these programs. Just make sure to select a group that embraces the philosophy of this book: not just managing conflict but using contention as a creative force.

Advanced Training for Coaches, Facilitators, and Mediators

After completing the basic training, those with the interest and ability to serve as coaches, facilitators, and mediators should go on to advanced training. This training would help people learn two skills: 1) providing confidential coaching to those in the midst of conflict and 2) serving as coaches, facilitators, and mediators for those who cannot creatively manage conflict themselves.

Organizations should consider training one coach/mediator for every 50 to 100 employees. This training would also be highly interactive, focusing on mediation and coaching skills beyond the basics. The training should take 2-1/2–5 days.

Once again, if the organization has skilled internal resources, they can develop these sessions. If not, make sure that the outside sources understand, and embrace, creative conflict.

Executive Briefing

Ideally, executives should take both levels of training since surveys show they spend at least one-fourth of their time resolving and mediating conflicts. At the least, executives should be briefed as to the basics of the program in a one to two hour session and receive a taste of the regular training.

Accountability

The last piece of the puzzle to creating a conflict-skilled organization is to focus on accountability. None of the other moves will create the level of cooperation, community, and teamwork you need in your organization without this important element.

For example, one of my clients is a large, world-class motor company. I was hired by the president, Helen, to conduct my conflict management workshop at their annual executive retreat. She'd told me one of their problems was that some people on the executive team used a pit bull style of conflict resolution while others triangulated conflict. The workshop was a success based on the feedback and participation; in fact, the executives wanted to expand the session to a full day class and bring it to all of their other managers. Over the next month, I conducted day-long workshops for their entire management team across the country. Again, the feedback was positive.

In my last meeting with Helen, she thanked me for making the workshops a success but lamented that—even though we'd provided the skills—one V.P. was still a problem. His behavior included incredible displays of rudeness, attacks, and constant criticism of the other executives and managers, yelling profanities, and a general inability to be a team player, even though he was good at his own substantive area of expertise.

"I just don't understand why he won't change," she sighed. I asked the obvious question: "Have you talked to him about his behavior?" Helen responded that she had, several times, but nothing changed.

I then went on to emphasize to her the difference between a talk about his behavior and making him accountable for his behavior. She'd never enforced any *consequences* for his inappropriate behavior. I suggested she needed to make improving his behavior a part of his performance plan, complete with consequences up to and including termination if he failed to meet those requirements. She revealed she was concerned about losing someone who was substantively good at what he does, yet Helen understood failure to do so would continue to undermine the entire executive team. Miraculously, when she followed my advice and included accountability for his behavior, he started to improve his skills.

You have the right and, indeed, the responsibility as a leader or manager to insist all of your workers make creative conflict management skills a part of their job description. Just giving them the skills may not be enough if you fail to follow through with significant consequences for their failure to act.

These kinds of behavioral change plans must be skillfully considered and managed. Be sure to include, in writing, behavioral specifics: what you want the person to say or do. If you use general language such as: "we need you to be less abrasive" or "we need you to not talk in a demeaning way to staff," they may not be able to change their behavior. Instead, use specific examples such as: "we need you to use a normal voice when you talk to staff," "we need you to not use profanity," "we need you to avoid sarcasm." Positive examples are also helpful. Chapter 13 explores more ways to offer constructive feedback.

How the System Works in Practice

With this system in place in a conflict-skilled organization, most conflicts would be resolved directly between the involved parties. If they are unable to do so, the participants could request individual coaching sessions from designated coaches. If that fails, they could then request mediation. Leaders could also refer associates to mediators to resolve disputes.

This approach allows an organization to take a systemic approach to creative conflict management and will result in significant savings in lost productivity, time, and energy. This system also prevents a rise in the negative spiral of unproductive and personal conflicts, lawsuits, and other costly conflicts. The time an organization invests in this system and training will bring dramatic results for all involved. Finally, this system will help you harness the power of a good fight to improve productivity and innovation.

Leadership and Storytelling

Much has been written in recent years about leadership in general and the need for all employees to become leaders, not just employees. These writers miss two significant nuances: the need to give people *meaning* in their work and the power of *story* as a tool for encouraging meaning and for serving as a model for the "why" behind conflict resolution. People must have common goals or resolution is not possible. Many organizational conflicts result from a lack of belief in or understanding about why the organization exists, does what it does, and what its true goals are. Skillfully using stories can help change this dynamic.

Futurist Rolf Jensen, Director of the Copenhagen Institute for Future Studies, writes:

> Storytellers will be the most valued workers in the 21st century. All professionals, including advertisers, teachers, entrepreneurs, politicians, athletes and religious leaders, will be valued for their ability to create stories that will captivate their audiences.

Jensen claims that in the years ahead we will move into what he calls the Dream Society:

> In today's Information Society, we prize those who can skillfully manipulate data; in tomorrow's Dream Society—focused on dreams, adventure, spirituality and feelings—we will most generously reward those who can tell stories. The highest-paid person in the first half of the next century will be the "storyteller." In the future, the notion that work should be no more than a means of obtaining something else will disappear. People will, of course, be paid for working, but money will not be the main reason for working. People will require meaning in their work.

Current surveys of Generation Xers place meaning high on the list of what they look for in a job. Aging baby boomers—having passed through their materialistic stage—will also demand meaning in their work, not just management.

Organizations will have to develop a collective meaning to survive and to resolve the ever-escalating conflicts. As Jensen writes:

> Today's business firm is rational, efficient and devoted to making profits, because it developed out of the Industrial Age and the Information Age. But this type of company will either adapt or disappear in the future. A Dream Society requires values—ethical, social or religious. A company obsessed with efficiency and working only for profit will be regarded as untrustworthy . . . in the Dream Society, companies will be more balanced. They will seek to earn a profit, but they will also want to achieve certain human values, i.e., kindness to animals, fairness to all or happiness for workers and their communities.

Leaders will be increasingly called upon to help give meaning to employees. Of course, before you can help others find meaning in their work, you have to find it in your own. Meaning fuels the sometimes challenging work of conflict resolution.

Can all honest, legal work have meaning, dignity, and value? Yes, I believe it can. If you doubt me, read Victor Frankle's classic work, *Man's Search for Meaning*, about finding meaning in his work as a prisoner in a Nazi concentration camp. There may be more difficult environments, but I can't imagine where or when.

Even if your current job doesn't fit your long-term passion, find meaning in the support the work provides as you plan for more passionate future work. Find meaning in doing what you do with excellence and integrity. Mother Teresa noted, "We do not do great things. We do small things with great love." Ultimately, if you can't find meaning in your work, leave. The dilemma is this: the future will require such a level of commitment that you will not be able to sustain your work with anything less than all-out dedication.

One way to give meaning to your work and to work of those you lead is through storytelling. As we moved into Jensen's Dream Society, in the later part of the 20th century, it's no accident we elected an actor, Ronald Reagan, as president of this country and a playwright, Vaclav Havel, as president of the Czech Republic.

How powerful are stories? "Everybody is a story," writes Dr. Naomi Remen in her book, *Kitchen Table Wisdom, Stories That Heal.*

> When I was a child, people sat around kitchen tables and told their stories. We don't do that so much anymore. Sitting around the table telling stories is not just a way of passing time, it is the way wisdom gets passed along. The stuff that helps us to live a life worth remembering. Despite the awesome powers of technology many of us still do not live very well. We may need to listen to one another's stories again.

Loneliness is the hidden wound of our time—the price many have paid for embracing such frontier values as independence, self-reliance, and competence. It's also a price paid by those who frequently change jobs. In the future, leaders will be increasingly called upon to remember we are all connected and can become a community, to help organizations work more cooperatively and to move toward goals with humor and meaning, with purpose and quality companionship. A good story provides a compass for a group's mission. Skillful conflict management builds trust and creates connections and helps a group work together to accomplish its mission.

As leaders, how do we discover and develop our own stories to inspire others? Look at your *wounds.* There is power in the wounded leader. As Nietzsche wrote, "life breaks all of us eventually, but some of us grow back stronger in the broken places." Ironically, our greatest strengths come from these wounds, from what makes us vulnerable, because our vulnerability also makes us human. And in our humanity lies our ability to connect with and lead others. At the heart of most wounds is a conflict. The healing of most wounds involves connection.

The ability to appropriately reveal our wounds, our vulnerability, makes the most powerful leaders. Bob Dole, despite his physical wounds, was not. It's why Clinton won a re-election (despite his many mishaps), and Hillary may not. It's why Marilyn Monroe, "the vulnerable blonde," is a timeless cultural icon, and Madonna never will be. (Unless, of course, parenthood brings Madonna to her knees, as it does most of us.)

How do we develop storytelling ability? After we look at our wounds, ask what we can teach from that place of wounding. What do you *know* because you bought that knowledge with your life?

Learn also from other great storytellers. Read and listen to a diverse collection of artists. Recently, for example, I've been inspired by such different sources as a novel by Haitian Edwidge Danticat, *Krik? Krak!*, and the academy award-winning documentary about Maya Lin, *A Strong Clear Vision*. Danticat evokes the conflict, terror, and heartache, along with the wonder, of her native Haiti, telling the story of a people who resist the brutality of their rulers through the powers of imagination and community. Through her work, those of us who find the news from Haiti too painful to hear, can understand the place more deeply than we ever thought possible. Out of her wounds, and the many conflicts in her country, Danticat weaves her life and culture into a powerful force to move us to understanding and action. Similarly, you can use your own life and culture to move your organization closer to its goals.

Maya Lin, the architect who at 20 beat out hundreds of more established architects to win the contest to design the Vietnam Veterans' Memorial, recounted how wounded she felt in the conflict when people attacked and misunderstood her design. Yet she found that out of that wound came the inspiration to design more and even greater work. Her story inspires us all.

Tell stories. Use them in your work. Search for the stories of others in songs, novels, poems, and dance. Practice them first if you must—in front of your kids, a Toastmasters' group, or your book club—but weave them into the memos and reports you write, the meetings and trainings you lead.

When you do, you will have taken an awesome step into the future toward leadership in conflict management through the power of storytelling. You will help your organization move forward to become a conflict-skilled organization.

Using storytelling skillfully is an essential eagle skill. If you're a baby boomer facing retirement, you may feel challenged to use stories effectively with younger workers who have been raised with MTV quick cuts and instant messaging. Yet if you pick the right time and venue, my experience is that these employees are hungry for stories that reveal the meaning behind the message. It is a powerful way to leave a legacy in your organization.

Summary

In this book, we've discussed the five major personality types and the importance of productively resolving conflict. Discussing conflict and using outstanding leadership skills to help your team be heard can avoid dangerous situations where ideas stall, and help the most creative and innovative ideas—and people willing to champion them—float to the top. You can also use these ideas to teach others these skills. Here are a few final traits to remember for organizations that foster creative conflict:

- The organization's mission, values, and priorities are clearly expressed and modeled through leaders who walk the talk and reinforce the culture through storytelling.
- Risk taking is encouraged, people take intelligent risks, and mistakes are viewed as learning opportunities.
- Diversity is welcomed and valued, workers are educated in diverse thinking and conflict styles.
- Decision-making is shared, people are encouraged to participate in making decisions in their area of expertise.
- Group wisdom is respected by making use of diverse teams to solve problems; because of a belief in the creative potential of the group, conflict is valued.
- Members of the group understand that conflict is a part of life and are trained in creative conflict management with the ability to disagree about issues instead of personalities; they understand we all have a piece of the truth.

If you yourself exhibit these traits and you teach others to do the same, you will be well on your way to success in today's competitive global environment. My final wish for you is that you will have only *good fights!*

Afterword

If there's one final piece of advice I could offer my executive clients it is this: unplug. Turn away from your email, voice mail, and "crackberry." Turn off your cell phone and listen for a higher call. Turn away from your monitor and face the line of visitors outside your door.

Sit with them; mentor them; challenge and offer them your skills on how to embrace conflict and build consensus as a creative force. If they're around the globe or working at home, pick up the phone and reconnect with their human voice. Let them hear the emotions behind your words: the fear, the anger, the celebration for a big win. Let them know you care and that you're there to cheer for them.

Let your email pile up or give it to an assistant. Demand that people sit through meetings without beeping watches, pagers, laptops, or camera cell phones. Force them to remember how to talk to each other. Let important strategic decisions stew, simmer, and boil over if you must but better to let them, like fine wine, ferment until they're the perfect vintage.

Give yourself time to think. I know I'm not the only one who shudders at the possibility of cell service on airplanes, our last bastion of private thinking time. Give yourself time to gain the 30,000 foot view, even if you have to leave the ground to do so. Constantly staying plugged into the network makes us all as twitchy as an eleven year old with attention deficit disorder. Let it go. Just let it go.

Leave your monitor and go for a run or a swim; hug your child or pet your dog. Brain researchers can now confirm what we've all know instinctively: the brain releases powerful chemicals when we exercise, spend time in nature, or connect with others, leading to increased energy, creativity, and innovation. Take advantage of that surge and model healthy attitudes for those you lead. Make sure they do the same.

Think about how you might pass these strategies and skills on to your team. This book has given you a framework to do just that. In today's competitive global environment, nothing else will do. Nothing less will lead you out of the thicket of unproductive conflict into good fights.

I wish you safe passage and success on your journey.

Lynne Eisaguirre
August 31, 2006
Golden, Colorado

Master Bibliography

Amabile, Teresa. "How to Kill Creativity." *Harvard Business Review.* September 1998.

Argyris, Chris. *Reasoning, Learning, and Action: Individual and Organizational.* San Francisco: Jossey-Bass, 1982.

Bellamy, Clayton. "Honesty Not the School Board Policy." *The Denver Post.* February 7, 2002.

Berendt, Joachim-Ernst. *The World is Sound: Nada Brohmn: Music and the Landscape of Consciousness.* Destiny Books; New Edition, 1991 Edition, 1987.

Bridges, William. *Jobshift: How To Prosper in a Workplace without Jobs.* Perseus Books Group; New Edition, 1995.

Bridges, William. *Transitions: Making Sense of Life's Changes.* Reading, MA: Addison-Wesley Publishing Company, 1980.

Charan, Ram. "Why CEOs Fail." *Fortune.* June 21, 1999, p.69.

Cloven, Geoffrey. "The Ultimate Manager." *Fortune.* November 22, 1999.

Collins, Jim. *Built to Last: Successful Habits of Visionary Companies.* Collins; 1st edition, 2002.

Edmondson, Amy, Richard Bohmer, and Gary Pisano. "Speeding Up Team Learning." *Harvard Business Review.* October 2001, p. 125.

Eisenhardt, Kathleen M., Jean L. Kahwajy, and L. J. Bourageois III. "How Management Teams Can Have a Good Fight." *Harvard Business Review.* July/August 97, Volume 75, Issue 4. Quotes and modified portions in Chapter 21 reprinted by permission. Copyright 1997 by Harvard Business School Publishing Corporation. All rights reserved.

Encyclopedia Brittanica. Encyclopedia Britannica Corporation; 15th edition, 2003.

Garvin, David A., and Michael A. Roberto. "What You Don't Know About Making Decisions." *Harvard Business Review.* September 2001.

Gilbert, Roberta. *Extraordinary Relationships.* New York: John Wiley & Sons, Inc., 1992.

Goleman, Daniel. *Emotional Intelligence: Why It Can Matter More Than IQ.* Bantam, Reprint Edition, 1997.

Grove, Andy. *Only The Paranoid Survive: How to Exploit the Crisis Points That Challenge Every Company.* Currency; 1st Currency paperback Edition, 1999.

Halgesen, Sally. *The Web of Inclusion: A New Architecture for Building Great Organizations*. New York: Currency/Doubleday, 1995.

Hallowell, Edward M. *Connect*. New York: Pantheon, 1999.

Hamel, Gary. *Leading the Revolution*. Boston: Harvard Business School Press, 2000.

Hauck, L. Christian, Rita M. Hauck, and Justin W. Schulz. "Sunflower Electric." *National World Electric Cooperative Association Journal of Management*. Summer 2001.

Hendricks, Gay. *A Year of Living Consciously*. San Francisco: Harper, 1990.

Hirshberg, Jerry. *The Creative Priority: Putting Innovation to Work in Your Business*. New York: HarperBusiness, 1999.

Hudson Institute. *Workforce 2020: Work and Workers for the 21ˢᵗ Century*. Indianapolis: Hudson Institute, 1997.

Jackson, Susan E. *Team Composition in Organizational Settings: Issues in Managing an Increasingly Diverse Work Force in Group Process and Productivity*. Beverly Hills: Safe, 1992.

Janis, Irving. *Groupthink: Psychological Studies of Policy Decisions and Fiascoes*. Boston: Houghton Mifflin, 1982.

Jensen, Rolf. *The Dream Society: How the Coming Shift from Information to Imagination Can Help Your Business*. McGraw-Hill, 1999.

Judge, Paul C. *Provocation 101*. Fast Company. January 2002, p. 110-111.

Judge, William Q., Gerald E. Fryxell, and Robert S. Dooley. "The New Task of R&D Management." *California Management Review*. 1997, Volume 39, Issue 3.

Kaner, Sam. *Facilitator's Guide to Participatory Decision-Making*. Gabriola Island, BC: New Society Publishing, 1996. Adapted with permission.

Kaye, Kenneth. *Workplace Wars and How to End Them: Turning Personal Conflicts into Productive Teamwork*. New York: AMACOM, 1994.

Landau, Sy, Barbara Landau, and Daryl Landau. *From Conflict to Creativity: How Resolving Workplace Disagreements Can Inspire Innovation and Productivity*. San Francisco: Jossey-Bass, 2001.

Leonard, Dorothy, and Walter Swap. *When Sparks Fly: Igniting Creativity in Groups*. Boston: Harvard Business School Press, 1999.

Michaels, Ed, Helen Handfiled-Jones, and Beth Axelrod. *The War for Talent*. Boston: Harvard Business School Press, 2001.

Miller, Gordon. *The Career Coach: Winning Strategies for Getting Ahead in Today's Job Market*. Currency; 1ˢᵗ edition. 2001.

Moore, C. *The Mediation Process: Practical Strategies for Resolving Conflict,* Second Edition. San Francisco: Jossey-Bass, 1996.

Moorhead, Gregory, Richard Ference, and Chris Neck. "Group Decision Fiascoes Continue." *Human Relations.* Volume 44, Number 1991.

Osborn, A. F. *Applied Imagination: Principles and Procedures of Creative Problem Solving.* New York: Scribner, 1963.

Packard, David. *The HP Way: How Bill Hewlett and I Built Our Company.* HarperBusiness, 1996.

Pascale, Richard Tanner. *Managing on the Edge: How the Smartest Companies Use Conflict to Stay Ahead.* New York: Simon & Schuster, 1990.

Peters, Tom. "Prometheus Barely Unbound."

Academy of Management Executives. 1990, Volume 4, Number 4.

Peters, Tomas, and Robert H. Waterman. *In Search of Excellence: Lessons from America's Best-Run Companies.* New York: Warner Books, 1982.

Remen, Naomi, M.D. *Kitchen Table Wisdom: Stories That Heal.* New York: Riverhead Books, 1996.

Rosenfeld, Jill. *She Stands on Common Ground.* Fast Company, January/February 2000.

Schlesinger, Jr., Arthur. *Robert Kennedy & His Times.* Houghton Mifflin, 1978.

"Smart Companies, Dumb Decisions." *Fast Company.* Issue 11, October 1997.

Sutton, Robert. "Weird Ideas That Work: 11[1/2] Practices for Promoting, Managing and Sustaining Innovation." *Harvard Business Review.* September 2001: p. 96–103.

Sternberg, Robert. *Successful Intelligence.* New York: Simon & Schuster, 1996.

Tannen, Deborah. *The Argument Culture: Stopping America's War of Words.* New York: Ballentine, 1999.

Tannen, Deborah. *You Just Don't Understand: Women and Men in Conversation.* New York: William Morrow, 1990.

Ury, William. *Getting To Peace.* Viking Adult, 1999.

Wheatley, Margaret. *Leadership and the New Science: Learning About Organizations from an Orderly Universe.* San Francisco: Berrett-Coehler Publishing, 1992.

Index

the COLOSSEUM

A day in the Flavian Amphitheatre

Figures speak for themselves: the major axis of its elliptical plan is 188 m long, the minor axis 156 m, and the walls in the outer ring rise to almost 52 m above ground; more than 100,000 cubic metres of travertine were used to build it (a special road, 6 m wide, had to be built in order to get such a large amount of travertine from the quarries in Tivoli to the building site) and even the metal cramps that held the blocks together must have weighed more than 300 tons.

Begun by Vespasian shortly after 70 A.D., the **Colosseum** – known in its day as the **Flavian Amphitheatre** – built where Nero had placed an artificial lake in the gardens of his *Domus Aurea*, was inaugurated by Titus in the year 80 A.D.

The Colosseum: detail of the second storey arcades.

The eighty arcades on the ground-floor were numbered (the number corresponding to that on the spectator's *tessera* or admission card) and led into 160 outlets (**vomitoria**) that took him to his seat on the steps of the cavea.

The interior of the Colosseum consisted of the **arena**, a wooden floor sustaining a bed of sand and of the stands or **cavea**, subdivided into three superposed tier sectors crowned on high by a "loggia" that housed a fourth order of steps, made of wood and providing standing room.

Reconstructed section of the Colosseum:

- Vth sector/loggia/*Maenianum Summum* (standing places for the plebians);
- IVth sector/ *Maenianum Secundum Summum*;
- IIIrd sector/ *Maenianum Secundum Imum*;
- IInd sector/ *Maenianum Primum* (reserved for the Equites or knights);
- Ist sector/*Podium* (reserved for the senators).

Each sector of steps was rigorously reserved for a particular class of citizens, the places on top being assigned to the least important, though all enjoyed free entry. Counting also the standing spectators, the amphitheatre could accomodate about 70,000 people, who came there to watch gladiatorial combats and wild beast hunts. There were also other shows, either as curtain raisers or as fill-in during intervals.

An enormous awning (**velarium**) protected the spectators from the heat of the sun; it was manoeuvered by a special detachment of sailors sent up from the naval base at Misenum, on the Gulf of Naples.

The interior of the Colosseum, reconstruction of the *cavea* and of the arena.

During shows the arena would be surrounded by a metal mesh carried on poles and spiked with elephant tusks; the top of the mesh was furbished with ivory rollers, so that animals could not get a foothold there and escape from the arena. Just in case, the niches in the podium of the bottom tier of steps were always full of archers.

Funerary relief depicting the parade (*pompa*) that took place before the gladiator games (Naples, National Museum).

A complex system of passages and underground rooms extended below the arena, used for services and to store the stage equipment for the shows: the scenery was often very elaborate, especially for the hunts, when the stage managers did not fight shy of creating hills, woods, and even small lakes.

For men and animals there were proper "elevators", operated by counterweights.

The animals were first driven along the corridors by "beaters" and made to enter cages arranged at the bottom of special shafts; each cage had a mechanism of its own capable of raising it to a higher level, where the cage would open onto a elevated wooden ramp, with a trap door at its upper end. When this door opened, the animal stepped out into the arena ready for the show.

We are told that on one occasion this system was used to bring a hundred lions into the arena at the same time: their combined roar was so loud that the noisy crowd was frightened into instant silence.

As to the gladiators, they could reach the arena direct from their main "barracks" (**Ludus Magnus**), which was situated by the side of the Colosseum, using a tunnel.

Spectacles in the amphitheater were not all that frequent nor did they take place at such regular intervals as, say, the games in a football league championship. But when they did take place they could go on for as long as three or four days, and sometimes much longer.

The spectacle which took place for the inauguration of the Flavian Amphitheatre lasted for 100 days and when Trajan celebrated his triumph over the Dacians in

The rigging to hoist the *velarium*.

107 A.D. the show went on for a whole 120 days, utlizing 10,000 gladiators and 11,000 wild beasts.

The programme of the event was announced and publicized by means of notices posted on walls, so that the right degree of anticipation would be created among the citizens.

The Colosseum: arcades of the outer ambulatory corridor.

The day got underway with a *pompa* (procession): the *editor* (the magistrate sponsoring the games – in the City of Rome often the emperor himself) paraded to the tune of trumpets, horns and organs, accompanied by *venatores* (hunters), prisoners who had been sentenced to death, gladiators, *primae rudes* and *secundae rudes* (first and second category umpires) and various other officials. The music continued throughout the whole spectacle: in the morning there were the *venationes* (hunts, or fights between gladiators and wild beasts), at lunch time the execution of those who had been condemned to death (which thus became a kind of spectacle in itself, albeit a disturbing one for us) and then in the afternoon the proper fighting took place.

Let us take a better look at these phases. For the *venationes*, not only elephants, but also tigers, hyenas, ostriches, rhinoceroses, hippopotamuses and crocodiles were employed with increasing frequency and at considerable expense: a lion could cost anything between 125,000 and 150,000 *sestertii*, a leopard between 75,000 and 100,000 and a bear between 20,000 and 25,000 (let us bear in mind that the average daily expenditure of a three-person household was about 6 *sestertii*). These high prices were the result of the many different operations involved, including the capture and transportation of the animals and then their housing and management in the run-up to the spectacle.

At lunchtime the execution of the condemned took place. Indeed, the death sentences handed down by Roman courts could be *ad bestias*, being mauled to death by wild beasts, or *ad gladium* ("by the sword"), in mortal combat with professional gladiators. This spectacle already bloodthirsty enough in its own right, was dressed up as a stage performance which played out some historical or mythical episode. After lunch, it was the turn of the gladiator fights. There were several "heats" consisting of duels which took place simultaneously. Sometimes the battles between the Romans and the Gauls were recreated and played out, employing several hundred combatants, and sometimes even famous sea battles, for which the arena was specially flooded.

These nautical games were stopped probably under Domitian because several large storage rooms were built beneath the arena which then could no longer contain the water as before.

It was easy to identify the *armaturae*, or different types of gladiator, from their equipment and fighting techniques: the *Thracian* with his gryphon-shaped crest and short sword with a curved blade (*sica*); the *Myrmillo* with his big, semi-cylindrical shield; the *Retiarius*, who would seek to snare his opponent in a net, and also carried a knife and trident; the *Secutor*, the adversary of the Retiarius, who wore a smooth, crestless helmet so that the latter couldn't get a hold; and so on. It is not true that a gladiator lived in constant risk of death. No combatant took part in the games more than two or three times a year, and sometimes he might be spared (*missus*) even when he had lost. Indeed, when one of the two combatants gave in it was up to the magistrate who had sponsored the games – though he might be swayed by the crowd – to decide whether or not his throat should be cut (*iugulatus*), and he could also opt to save him.

THE GLADIATORS

SCISSOR   MURMILLO   SECUTOR   RETIARIUS   THRAEX

Obviously, the risks remained high.

The gladiator's tension would build up over the course of the day, not just at the moment of the fight. Before entering the arena, the gladiator awaited his turn in the underground parts of the amphitheater.

We have already mentioned the extensive facilities – corridors, rooms and storage areas for ladders and pulleys. Now they are open to the sky (indeed, access has recently been extended to visitors), but in ancient times they were covered by floorboards strewn with the bed of sand upon which the games took place. Imagine the gladiators waiting down there. The atmosphere must have been almost unbearable: hot and stuffy, with the sand trickling down between the gaps in the floorboards.

Gladiator's helmet found in Pompeii (Naples, National Museum).

the Square of
the COLOSSEUM

Overshadowed by the immense mass of the amphitheatre, the great square of the Colosseum assumed its final monumental appearance with the building of the **Temple of Venus and Rome** and this layout has been substantially preserved right down to our own day. Willed and possibly also designed by Hadrian, this temple, dedicated to the divine ancestress of the Julian family and to the city, mistress of the world, was inaugurated in A.D. 135 and then reconstructed by Maxentius round about 310, after it had been destroyed by fire. It had two apses, standing back to back at the centre of a broad terrace on the Velian hill (which at that time stretched beyond today's Via dei Fori Imperiali, from the Palatine hill towards the Esquiline) and was surrounded on at least two sides by porticoes.

The remains of the "vestibule" of Nero's *Domus Aurea* were torn down to make room for this temple and even the **Colossus of Nero** had to be shifted. Twelve pairs of elephants were used to move it.

At the entrance of the Via Sacra, where it leaves the Square of the Colosseum to run down into the Forum, there was a fountain built in the middle of the 1st century A.D., which had a shape rather like one of the *metae* or turning points in the Circus that the chariots had to race around: it therefore came to be known as **Meta Sudans**, the Turn of Sweat.

The last monument added to adorn this great square was the **Arch of Costantine**. As its inscription records, it was erected in A.D. 312 by the Senate and People of Rome in honour of the Emperor who had liberated the city and the state from the "tyrant" Maxentius by his victory in the battle of the Milvan Bridge.

The arch was richly decorated with sculpture taken from earlier monuments erected by Trajan, Hadrian and Marcus Aurelius in the second century, and only the small reliefs which run round the whole monument actually depict events in which Constantine himself was involved.

Square of the Colosseum: the *Meta Sudans* in the middle, the Colossus of Nero on the right, the Temple of Venus and Rome in the background.

The exterior of the Colosseum, reconstruction.

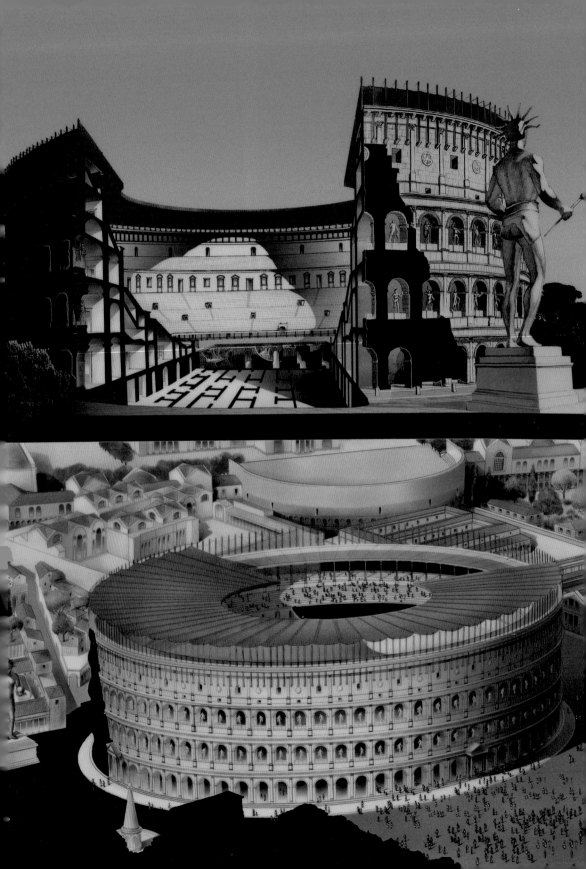

Rome of the Caesars
IMPERIAL Fora
the Forum of CAESAR

In the twenty years after the death of Sulla (78 A.D.), and as soon as the civil war bloodbath was over, the population of the city of Rome increased significantly owing to the arrival of people from new provinces, veterans and small landowners ruined by the conflict and looking for a way to survive in the city. The structures of the Roman Forum, above all, the ones for the administration of justice, were no longer adequate; that was one of the effects of such population increase. For this reason, Julius Caesar (102-44 B.C.) decided to construct a large complex, which he opened in 46 B.C.; officially, it was an extension of the old Forum, but in practice, it was a stage for the history of his family, the gens Julia, and indirectly, for himself; this self-representation originated from the splendour of the courts of Grecian-Hellenic sovereigns becoming part of Roman dominion just a few decades earlier. Caesar expropriated the area for building his Forum by paying with his own money a very high sum to private citizens, ranging from sixty to one hundred million sesterces according to ancient authors.

Basalt bust of Gaius Julius Caesar (Berlin, Staatmuseum).

The Forum of Caesar, today.

Reconstruction of the Forum of Caesar (A. Delfino/V. Di Cola/Inklink).

Forum of Caesar: the remaining columns of the Venus Genitrix temple (right) and those of the piazza's western portico (left) (Photo E. Bianchi).

The square was paved with travertine, with two-floor porticoes on three sides, and with double rows of Corinthian columns of white marble from Luni (Carrara, today) on the ground floor. The **Temple of Venus Genetrix** was located at the centre of its northern side; this Goddess was regarded as the mythical progenitor of the gens Julia, for Aeneas was born from her love for Anchises. In turn, Aeneas generated Iulus (alias Ascanius), who was the origin of the family's name. Today, of the Temple reconstructed by Trajan in 113 A.D., three of the very tall lateral Corinthian columns are left; they were lifted up again in 1933; the Forum of Caesar is the only fully visible one of the five existing, thanks to the excavations carried out by the City of Rome in 1932-1933, and from 1998 to 2008.

the Forum of AUGUSTUS

Two years after the murder of Caesar, occurred at the Ides of March (on March 15th, today) in 44 B.C., the troops of the conspirators headed by Cassius and Brutus, and the troops headed by the young Gaius Octavius, foster son of Caesar, clashed in Philippi (42 B.C.) in a decisive battle.

On that occasion, the future first Emperor Octavius Augustus (23 B.C.-14 A.D.) made a vow to erect in case of victory a Temple dedicated to Mars Ultor, that is, Avenger of Caesar's assassination.

Forum of Augustus: the Temple of Mars Ultor.

Reconstruction of the Forum of Augustus
and of the Temple of Mars Ultor
(R. Meneghini/Inklink).

The God was favourable to Augustus. Once he had won and become Emperor, he kept his vow and bought the private properties in the area between the Forum of Caesar and Suburra, and those properties were demolished to make room for building the new Forum, which was inaugurated in 2 B.C. It was a further extension of the areas for the administration of justice in the Roman Forum and in the Forum of Caesar, which were not enough to grant the proper working of the imposing judicial machine of the Empire.

The Forum of Augustus was thus a huge courthouse; the big hemicycles with their column porticoes along the major sides of the square hosted tribunals presided over by the praetors resolving controversies between Roman citizens (*Praetor Urbanus*), or between them and foreigners (*Praetor Peregrinus*). Portrait statues of famous men (*summi viri*) with descriptions of their deeds were located in the niches and between portico columns. It was a real gallery of the glories of Roman history. The **Temple of Mars Ultor** was in the eastern side. It was a huge temple with eight columns of white marble from Luni in its facade, 15 metres tall, surmounted by a pediment decorated with a thick group of painted statues, at the centre of which the statues of Mars and Venus stood out, the mythic progenitors of the Roman stock and the gens Julia.

Today, after the excavations in 1932 and 2004-2007 by the City of Rome, about one half of the whole complex – marked by the high tufa block wall separating it from Suburra, and by the three columns of the temple left – is visible, while the other half is still buried under Via Alessandrina and Via dei Fori Imperiali.

To the left reconstruction of the Temple of Peace with the *Forma Urbis* marble slabs; to the right Via dei Fori Imperiali between the Basilica of Maxentius and the Church of Saints Cosmas and Damian, where stood the Temple of Peace.

the Forum or TEMPLE of PEACE

In 70 A.D., after the bloody civil war through which the Flavian dynasty took power, and at the end of the tragic repression of the Judaic revolt, Emperor Vespasian (69-79 A.D.) started building the new monumental complex dedicated to Peace, which was inaugurated in 75 A.D. It was not a forum in the strict sense of the word, since no activities connected to justice administration or trade took place in there; for the ancient, it was a *templum* (temple), that is, just a sacred place to celebrate Empire pacification. The square looked like a big garden, paved with beaten earth most of all, with raised water channels (*euripi*) bordered by rose bushes with several statues of famous Grecian sculptors placed on the high plinths located in the porticoes, too. The centre of the southern side of the **Templum Pacis** hosted the chamber of worship of Peace, whose wonderful marble floor has been brought to light recently. The side rooms hosted a famous library (**Bibliotheca Pacis**) and offices of the Urban Prefecture. The old brick wall with the holes of the cramps fixing the covering plates, still up on the left of the entrance to the Basilica of Saints Cosmas and Damian, proves that the big marble map of Rome (**forma Urbis**) placed under Septimius Severus (193-211 A.D.) was hanging there, and was located inside an office in charge of the City cadastre. The excavations of the City of Rome brought back to light a large portion of the complex corresponding to the Western sector of the square with the ruins of the portico opening on that side from 1998 to 2001.

Reconstruction of the *Forma Urbis* hall (R. Meneghini/Inklink).
Temple of Peace: the wall where in antiquity the marble plan of Rome (the *Forma Urbis*) was displayed; on the right the entrance to the church of Saints Cosmas and Damian can be seen (Photo R. Meneghini).

When Emperor Domitian (81-96 A.D.) started ruling, the redevelopment area within
the three Fora of Caesar, Augustus and
Peace was still full of the ruins of the residential quarter before the Imperial Fora
(*Argiletum*), not used from the architectonic

the Forum of
NERVA

point of view. Domi-
tian himself started
works on it to make
the Forum's fourth
square acting as
connection for the
others, as well as
link of the Roman
Forum with the pop-
ulous Suburra.
Owing to lack of
space, the tradition-
al porticos could not
be erected along
the borders of the
square; therefore,
they just placed 44

Reconstruction of the Forum of Nerva and
of the Temple of Minerva (R. Meneghini/Inklink).

tall columns against the perimeter walls.
The fluted columns jutted out of the wall
together with the entablature. Two of those
columns escaping medieval demolition
have been standing until now; since they
are actually ruins, the people call them the
"**Colonnacce**" (bad columns).
On the attic, in the rooms in between each
pair of columns, there was a marble panel
with the personification of a province or a
people subjected to the Romans (just one is
left, traditionally understood as the image
of Minerva); and this Forum was a real gallery of the triumphs and conquests of the
Empire. On the east side of the square, nar-

row and long, Domitian placed a **temple
dedicated to Minerva**, his tutelary deity,
which perfectly survived actually until 1606,
when it was demolished by Pope Paul V in
order to get building material. Today, only
the core of its concrete basement is left.
The name of the Forum originates from
Emperor Nerva (96-98 A.D.), successor of
Domitian, who inaugurated it.
Today, only the east and west sectors of it
can be seen, brought back to light after two
excavation operations by the City of Rome
in 1940-1941 and 1995-1996; on the other
hand, the central portion is still buried under Via dei Fori Imperiali.

Forum of Nerva: (right) the so-called "Colonnacce"
and (left) the Torre dei Conti (Photo R. Meneghini).

1 Basilica Ulpia
2 Forum of Trajan
3 Trajan's Market
4 Forum of Caesar
5 Forum of Augustus
6 Forum of Nerva
7 Forum or
Temple of Peace

Reconstruction of the Imperial Fora in the 2nd century B.C.

Caesar's Forum and the Temple of Venus Genetrix.

Trajan's column.

the Forum of
TRAJAN

At the time of Emperor Trajan (98-117 A.D.), the Roman Empire reached the height of success and territorial extension, with the effect of a further remarkable increase in the administration and judicial activities in the Capital: again, it was necessary to extend the structures meant for justice administration and relations with the provinces.

The Emperor used the huge war chest originating from the wars against the Dacians (101-102/105-106 A.D.), a people settled in the area currently occupied by Romania, to carry out the Forum with his name on a flat land obtained by Domitian by pulling down a hillside of the Quirinal, north of the Forum of Augustus. The new complex, inaugurated in 112 A.D. was characterised by innovative architecture: on one of the short sides of the Forum, they actually did not build a temple in accordance with the old Italic custom, but a civil building, the Basilica Ulpia (after *Marcus Ulpius Traianus*) meant to conduct trials. On the opposite side, a monumental architectonic elevation with coloured marble columns framed the bronze equestrian statue of Trajan (the *Equus Traiani*), erected almost at the centre of the square, and from 10 to 15 metres tall. Two huge hemicycles opened at the side porticoes; they hosted more tribunals as well as a remarkable gallery of statues and portraits of famous men and of members of the imperial dynasty, the ideal continuation of the one existing in the nearby Forum of Augustus.

Frieze with Victories from the main nave of the Basilica Ulpia.

14

Trajan's Forum: the unearthing of one of the white marble statues of Dacian prisoners during the 1998 excavations by Rome's Municipality's Cultural heritage Superintendence (Photo R. Meneghini).

On the other hand, the attic surmounting the portico colonnade was decorated with the famous marble statues of Dacian captive warriors.

The ruins of the eastern hemicycle, the only one brought back to light until now together with its portico, in 1932, can still be seen at the foot of the monumental semi-circular elevation of the Trajan's Market. The **Basilica Ulpia** was a grandiose courthouse with five naves separated by rows of grey granite columns, with two inner floors superimposed, and with the height of almost 30 metres; it prevented the Storied Column from being seen from the Forum square. A couple of opposing buildings traditionally identified with two libraries leaned against the Basilica; in between them, in a narrow yard, the **Historiated Column** stood; it was also called the **Centenary column** because it was 100 Roman feet tall (about 30 metres), with its marble shaft decorated with a spiral frieze 200 metres long, and with bas-reliefs representing the main episodes of the two Dacian wars. The complex was finished by Emperor Hadrian (117-138 A.D.) with the construction of a temple dedicated to Trajan and his wife Pompeia Plotina, both of them deified, traditionally placed north of the Column, in the subsoil of the palace now hosting the Province of Rome.

The Basilica Ulpia in Trajan's Forum.

Trajan's Market: the "via Biberatica" and the Central Body.

TRAJAN'S
Market

TRAJAN'S MARKET:
Romans, great builders!

At the beginning of Via dei Fori Imperiali, after Trajan's Column, our attention is captured by a scenic brick backdrop with a characteristic semi-circular shape, dominated by a polygonal-shaped building and by the highest medieval tower in the city, namely Torre delle Milizie. It is the monumental complex known with the modern name of "**Trajan's Market**", which stretches out all the way to Largo Magnanapoli towards via Nazionale.

Bust of emperor Trajan (Ankara, Archaeological Museum).

View of the Trajan markets' area.

Commissioned by Trajan at the beginning of the 2nd century A.D. and attributed to Apollodorus of Damascus (an architect of Syrian origins), the complex stands like a hinge between the ancient and popular *Subura* quarter (today known as rione Monti) and the valley of the Fora. On one side it served as a support and a lining for the outer slopes of the Quirinal Hill, which were excavated to make room for **Trajan's Forum**; while on the other it served to

The skylight inside the Great Hall.
At the upper level: Vault with frescoes of the 16th century.

Trajan's Market, the Great Hemicycle.

overcome a difference of altitude equal to 40 metres with its bold engineering solution. It was made using the ductile Roman concrete technique and all types of vaulted roofing systems.

The "Market" is organized over six levels distributed through two sectors: the bottom one includes the **Great Hemicycle with two frontal halls with semicircular domes** and a **Small Hemicycle**; the highest one with the **Central Body** and the **Great Hall**. Communication took place horizontally through three flagstone but pedestrian roads, wedged between the tall buildings; while a complicated system of internal stairs and an outdoor urban stairway to the side of the Great Hemicycle served for vertical communication.

Axonometric vertical section of Trajan's Markets (Inklink).

The blocks are independent ones with controlled accesses: they most probably served as a "multipurpose centre" with activities mainly involving the administrative aspect for the administration and functioning of Trajan's Forum, which was headed by a public official (*procurator Fori Traiani*) according to an inscription discovered during recent excavations.

Its topographic position and the availability of space (that is remarkable for its quantity and quality) have fostered the constant reemployment of the "Market" with effects not only involving "wear" and tampering to the structures, but also its "preservation" as its testifying to the transformations the city has been subjected to over nearly two-thousand years of history. From being the premises of prestigious Roman families to *Castellum Miliciae*, with the multi-stage construction of the massive **Torre delle Milizie** (Pope Boniface VIII had a fundamental role around the year 1300), to its complete transformation into a **convent** of the Dominican Order of **St. Catherine of Siena** (last decades of the 16th century), all the way to its reoccupation (after Rome was appointed capital) with a **military barracks** (after 1870), and to its rediscovery at the beginning of the 20th century (1926-1934) when the structures (considered "the first shopping centre of Ancient Rome") were denominated "Tra-jan's Market". Even we as contemporaries have established a new use for the complex as premises of the **Museum of the Imperial Fora**. Therefore in addition to the many signs left behind by the most ancient transformations, today there are those introduced for its safeguarding and enhancement: such as the protection of the Great Hall from pollutants thanks to Plexiglas panels; safeguarding the buildings using anti-seismic measures; positioning a hydraulic elevator and a platform lift serving the Great Hall, the Central Body and via Biberatica, connected through a system of ramps and walkways.

The complicated tour itinerary is complemented by panels and by the "**Window over History**" video-panel that offers an excellent illustration of the Market's liveliness and constant relationship with the city.

Our rapid itinerary begins at the entrance in via Quattro Novembre and then on to the **Great Hall** with a large central rectangular space (32 m x 8 m) today lacking its probable plastering, which opens up towards rectangular rooms located on three levels. The ceiling of the hall, made up of six large cross-vaults in Roman concrete (approximately 2,800 tons), relieves its mass onto the dividing walls off to the side and on brick piers with travertine lintels.

Trajan's Market, the Great Hall.

Two of the entrances were controlled, namely the main entrance on via Biberatica and the one corresponding to the present via Quattro Novembre; a third entrance, towards the Militia Garden, was turned into a window subsequent to modifications made to what was once a stairway belonging to the S. Caterina da Siena convent.

Originally the Great Hall and the Central Body were independent and non-communicating buildings; the latter rises narrow and tall between via Biberatica and the Militia Garden; the first floor contains an apsed room that must have once been the office of the *procurator Fori Traiani*.

The principal facade located on via Biberatica has witnessed the transformations of the building as the *opus latericium* was accosted and superimposed by brickwork obtained from debris, whereas the southern part has square-shaped bricks of tuff that outline a merlon (interventions during medieval times). The basalt road called "**via della Torre**" is above the Central Body and the Great Hall, which today ends in a beautiful panoramic terrace over the Imperial Fora (called "**Belvedere**").

The promenade along "**via Biberatica**" (perhaps from the Late Latin *bibere* = drink), especially along the straight northern stretch, once again recalls an urban road of an ancient city such as Ostia or Pompeii: the rooms to the sides still preserve their original thresholds, lintels and jambs in travertine. The central stretch offers a panorama over the city that does not correspond to the situation during the Roman Age, when the rooms belonging to the third level of the Great Hemicycle were preserved in an elevated position. Further on, a **large arch** stands above the road; it was later added as a buttress to the southern part of the Central Body.

The lower sector of the **Great Hemicycle with two large halls with semicircular domes**, because of its decorative characteristics and the articulation of the spaces, gravitates towards the Forum and was most probably used for cultural functions. The facade with its alternating triangular, semi-circular and broken tympanums above the first floor windows would become a model for Renaissance buildings.

Night view of the Torre delle Milizie from the south.

The big arch overlooking the via Biberatica in Trajan's markets.

↑ Axonometric section of the Great Hemicycle with the reconstruction of the rooms opening onto Via Biberatica.

👁 Proposed reconstruction of the Via Biberatica: on the left the Great Hall building.

↓

The floors on the ground level rooms are black and white mosaics with geometrical designs, the walls are all frescoed and date back to a general restoration carried out at the beginning of the 3rd century A.D.; on the floor above, 11 radial rooms face onto a ring-shaped corridor with barrel vault; some of the original flooring is still preserved, paved in small bricks arranged in a herring-bone pattern; on the third level stands a terrace of service, where some radial rooms were turned towards via Biberatica. The two **Halls with semicircular domes**, rectilinear facade and a semi-domed ceiling presented wall coverings and marble floorings within.

The **Small Hemicycle** sector, at the various levels, represented a type of hinge and communication trench between the various parts of the complex and its development northwards.

The Imperial Fora Museum: the tale of architecture!

Narrating **Roman architecture**, of a monumental nature, no longer existing, that of its greatest achievements, the Imperial Fora, where grandiose architectural orders, spaces with vertical development even of an exasperated nature, host refined sculptural cycles that were authentic manifestoes of the power and ideologies of imperial clients. This is the challenge of the Imperial Fora Museum with its 3D physical reconstructions that join together splendid fragments in casts and integrations to these in order to of-

Recomposition of the attic storey of the portico of Augustus's Forum with the plaster casting of a Caryatid (Rome, Imperial Fora Museum, Great Hall).

Gilded bronze foot from a flying Victory's statue found in the Forum of Augustus (Rome, Imperial Fora Museum).

fer the public a unified vision in a 1:1 scale of complex architectural and sculptural parts. An innovative system of integrated communication has been studied for the first time, using video-panels, traditional bilingual panels and watercolour views that "lead" visitors through the space and time of the materials on display.

The rooms serving as an introduction to the entire Fora complex present some of the most significant findings from the five Fora, then two sectors dedicated to the Forum of Caesar and the Forum of Augustus have been developed.

The choice of exhibits leads visitors amidst very rare and precious material, such as the **guilded bronze foot** that belonged to a winged Victory in flight, probable acroteria (statue on the peak of a roof) from the Temple of Mars Ultor in the Forum of Augustus; in addition to great architectural reconstructions such as the portion of the **attic of the lateral porticos of the Forum** itself, a prototype of the Museum, with the original fragments completed by stone integrations and the cast of a delicate female figure, a Caryatid alongside the tormented head of a barbarian.

the ROMAN
Forum

Aerial view of the Roman Forum.

The heart of the city

For centuries, the narrow valley between the Palatine and the Capitoline Hill, the result of the multi-millenary erosion of a small tributary of the Tiber, the *Velabrum*, has been part of a very old communication route between the river port of call in the Tiber Island and the original layout of Via Salaria. The area was then used as necropolis by the small communities living on the two hills, starting from the 10th century B.C.

At the beginning of the 20th century, a few tombs of this cemetery were excavated at the Temple of Antoninus and Faustina, while others, slightly older (11th-10th century B.C.) but belonging to the same human groups, were found at the Forum of Caesar during 1998-2008 excavations. During the first half of the 8th century B.C., the coexistence of those and other groups – clearly more and more numerous – led to the shaping of the first urban centre (city foundation traditional date: 21 April 753 B.C.).

The first beaten earth paving of the one which has become the main square of the built-up area crossed by the Cloaca Maxima dates back to 600 B.C., approximately; the Cloaca Maxima was one of the most important urban works carried out by King Tarquinius Priscus a few years earlier. This sewage channel still flowing in the subsoil of the Forum collected the old *Velabrum* stream and carried the waste of whole quarters to the Tiber. Since then, the most ancient and sacred buildings or temples of the city started being built, or re-built, around the square. The northern corner was actually dedicated to the **Comitium**, with political and judiciary functions; sporadic ruins were found of it.

During 1899 excavations, a small area paved with black marble (*Niger Lapis*) was actually brought to light; it was mentioned by an ancient writer (Festus), who described it as part of the Comitium, and related it to the death of Romulus. They are the still visible traces of a small sanctuary, probably erected at the point where Romulus was killed; from excavation materials, it may be said that its foundation dates back to the 6th century B.C. At the end of the same century, at the eastern end of the Forum, the **Regia** was reconstructed.

The Roman Forum, the *Lapis Niger*.

The Temple of Vesta, the Arch of Augustus and the Temple of Castor and Pollux; in the background the Palatine: past & present.

Traditionally identified with the dwelling of King Numa Pompilius, its ruins are still visible. During the early years of the Republican period, starting from 509 B.C., the **Temple of Castor and Pollux** and the **Temple of Saturn** were erected along the southern side of the square. The first building was connected to the victory of republic over monarchy, because Castor and Pollux, the mythic twins born from the love of Jupiter and Leda, miraculously appeared in the Forum in 496 B.C., while the Battle of Lake Regillus was going on against the Tarquins and the Latins, their allies, announcing the victory of the Romans, following a legend handed down by some ancient historians (Livy, Dionisyus of Halicarnassus, Ovid and Plutarch). On that occasion, dictator Postumius devoted a temple to the divine twins, which was completed and inaugurated by his son in 484. In the following centuries, the building was reconstructed several times, until rebuilding by Tiberius in 6 A.D., under the kingdom of Augustus, at the time when the three famous surviving columns were elected. On the other hand, perhaps the **Temple of Saturn** was devoted by Tarquinius Superbus, but it was finished and dedicated by one of the consuls in the very early years of the Republic, from 501 to 497 B.C. The *Aerarium*, the public treasury, was preserved in the Temple together with state archives and the regalia. Today, the surviving portions of the buildings are: part of the tall podium, dating back to the 42 B.C. rebuilding by Munatius Plancus, and the front colonnade reconstructed in the second half of the 4th century A.D. after arson.

Portrait statue of Emperor Augustus found at Prima Porta, to the north of Rome (Vatican Museum).

Roman Forum, the Basilica Julia.

The large pedestal visible under the right corner of the **Tabularium** – the monumental state archives with arch facade build in 78 B.C., the background for this side of the Forum – is the surviving portion of the **Temple of Concord**, traditionally assigned to Furius Camillus, who erected it to celebrate the end of the fight between Patrician and Plebeian classes in 367 B.C. From the 2nd to the 1st century B.C., on the north and south sides of the square, two big basilicas were built, Emilia and Julia, where justice was administered. The **Basilica Emilia** was erected in 179 B.C.; now it is the outcome of several rebuilding operations by members of the gens with the same name, from 80 to 14 B.C., until the one of Tiberius in 22 A.D. On the other hand, the **Basilica Julia** was started by Caesar in 54 B.C. and was named after his family. On the eastern side of the Forum, Augustus erected the **Temple of Caesar** in 29 B.C., in the memory of Caesar, deified after his murder; today, only the plinth with the big frontal semicircular niche is left of the building. Augustus completed also the Caesar construction of the

Coin of Emperor Tiberius showing the Temple of Concord in the Roman Forum.

Rostra, the ancient tribunal of the speakers decorated with the metal rams (*rostra*) of the ships captured in the Battle of Antium in 338 B.C., during the Latin War.

Basilica Emilia, entrance arch.

Roman Forum, reconstruction of the Temple of Caesar.

Roman Forum, the Temple of Antoninus and Faustina.

At the foot of the Capital Hill, beside the Temple of the Concord, three columns are left, with a portion of the entablature of the **Temple of Vespasian and Titus** deified, completed by Emperor Domitian.

In the 2nd century A.D., other buildings were included in the forum's complex, including the facade with six columns, still standing, of the **Temple of Antoninus and Faustina**, initially dedicated to the only Empress deified, in 141 A.D., and then to Antoninus Pius (138-161) himself, after his death. The big **Triumphal Arch** with three fornices, still perfectly preserved, closes the western side of the square; it was erected in honour of Septimius Severus and his son Caracalla (211-217 A.D.) in 203 A.D., following the victory in the war against the Parthians, the ancient people in the Iranian plateau, arch enemies of the Roman Empire.

Roman Forum, the Temple of Vesta.

Septimius Severus's wife, Empress Julia Domna provided also for rebuilding the ancient **Temple of Vesta**, a small circular sacellum in which the oldest cult objects of Rome were preserved, as well as the perpetual sacred flame of the goddess; a section is still visible after the modern restoration. Along the southern side of the Forum, exactly in front of the facade line of the Basilica Julia, the bases of seven columns (the **Honorary Columns**) are still standing (two of which have been re-erected); they were meant to uphold honorary statues in the Diocletian era (284-305 A.D.).

Emperor Diocletian rebuilt also the **Curia**, the historical seat of the Senate, destroyed by fire in 283 A.D.; it is still up, almost intact, for it was changed into the church of St. Hadrian during the 7th century.

Roman Forum, the Arch of Septimius Severus.

The Diocletian Curia, brought back to its original condition through the excavation and demolition works carried out in the middle of the 20th century, replaced the **Curia Iulia**, planned by Caesar and built in the same place by Augustus in 29 B.C.; in turn, Augustus replaced the very old **Curia Hostilia**, founded by King Tullus Hostilius. The latest monument in the Forum was made on the threshold of the Middle Ages: a tall column on a step plinth, probably already existing earlier, but replaced by the summit statue, which was dedicated to Byzantine Emperor **Phocas** in 608 A.D.

↑ The Square of the Roman Forum, reconstruction.

👁

👁 The Temples of Saturn and of Concord, ↓ reconstruction.

CAMPIDOGLIO
The Capitoline Hill, this unknown stranger!

A mandatory visit during our itinerary, it is the smallest yet most important hill of the ancient city. The Capitoline Hill, a name that refers to the heart of politics even at present, not only in Rome, but also in many other places around the world (i.e. Capitol Hill in Washington, D.C.). This area originally had two peaks (up to approx. 50 metres in height) named *Arx*, **Arce**, **fortress**, and *Capitolium*, **Capitoline Hill**, whose strategic and very defendable position by the river determined its early and continuous occupation, from the Bronze Age to present times.

The Piazza del Campidoglio, at night.

Between the two peaks, a deep wooded valley (today no longer visible) was called *Asylum* (shelter), in memory of hospitality allegedly offered by Romulus (the legendary founder of Rome) to the "political" refugees from back then! Today one usually walks up to the Capitoline Hill on the "**cordonata**", which is the monumental stairway designed by Michelangelo. But wishing to visit the ancient hill with our imagination, we have to climb up the opposite side, from the *clivus capitolinus*, namely from the valley of the Roman Forum, towards which activities and buildings were projected.

To the right rose the *Arx*, where the **S. Maria in Aracoeli** church stands today; to the left the *Capitolium*, where **Palazzo dei Conservatori** and **Palazzo Caffarelli** are presently located. Here investigations conducted by archaeologists over the last few years have brought to light a very ancient **settlement** dating back to the **17-16th centuries B.C.**, which testifies to a community organized over approximately one hectare of land with no more than 200 individuals, not dominating yet prevailing over other communities due to the favourable position for exchange and production.

While visiting the **Capitoline Museums** in the two Palazzi, we will see that this area stretched out into the "**Roman Garden**" that today is part of the museum layout.

The decisive moment for the development of the hill was the age of the Etruscan kings, the Tarquins, between the end of the 7th and the end of the 6th centuries B.C., when the massive **Temple of Jupiter Capitolinus** was built (approximately 60 metres in length and wide slightly less), dedicated to the three most important divinities of the Roman Olympus: Jupiter, Juno and Minerva.

A human skull was discovered in the foundations during construction, therefore the toponym *a capite Olii* that led to *Capitolium*. For centuries the history of the city was the history of the hill, the stage for bloody and epochal clashes, for legendary deeds and great achievements.

In the year **460 B.C.,** when Romans still had not established their control over the entire territory, the hill was occupied by the Sabines stationed on the Quirinal Hill.

According to legend, this took place due to the betrayal of a young Roman woman named Tarpea (whose name derived from the ancient name of the Capitoline Hill, **Mons Tarpeius**), who was punished by the Sabines themselves: the area called **Rupe Tarpea** is still the steepest slope of the hill (towards the present via della Consolazione) where traitors once used to be flung. During the invasion of the Gauls in **386 B.C.**, Capitoline Hill was the stronghold of Roman resistance, defending it to the bitter end as it was *sedes deorum* = **home of the gods**. Again there is another legendary episode involving some geese in a pen close to a sacred altar dedicated to Juno on the Arx, that suddenly began squawking and thus warned of the presence of enemies.

This is connected to another important epithet: the **temple of Juno Moneta** (namely which cautions, warns) where the first mint was to be located (from which the modern term "money" derives). Amongst the other important sacred buildings, we have another **temple dedicated to Vejovis** (young infernal deity), some remains of which can be viewed during the visit to the museum complex, as it was built in the valley area between the two peaks of the Capitolium.

According to literature and archaeological remains scattered in the area, many other sacred buildings were built. But all of their raised sectors were destroyed during addi-

Reconstruction of the Capitolium with the Temple of Jupiter Capitolinus, 6th century B.C. (Inklink).

tional violent episodes such as the fire that broke out in **83 B.C.**, as a result of which massive substruction works were carried out. For instance these substruction works were done on the *Tabularium* (that was built in 78 B.C. overlooking the *Asylum*) which was the first **State Archives of Rome** (laws and treaties were written on the *tabulae* = tablets, documents), that was becoming a vast empire.

Today we can still see the massive substruction works in tuff blocks underneath **Palazzo Senatorio** that can be viewed during the visit to the **Capitoline Museums**.

The arcades of the *Tabularium*, the first State Archives of Rome.

The turbulent expansion of the city led to intensive construction of private dwellings along the slopes, as testified by the remains of a 2nd century A.D. *insula*, namely "public housing" complex that must have counted at least six floors for a total of 400 tenants! Substantial remains of the building can still be seen between Il Vittoriano and the stairway that leads up to S. Maria in Aracoeli.

The civil war that raged in **89 A.D.** was to cause more destruction. The war lasted one long year and witnessed the victory of Vespasian, who began the Flavian dynasty and subsequently led the area to its brilliant resurgence.

During the Middle Ages, Capitoline Hill became the "periphery" of the new centre of religious power which was St. Peter's in the Vatican and the medieval settlement; all the buildings and activities on the hill were progressively directed towards them. There was the prevalence of agriculture and trade (new denominations such as Campo Vaccino and Campo Caprino also derived from the presence of the **market**); and although the wooded area on the Arce housed a church dedicated to the Virgin Mary as early as the 4th century A.D. (initially S. Maria in Capitolio, then the **S. Maria in Aracoeli Church** of the Franciscan order, in continuity with the temple dedicated to Juno Moneta), the other peak was the site where executions were staged!

The *Tabularium*, like many other Roman buildings, was reemployed as a fortified residence of the important aristocratic Corsi family (end 11th - beginning 12th century). But in 1143 the building became the premises of the libero Comune di Roma and the early Senators, hence the name **Palazzo Senatorio**. While visiting the Hall of the City Council, also known as the Julius Caesar Hall (named after an ancient statue), one can still clearly distinguish the columns and other signs of the medieval open gallery belonging to Palazzo.

When a new form of government made its way into the city (1363) with only one Senator and three magistrates being elected (the Conservatives), a small old building to the right of the Senatorio became **Palazzo dei Conservatori**. It originally had a long portico and rooms that housed the premises of arts and crafts guilds whose in-

Side entrance portal to S. Maria in Aracoeli with a fresco showing the Madonna and Child between two angels.

scriptions can be read on the lintels of the doorways.

This building was entrusted with the task of "narrating" the legendary origins of Rome and exalting the examples of virtue and bravery in the Republic already at the beginning of the 15th century. In the meantime Pope Sixtus IV (1471) presented the people of Rome with the first group of bronze statues that still symbolize the city and represent the first public museum in the world.

The growing importance of the hill called for a new town-planning and architectural layout, which the very powerful Pope Paul III Farnese entrusted to Michelangelo Buonarroti. He had already transformed the esplanade in 1538, with the creation of a central focal point: **the equestrian statue of Marcus Aurelius**, a symbol of Christian Rome (it was then thought that this statue portrayed Constantine, the first Christian Emperor).

Colossal portrait of emperor Constantine (Rome, Palazzo dei Conservatori).

Then the facades of **Palazzo Senatorio** and **Palazzo dei Conservatori** were redesigned, which were joined by **Palazzo Nuovo** (built at a later date). The **facades** are articulated by a giant order that gives a sense of urban monumentality in a relatively compressed space. Ascending from the **cordonata**, one follows the vertical line that focalizes on the **statue** (presently a copy) and comes to an end at the **tower of Palazzo Senatorio**. The square layout has remained the same until today. Palazzo Senatorio is still the premises for the highest office in the city, namely the Mayor and the City Council.

The Capitoline collections: the most ancient museum in the world!

The tour begins in **Palazzo dei Conservatori**. The Courtyard holds some impressive fragments from the colossal marble statue of **Constantine**, which were discovered close to the Basilica of Maxentius during the 15th century.

Equestrian statue of the emperor Marcus Aurelius.

We walk across the **Apartment** on the first floor, where the **Hall of the Horatii and Curiatii** houses some massive frescoes (1595) by Giuseppe Cesari, better known as **Cavaliere d'Arpino**, that hang like tapestries on the walls. They depict some important episodes regarding the origins of Rome. While other halls contain bronze statues that are the historical core of the museums: beginning with the "**La Lupa**" ("She-Wolf"), the very famous sculpture that is the symbol of Rome; the delicate "**Spinario**" ("Boy with Thorn"), depicting a young boy as he removes a thorn from his foot); the intriguing portrait of a man known as "**Bruto**" ("Brutus") that was donated to the Museum in 1564.

The visit continues with the recent renovation of the wing that connects Palazzo dei Conservatori to Palazzo Caffarelli. The historical **Roman Garden** has been subjected to archaeological excavations: today we can admire the remains of the **Temple of Jupiter Capitolinus** in an exhibition area involving a large glassed-in exedra that was especially created to house the bronze statue of **Marcus Aurelius** and thereby protect it from the elements that were threatening its integrity. Before leaving Palazzo dei Conservatori, one must pay a visit to the **Capitoline Picture Gallery**.

It is a fine example of the wise acquisition of private collections made by Pope Benedict XIV during the 18th century.

Here we can find the most outstanding names from the 16th and 17th centuries: **Titian** with his "Baptism of Christ", **Caravaggio** with "The Fortune Teller" and "John the Baptist", **Guercino** with the enormous "St. Petronilla Altarpiece", **Guido Reni**'s "St. Sebastian" and the largest hall

"The rape of the Sabines" by Cavaliere d'Arpino, 1636-1640 (Rome, Palazzo dei Conservatori).

dedicated to **Pietro da Cortona**, just to mention a few. Returning to the ground floor of Palazzo dei Conservatori, our tour through History continues into the bowels... of the square! We shall be walking through the **Galleria Lapidaria**, an underground junction that houses the extraordinary collection of ancient Latin and Greek inscriptions that have been made legible and comprehensible. We will ultimately be reaching the *Tabularium* and one of the most spectacular views of Rome: at our feet lies the valley of the Roman Forum, the Imperial Fora and the Palatine Hill in perspective. Hence our tour will be complete with a visit to **Palazzo Nuovo**, where we should not be intimidated by the many sculptures, but discover their charm: the story of legends such as the **statue of Marphurius** in the courtyard; the **Capitoline Venus** that stands in a small precious hall; the **Wounded Amazon** on display in the Hall; historical references made through the splendid **portraits of the emperors**; and the complex sculptural groups such as **The Dying Gaul**, which is one of the most famous statues of antiquity (either pertinent or a copy of the great monument in the city of Pergamon in Asia Minor).

"The Spinario", small sculpture of a boy removing a thorn from his foot (Rome, Palazzo dei Conservatori).

Visiting the Capitoline Museums must envisage a tour of **Centrale Montemartini**, which can easily be reached with the underground B line (Garbatella stop).

It is much more than a "branch" of the Capitoline Museums"! It is actually one of the most successful examples of industrial archaeology transformed into a prestigious art venue: since 1997, the first (1912) power station in Rome has been the premises of a superb collection of sculptures and archaeological material discovered in excavations conducted post-Roma Capitale (1870) and during the 1930ˢ.

"The fortune teller" by Caravaggio, around 1595 (Rome, Capitoline Picture Gallery).

The Capitoline Wolf, the city's symbol (Rome, Palazzo dei Conservatori).

The relation between **machines and... the gods** culminates in the sculptures that decorated the pediment of the **Temple of Apollo Sosianus, with the battle scene between the Greeks and the Amazons**, rediscovered... digging inside archaeological deposits, reassembling real excellence of Greek sculpture dating back to 450-425 B.C. originally from Eretria and transported to Rome during the last decades of the 1st century B.C. This is one of the many "discoveries" that this extraordinary place reserves as an industrial container and as artistic content: we must recall, amidst the many treasures, a **bed coated with silver and copper sheets** that dates back to between the 1st century B.C. and the 1st century A.D., from a tomb in Amiternum; the statue depicting the gentle **muse** named **Polyhymnia**; the splendid **mosaic floor** that is a truly great carpet made up of bright multicolored tiles illustrating lively hunting scenes, dating back to the 4th century A.D., that was discovered close to the S. Bibiana church.

Statue of the "Dying Gaul", (Rome, Capitoline Museum, Palazzo Nuovo).

Detail of a mosaic with hunting scenes from the Horti Liciniani- near Santa Bibiana- 4th century A.D. (Rome, Centrale Montemartini museum).

The "Capitoline Venus", showing the goddess rising from her bath (Rome, Capitoline Museum, Palazzo Nuovo).

Statue of Polyhymnia, 2nd century A.D. (Rome, Centrale Montemartini museum).

Statue dressed in a peplum in front of a diesel engine (Rome, engine hall of the Centrale Montemartini museum).

QR CODED
3D VIDEO

The Colosseum

Trajan's Market

The Imperial Fora

The Basilica Ulpia

inside IMPERIAL ROME

FROM LIONS TO GODS

WITH RECONSTRUCTIONS

EDIZIONE INGLESE

IN THE FOOTSTEPS OF EMPERORS:
THE COLOSSEUM AND ITS SQUARE, THE IMPERIAL FORA,
THE ROMAN FORUM , THE CAPITOLINE HILL AND ITS MUSEUMS.

978-88-8162-320-4

9 788881 623204

€ 6,00 IVA INCLUSA

VISION
ROMA
PAST & PRESENT

PQL312410

Printed in the United States
62464LVS00002B/4-51

9 781933 669052